KU-033-435

FRANCE

ON

BACKROADS

FRANCE
ON
BACKROADS

THE MOTORIST'S GUIDE TO THE FRENCH COUNTRYSIDE

PAN BOOKS

First published 1986 by Pan Books Ltd, Cavaye Place, London SW10 9PG.
987654321

Conceived, edited and designed by Duncan Petersen Publishing Ltd, 5 Botts
Mews, Chepstow Road, London W2 5AG.

© Duncan Petersen Publishing Ltd, 1986
© Tours text, individual contributors as listed
© Maps, Institut Géographique National, (French Official Survey)
authorization number 701036
107 Rue la Boétie, 75008 Paris

ISBN 0 330 29383 4 (paperback)
     0 330 29742 2 (hardback)

Typeset and originated in Great Britain by Modern Reprographics Ltd, Hull.

Printed and bound in Italy by G. Canale and C. SpA, Turin.

This book is sold subject to the condition that it shall not, by way of trade or
otherwise, be lent, re-sold, hired out or otherwise circulated without the
publisher's prior consent in any form of binding or cover other than that in which
it is published and without a similar condition being imposed on the subsequent
purchaser.

■ All routes described in this book are undertaken at the individual's own risk.
The publisher and copyright owners accept no responsibility for any
consequences arising out of use of this book, including misinterpretation of the
maps and directions.

■ Information on opening and closing times, and telephone numbers, was
correct at time of publication, but those who run hotels, restaurants and tourist
attractions are sometimes obliged to change times at short notice. If your
enjoyment of a day out is going to depend on seeing, or eating at a certain
place, it makes sense to check beforehand that you will gain admission.

■ Many of the roads used for tours in this book are country lanes in the true
sense: they have zero visibility at corners, they are too narrow for oncoming
cars to pass, and they include hairpin bends and precarious mountain roads with
sheer drops. Please drive with due care and attention, and at suitable speeds.

■ Many of the roads used for tours in this book are in upland areas. During
winter, they could be closed by snow. Consult a motoring organization or local
tourist office if in doubt.

The authors

Every kilometre of *France on Backroads* was not only planned, and written, but driven by a team of dedicated Francophile travel writers:

Ile de France, Alsace, the three Loire tours, and the Jura and Burgundy tours are by **Leslie and Adrian Gardiner.** Leslie Gardiner first visited France in a minesweeper and came to know the small harbours of the Channel and Biscay coasts intimately. Later, as a travel writer and correspondent of the *Guardian* and *The Times*, he undertook many motoring, walking and boating tours of the hinterland when writing about French life and leisure in his books on Western European travel and transport. His son Adrian has lived and worked in the Loire and Pyrenees regions and makes annual visits to other parts of the country.

Dordogne: Périgord Blanc, both the Auvergne tours, Gorges du Tarn, Northern Ardèche, both Pyrenees tours, The *Bastides* of Gascony, Lower Rhône and Provence are by **Peter Graham,** who has lived in France since 1962. He contributes articles on food, wine and travel to *The Sunday Times* magazine, the *Guardian* and *The International Herald Tribune.* He was a major contributor to the *American Express/Mitchell Beazley Pocket Guide to Paris* and wrote *The International Herald Tribune Guide to Business Travel and Entertainment.*

The Brittany and Normandy tours (except for Rouen and the Seine Valley) are by **Stephen Brough,** editorial director of the *Economist Business Traveller's Guides* and formerly Deputy Editor of *Holiday Which.*

Dordogne: Vineyards, Rivers and *Bastides*, Languedoc and Côte d'Azur are by **Fiona Duncan,** author, travel writer and editor of the *American Express/Mitchell Beazley Pocket Guides* to *Paris* and the *South of France.*

The two Alps tours are by **Christopher Gill,** formerly editor of *Holiday Which* and co-editor of *The Good Bath Guide.*

Normandy: Rouen and the Seine Valley is by **Anthony Abrahams,** Oxford doctor and childrens' author, and by **Joy Abrahams;** Eastern Picardy is by **John Farndon,** journalist and writer on an encyclopaedic range of subjects.

Contents

The tours are arranged in a north-south sequence, beginning in Picardy, north of Paris, and ending with the south-eastern corner of the Pyrenees. Where several tours fall within the same region, for example Normandy, Brittany, the Auvergne or the Dordogne, these are grouped together, even if it means deviating temporarily from the north-south sequence.

Contents

Touring with *France on Backroads*

Meandering on sleepy French country roads from restaurant to shady café, stopping here and there to take in a dignified château, a charming old village, or simply pausing to admire the view: for many, life has few greater pleasures, and this book is made for them. But it is also very much a book for those who have not yet discovered the unequalled delights of the French countryside, indeed for anyone with a day or two to spare in France and the urge to explore.

Whichever the case, you will get most pleasure from *France on Backroads* if you read these two pages.

The routes

The figure-8s are designed to be driven in either two days or one. But you will enjoy the tours most if you drive them in two, or more, days. On every tour there is so much to see and enjoy that it would be a shame, unless you are short of time, to take them any faster.

Even taking them at this pace, you are not intended to stop at every point of interest described, merely the ones that interest you. Regard the routes as frameworks for exploration, not as exercises to be undertaken exactly as the manual instructs. It is far more important to enjoy them, at whatever pace suits you, and indeed to modify the routes according to your needs, than to complete them in a given space of time.

There are, however, occasions when one finds oneself in a locality with limited time, and the desire to see at least something of it. With an average length of about 160 km, all the figure-8s can be driven inside a day, and approaching a tour in this way is perfectly viable, and, in its way, an interesting undertaking. You won't be able to make many stops, but because the two loops making up a figure-8 are usually devised to take in contrasting landscapes, driving them gives an excellent overall feel for an area.

The tours are in 30 locations all round France (see map on page 6). The locations are chosen for a combination of qualities: interesting backroads; beautiful landscape, seen to advantage on country roads; interesting towns and villages; strong local identity, including, naturally, cuisine and wine; and, sometimes, major tourist attractions. Several of the tours take in important sights where you will temporarily be forced to forget the peace of the backwaters through which you have just driven; don't be disheartened - the crowds are soon left behind once more. By contrast, some of the tours are located in the vicinity of major tourist destinations but don't actually take them in, usually because this would compromise the route, and in any case the place in question is best tackled on a special visit.

The roads

France on Backroads is about country roads, warts and all: expect some terrible surfaces. In upland areas, be prepared to creep through terrifying hair-pin bends, and to edge past unprotected verges, wheels centimetres from the void. In some country areas, be ready for blind corners, slow farm vehicles and poor signposting.

The maps The routes are featured on the Institut Géographique National's *Serie Rouge* maps: general-purpose motoring maps at a scale of 1:250,000.

The IGN is the French official survey, and its cartography is the product of meticulous surveys - accurate measurement of the ground combined with aerial photography. The result is a precision product on which all other mapping of France ultimately derives. The 1:250,000 maps used in *France on Backroads* carry, moreover, plenty of helpful extra information for the tourist and road user. The scale allows road bends as close as 250 metres apart to show up; and the 'white' roads, with no coloured infill, are a faithful representation of the network of country lanes. However, in common with all other maps at this scale, not every single minor road is featured (indeed the tours occasionally use short stretches of unmarked road - see below under **Route Directions**) and the names of some small settlements are omitted.

Road numbers In recent years, many of the 'D' (Département) and 'N' (National) designations of French roads have been changed. In some localities, the signposts do not yet reflect the change. Thus map, and what you read on signposts, may differ. In practice this is not as confusing as it sounds; and in the interests of consistency, the text uses the version given on the map.

Some place name spellings also differ on the map and on the ground; once again, the text follows the IGN version.

Hints on map-reading If you are not an expert map-reader, it is worth acquainting yourself with IGN mapping's conventional symbols by looking at the key on any *Serie Rouge* folded sheet. But above all, when on the road, map-read *actively*, rather than passively.

This comes down to knowing where you are on the map *all* the time. Understanding the implications of scale is, therefore, essential. On 1:250,000 mapping, one centimetre on the map represents two-and-a-half kilometres on the ground. So for every kilometre you travel, you should mentally tick off the appropriate portion of map. To do that, of course, you need a point of reference from which to start. This is generally easy: obvious landmarks present themselves continuously in the form of villages and road junctions.

Don't forget that IGN produces maps at the larger scale of 1:100,000 which can be useful in conjunction with *France on Backroads*; and indeed walking maps at the scale of 1:50,000.

The route directions Printed in italics, these are an aid to trouble-free navigation, *not* a complete set of instructions for getting round the routes. You will find that they are most detailed on tricky backroads stretches, and especially so on the odd occasion where your route follows a road not actually marked on the map. It is of course particularly important to follow the directions carefully on such stretches. The text does not always draw your attention to the fact that a road is not marked.

Food

Our contributors set out not only to make each tour an interesting drive, but to find good restaurants on or near the routes. Some areas are not, however, as well endowed with restaurants as others, and this is reflected in the varying numbers of recommendations.

The restaurants mentioned are not by any means the only ones you will find on or near the routes: but they will be particularly interesting for some or all of the following reasons: value, food and wine, ambience, friendly service and for being representative of the local *cuisine*. They are generally, but not always, in the middle-to-lower price bracket. Although they have been chosen with the lunchtime stop in mind, they are usually excellent places for an evening meal as well.

Recommendations come in two forms: a main recommendation, with essential details such as telephone number and closing times; and a passing mention, intended as a helpful extra, with minimum details, usually just a telephone number. Although the restaurant information was accurate at time of going to press, remember that opening and closing times change. Where no closing time is given, assume the restaurant is always open; assume also that some but not all establishments will be closed on national holidays. **To avoid disappointment, book in advance whenever possible.**

Hotels

Like the restaurant recommendations, these are not exhaustive. They are a selection of interesting accommodation at sound value prices which link in with the routes. No opening and closing times are given.

Recommendations are in two forms: main, and passing.

Fuel

In some parts of France, and particularly on the minor roads used for the tours, filling stations can be scarce. Try to think ahead, therefore, and preferably fill up before starting. (Best prices are to be found at giant supermarket pumps.)

Fuel stops are mentioned specifically on some tours where there is a marked shortage. Once again, the mentions are selective, rather than exhaustive; there will be other filling stations on the routes.

Picnic places In a country where such a wealth of instant picnic materials is available, no one wants always to eat in restaurants. A selection, rather than an exhaustive survey, of useful picnic stops is given for most tours. You can assume that they are representative of the best, but not the only places to picnic on a route.

National holidays New Year's Day; Easter Monday; 1 May (Labour Day); 8 May (Victory in Europe Day); Ascension Day (the sixth Thurs. after Easter); Whit Monday (the second Mon after Ascension); 14 July (Bastille Day); 15 Aug (Assumption); 1 Nov (All Saints Day); 11 Nov (Remembrance Day); Christmas Day.

Shopping hours In the north, department stores and supermarkets are generally open from 9.30-6.30 (not closing for lunch) Mon-Sat; some open late on Wed. Smaller shops generally open 10-6, Mon-Sat, some closing for lunch, some not.
In the south, shops tend to open early, 7 or 8, and close for the siesta, 12-3, opening again until quite late in the evening - 7 or 8.
In north and south, many shops close on Mon, though some may open during the afternoon.

Time France is one hour ahead of Greenwich Mean Time in winter and two hours ahead in summer.

THE PRICE BANDS

To give an indication of cost, four restaurant price bands are quoted. They represent approximate prices for lunch, typically three courses, service but no wine included.

Price band A	Under 60 francs
Price band B	60-100 francs
Price band C	100-150 francs
Price band D	over 150 francs

Price band D necessarily covers the large price differentials found in the top range: it is easy to find yourself with a bill of 350-600 francs a head or more for dinner in a famed restaurant.

The prices quoted were correct at time of printing, but liable, of course, to increase. In most cases, however, increases will remain in proportion, so that the price banding system is likely to remain useful. Note that the price banding system does not apply to accommodation, even when rooms are available at the same establishment.

Eastern Picardy:

SOISSONS, LAON AND COMPIÈGNE

Speeding south on the *autoroute* to Paris from the Channel ports, you may catch a glimpse of this region in the distance. Mile upon mile of ancient forest - Compiègne, St-Gobain, Retz - made the country around Soissons the playground of the kings of France: a place to hunt stag and wild boar, to ride, and to romance. The kings are long gone, but the châteaux they built, and the forests, remain.

It is a richly varied land. Royal hunting forests run down to green river valleys, or give way to endless plains of wheat. The Aisne, Ailette and Oise rivers cut deep into limestone plateaux on their way to join the Seine.

Route One explores the countryside between Soissons and Laon, the ancient capital of France, heading north through Coucy and the Fôret de St-Gobain, then down through Laon into the rolling hills of the Côte Laonnois. The second route meanders through the Retz and Compiègne forests before heading back along the Aisne valley.

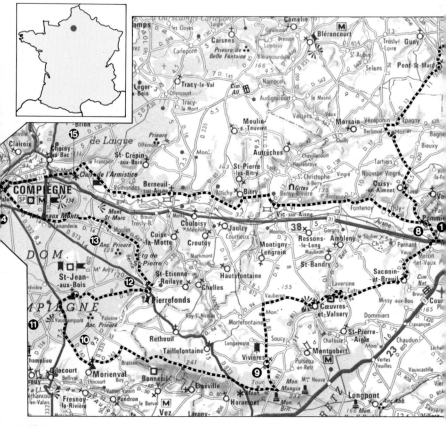

ROUTE ONE: 116 KM

Soissons -
Coucy-le-
Château

① *Leave Soissons on the main road to Compiègne - the N31 - and after 2 km turn left on to the D6 to Pommiers. In Vézaponin, turn right on to the D13 for Coucy. A short climb from the marshy Aisne valley brings you out on to a wide open plateau.*

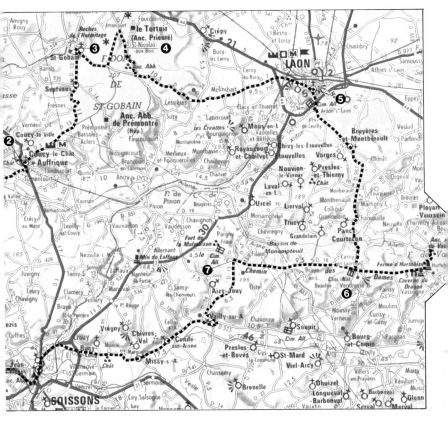

Coucy-le-
Château

Straddled right across its commanding hilltop site, the castle of the lords of Coucy was once the greatest medieval fortress in Europe. There is not much left except for the ramparts and a vast pile of rubble: the demolition Cardinal Mazarin failed to complete in 1652 was thoroughly accomplished by the Germans in 1917. Yet it is still worth paying to wander around the ruins, and the view from the ramparts is splendid. Park in the village square by the lions and follow the signs to the entrance. In her classic history of 14thC France, Barbara Tuchmann gives a fascinating account of the Coucy dynasty, and in particular of the

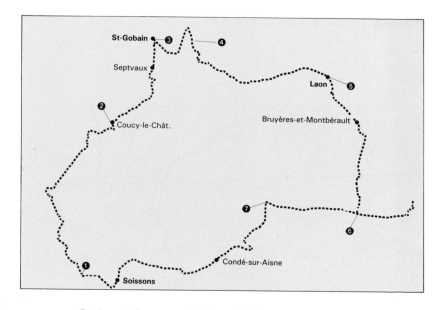

flamboyant Enguerrand VII, last of this powerful line. Their motto proclaimed: *'Roi ne suis, ne prince ne duc ne comte aussi; je suis le sire de Coucy'*. Few argued. *Open am and pm all year; closed Tues, Wed.*

Hotel Belle Vue *(restaurant, Coucy)*	You can lunch pleasantly at the Hotel Belle Vue; or sip a beer in the garden opposite. The Belle Vue do particularly fine *ficelles Picardes* - the pancakes with ham in mushroom sauce that are a speciality of Picardy. *Just off the Place du Marché; price band C.* ② *Leave Coucy through the narrow Porte de Laon on the D5; after about one km, bear left along the D13 signposted St-Gobain.*
Coucy - Laon	Wonderful driving through the ancient Forest of St-Gobain, famous for its wild mushrooms, though most are now grown in *champignonnières*.
St-Gobain	St-Gobain's royal glass works, established by Marie de Luxemburg in the 17thC, is a working factory and visitors are not encouraged. ③ *Leave St-Gobain by the D7 for Laon and, after 2.5 km, turn left at the mini roundabout, following the sign to* Centre du Recreations. *At the crossroads, turn sharp right signposted Anizy and St-Nicolas, and then left on to the D556.*
Roches de l'Hermitage	About 0.5 km past the mini-roundabout, a small sign on the left indicates the footpath to the Roches de l'Hermitage of St-Gobain, a 7thC Irish martyr. A fine 20-minute stroll through the trees brings you to the rocks where he had his hideaway - a useful picnic spot.

*The abbey.
St-Nicolas-
aux-Bois.*

**St-
Nicolas-
aux-Bois**

This Benedictine abbey is set in an enchanting woodland glade and has a mysterious, magical atmosphere. Sadly, the occupants do not welcome visitors; you can only peer through the trees from the road.

④ *Continue on the D55, then the D7 for Laon.*

Laon

Tumbling over a hill that rises steeply from the surrounding plain, the walled medieval town of Laon persuaded Victor Hugo to exclaim, 'In Laon, everything is beautiful - the churches, the houses, the countryside, everything.' Today, chic shops and pedestrian precincts have eroded some of the charm, but the narrow streets and crumbling old houses still give you a tremendous sense of the town's long and chequered history.

The cathedral is not to be missed: it is one of the loveliest in France, especially late in the day when the sun catches the stonework on the west front - the stone oxen peering from the towers are said to commemorate the poor beasts who had to drag the stone for the cathedral all the way up the hill. If the cathedral is crowded, you can escape to the chapel founded by Knights Templar, grateful for their safe return from the Crusades - the garden is a welcome oasis from the bustle of the town (closed Tuesday). From here it is just a step to the ramparts with their superb views over the Laonnois countryside.

Park in the lower town near the station and catch the Poma 2000 monorail up to the old town. As you walk up to the cathedral, you may be tempted by the shops. If you weaken, try the local caramels or the superb *fromagerie* on Rue Châtelaine.

La Bannière de France
(restaurant, Laon)

Superb regional dishes from the best local ingredients in a 17thC coaching inn: the restaurant is famed for its *rognons de veau au Bouzy* - veal kidneys cooked in Bouzy, the still red wine from nearby Champagne - and its delicious desserts, but the cost will rise steeply unless you stick to the excellent value three-course menu. *11 Rue Franklin Roosevelt (near the town hall); closed 20th Dec-20th Jan; tel 23.23.21.44; price band B.*

⑤ *Descend from Laon near the Porte d'Ardon and head out on the D967 signposted Bruyères-et-Montbérault. Continue on this road through Chamouille to Cerny-en-Laonnois. At Cerny* ⑥ *turn right on to the D18 signposted Soissons. Or make this recommended detour.*

Caverne du Dragon
(detour)

Turn left at ⑥ *along the D18 signposted Caverne du Dragon, which is reached in about 4.5 km.* Old field guns and armoured cars from both World Wars mark the entrance to this grim underground museum to the Chemin des Dames offensive. Expect to leave angry and depressed: the horror of war is chillingly brought home. In this very cavern 6,000 German troops were holed up during the April 1917 offensive; and many French and German troops died here. Some recent entries in the visitors' book are heart-rending. *Open all day, April-Oct.*

Ferme d'Hurtebise
(detour)

From the Caverne, continue on the D18 another 0.5 km. The strategically-placed Ferme d'Hurtebise was at stake in the Battle of Craonne in March 1814, a fierce engagement in Napoleon's dazzling but forlorn defensive manoeuvres against the advancing Prussian armies. A hundred years later, the farm was again at stake in September 1914.

Abbaye de Vauclair
(detour)

From the Ferme d'Hurtebise turn left on to the D886. Continue one km. If you are at all interested in medicinal herbs, stop at this ruined Cistercian abbey: it has one of the best herb gardens in France. *Open all day until 10 pm in summer. Retrace to* ⑥.

Le Chemin des Dames

From Cerny, this road runs straight as an arrow along the Chemin des Dames on the crest of a ridge with superb views either side over the Aisne and Ailette valleys. The road is an old Roman road, but is called le Chemin des Dames after the daughters of Louis XV, who used to hurtle along here on their way to the Château Bove. The peaceful scene gives no reminder of the terrible day in April 1917 when the French tried to break through the German front here. The pointless slaughter precipitated mutiny in the French army.

Hostellerie du Château
(detour to rest., Fère-en-Tardenois)

Turn off the Chemin des Dames on to the D967 in the direction of Bourg and Fismes for what could be the gourmet experience of a lifetime. It is expensive, but the food, lovingly prepared by Patrick Michelon, is unforgettable, and the setting, an old château, is magnificent. *Three km from Fère-en-Tardenois on the D967; tel 23.82.21.13; closed Jan and Feb, last bookings 9pm; price band D.*

ROUTE TWO: 109 KM

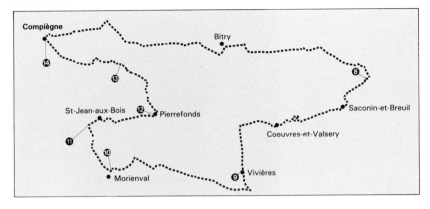

⑦ *Turn left on to the D15, signposted Vailly. In Vailly, turn right along the D925 to return to Soissons.*

Soissons - Vivières

Leave Soissons on the main road to Compiègne - the N31 - and after about 3.5 km, ⑧ *turn left on to the D94, signposted Saconin-et-Breuil. Continue on the D94 through Saconin and Coeuvres and, 4 km beyond Coeuvres, turn left on to the D81 to Vivières.* You now have a leisurely drive across the Soissonais plateau.

Vivières

An unspoiled village of ancient stone cottages in the local style, Vivières deserves at least a brief stop. Park near the crossroads by the Ecole Communale and wander through the quiet lanes up to the right towards the 17thC château (not open to visitors).

⑨ *Continue on the D81 until you pass the D811, then hairpin right on the tiny road to Forêt de Compiègne. Pick up this road again after a short spell on the D973. Once you emerge from the trees turn left and, soon after, left again, signposted Fossemont.*

Vivières - Morienval

This is a ridge-top route through the beautiful Forêt de Retz. The broad swathe through the trees opposite the telecommunications tower is the Allée Royale, which leads to the château in Villars-Cotteret, 4 km away.

Morienval

The original 9thC abbey of Morienval had the dubious distinction of housing both monks and nuns under the same roof; the present abbey, dating from the 11thC, can claim to be the finest Romanesque building in France. Students of architecture will find the place fascinating.

⑩ *Turn left on to the D335, then almost immediately turn sharp right, by the Elf garage, on to the D163 to Compiègne. At the D332, turn right for Vaudrampoint.*

Morienval - Here the road runs by the Forêt de Compiègne, less wild St-Gobain,
Compiègne but equally beautiful. Felled trees and broad clearings show the ancient
forest is exploited for its wood as well as its scenery; but careful
management ensures the forest will always regenerate.

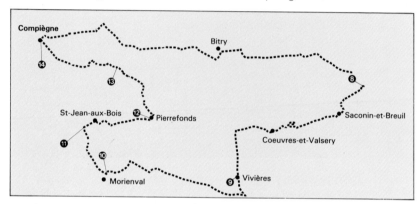

Auberge Idyllic country inn atmosphere and excellent food make this the place
du Bon for a long, extravagant lunch; for a cheaper lunch, go on to St-Jean-aux-
Accueil Bois. You can stay here, too. *On the road from Morienval to*
(restaurant, *Vaudrampont; tel 44.42.84.04; price band C; closed February, Monday*
Vaudram- *evenings, Tuesday.*
pont) ⑪ *Soon after the Bon Accueil, turn right for St-Jean-aux-Bois.*

St-Jean- An attractive old hamlet of stone houses clustered around a 12thC
aux-Bois abbey, right in the heart of Compiègne forest.

Pierre- Avoid the château tour: the rooms are gloomy, the tour long and
fonds costly, and there is no way to escape from the noisy crowds and the
guide's rambling monologue - they lock you securely in each room.
Much better to park down by the lake, relax with a drink in the garden
of the Hôtel l'Etranger, and admire the château from a distance. It was
completely rebuilt from a medieval ruin in the 19thC by the famous
restorer and architect, Viollet-le-Duc. *Open am and pm all year; closed*
Tues in summer, Tues and Wed in winter.
⑫ *Head out of Pierrefonds on the D335 in the direction of Attichy; just*
after the Fontenoy brasserie, turn sharp left on to the D547 for Compiègne.

Etang de This serene lake in the forest is a fine picnic site on weekdays, with
St-Pierre - pleasant walks in all directions. At weekends, it is overrun with day
Mont St- trippers. The same goes for the charming village of Vieux Moulin just up
Marc the road. But you can park by the Auberge du Mont St-Marc and walk
up through the trees, away from the crowds. *After the Auberge du Mont*
St-Marc, bear right ⑬ *and, at the next crossroads, turn left (not*

signposted) and then right. Turn left at the next crossroads, and follow signs to Compiègne.

Com-piègne
The grandiose royal palace of Louis XV stands on the eastern edge, its formal gardens merging into the wilderness of Compiègne forest. At weekends, the palace is packed with tourists, and the tour can be a real ordeal - but there are compensations. Some of the rooms are magnificent, and the Musée du Second Empire recalls the glittering days when Napoleon III and his Empress, Eugénie, presided over extravagant house parties here - the *Series de Compiègne* - attended by such celebrities as Verdi, Meyerbeer, Gounod, Flaubert, Dumas, Pasteur and Prosper Merimée. The entry price also includes the Musée de la Voiture; entry to the gardens is free; *open 9.30-11.15, 1.30-4.30 daily.*

If, however, your visit to Compiègne is brief, give the palace a miss and sample some of the town's less obvious attractions. It was outside the walls of Compiègne that Joan of Arc was finally captured, and in the Place St-Jacques you can see the church where the Maid of Orléans prayed that very day in May 1430; but there is no truth in the story that she was then incarcerated in the (misnamed) Tour Jeanne d'Arc near the river. Near the tower is the Musée de Vivenel *(open am and pm, except Tues)* with a fascinating collection of Greek and Roman pottery, Dürer drawings and local folk art, and just outside the museum is the best picnic spot in town - the atmospheric Parc de Songeons between the River Oise and the old Hotel-Dieu (a 12thC hospital). You can buy delicious food for a picnic in the delicatessen in the little street just off Rue Magenta to the right past the Hotel de Ville.

The Hotel de Ville itself is one of the highlights of the town, a 15thC gothic masterpice with a façade described by R. L. Stevenson as 'all turreted and gargoyled and slashed and bedizened with half a score of architectural fancies.' There is a flower market outside on Saturday.
⑭ *Leave Compiègne on the Soissons road (N31), and turn left just past the traffic lights, signposted Clairière de l'Armistice.*

Clairière
The armistice which ended World War I was signed in a railway carriage in the middle of Compiègne forest on 11 November 1918. Hitler insisted on using the same carriage again when the defeated French came to terms in 1940. The Führer danced a jig beneath the trees outside. An identical carriage is on display, with the original contents. *Open am and pm all year, except Tues. 15 Leaving the Clairière on the road to Choisy, at le Mancport turn right on to the D81 for Rethondes. Continue to Vic-sur-Aisne, where continue on the D91 for Soissons,* a pleasant winding drive, with views, along the Aisne valley.

Auberge au Bord de l'Eau
About 0.5 km off to the right on to the D17 in Port Fontenoy, this bar with a garden on the banks of the Aisne is perfect for a late drink to round off the day.

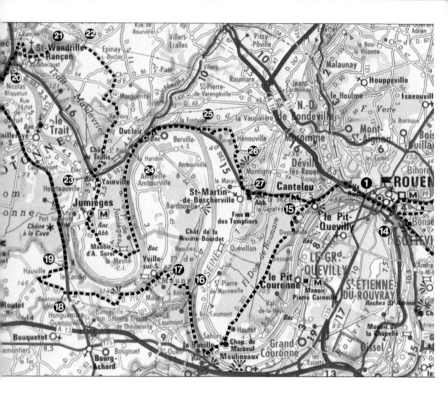

Rouen, the hub of this tour, is a cheerful, busy city, much damaged by bombs in World War II but superbly restored to its former glory. Streets lined with half-timbered houses, the Gothic cathedral (often painted by Monet), and several fine churches and museums all demand attention; but Rouen is only the start.

Route One includes pleasant châteaux, rural churches, a fortress with a view and a peep-show collection. For many, however, the highlight will be the modern art exhibition set in the garden of an enchanting château.

Route Two crosses the River Seine by road and by water, and goes in search of abbeys both ruined and flourishing - solemn legacies of Norman grandees.

Food is simple but plentiful - few signs of *nouvelle cuisine* here - and every menu includes the ubiquitous apple, as well as cream or cheese from Normandy's own breed of cow, whose brown and white colouring is enhanced by the dappled light of the orchards where it is so often seen grazing. The apple trees are in blossom from April to May, and of all seasons spring must be the best for exploring these charming parts.

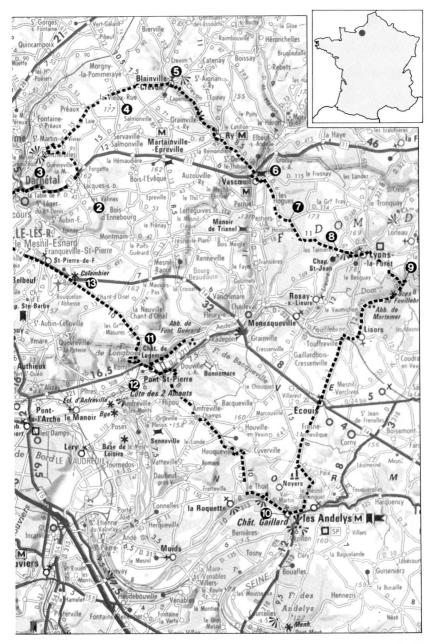

■ **ROUTE ONE 107 KM**

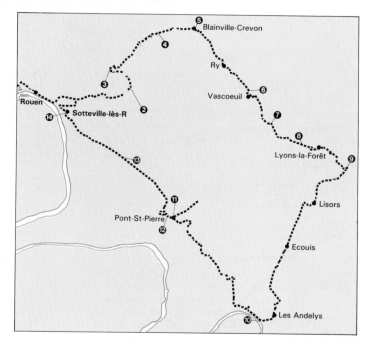

Rouen   Apart from the cathedral, be sure to take in the market place, with its medieval and modern architecture, where St Joan was martyred in 1432. By the side of the Cross of Rehabilitation, where the stake once stood, is the church of Joan of Arc, like a great ship in full sail, with side windows shaped like fishes swimming past, and the curved, green-crested roofs of the market the waves on which it rides. Inside, you must see the 16thC stained-glass windows rising from floor to ceiling.
① *Leave Rouen on the right bank of the river, following Beauvais/Amiens signs on to the N31.*
② *In 10 km (just before Forgette) slow down when you see on the left a large white silo, with a hexagonal tiled roof; immediately before the silo turn left on to a minor unsignposted road.*

Roncher-   ③ *Follow the D15 to the far end of the village.* At the *Cidre bouché*
olles   *fermier* sign, go down the drive to the farm, where M. Poixblanc will welcome you with a grin, a torrent of French, and copious tastings of his delicious cider, and also *poiré* (perry) grown from 200-year-old trees. Inspect the oak vats where the cider matures, then compare the sweet *cidre doux* with the dry *cidre bouché* before buying at very fair prices.
    Continue to La Vieux-Rue, passing several small charming châteaux.

La Vieux- ④ *At crossroads go straight ahead on the D61*. Pause to admire the tiny
Rue - Ry church, with its old wooden porch and new spire topped by an
amazingly lifelike red-crested cockerel.
Just beyond Gruchy (not on map) turn right at T-junction on to the D12.
⑤ *In central Blainville-Crevon, at crossroads, turn left on to the D7, then
turn right immediately on to the D12, signposted Ry*. Drive along the
valley, through which the tiny Crevon meanders peacefully. In 4 km the
wide verge, on the right by an uphill path, makes a good picnic spot.

Ry *Turn left at main crossroads* to visit the Madame Bovary Museum
(*Gallerie d'Automates*). As a tribute to Flaubert's famous novel, which
was was set in the village, M. Burgaud has made several hundred
miniature automatons, which act out scenes from *Madame Bovary*;
other subjects, including cowboys and eskimos, will appeal to children,
while Flaubert lovers may prefer the carefully restored Ry pharmacy,
also in the museum. *Open Easter to Oct, Sat-Mon.*

Auberge Next to the museum, this picturesque but comfortable inn (built in
la 1634) has four bedrooms and four dining rooms. Choose from the
Crevon- cheapest menu, for good plain cooking - the trout from the stream
nière running through the hotel grounds is particularly recommended; *tel
(hotel-* *35.23.60.52; closed Aug, Tues evening and Wed; price band B*. If you
restaurant, have time to spare before your meal, walk to the church to see the
Ry) rustic carved wooden porch (interior not worth visiting).
Rejoin the D12, signposted Vascoeuil.

⑥ *At the junction with the N31, turn right across bridge, then
immediately turn left*. Car park for Château de Vascoeuil on right.

Château This little-known château is one of the most charming in France.
de Lovingly restored to become a modern art collection, the works of art
Vascoeuil not only fill the château, but overflow into the informal gardens, where
sculptures and mosaics (Calder, Leger, Braque and others) grow
between trees. Important summer exhibitions, ranging from Dali to
Lurgat add to the permanent collection, and overflow into the elegant
stone dovecote usually devoted to tapestries. *Open Mar-Nov, 2.30-6.30.*

Vascoeuil - The route now continues through the remains of the great forest of
Lyons-la- Lyons, where dukes of Normandy once hunted. The tradition continues
Forêt still. From late autumn until spring, during the season of *la chasse*,
sportsmen aim at most things that move, so the numerous and lovely
walks are best enjoyed Apr-Oct.
⑦ *Beyond Les Hogues go over crossroads and in about 0.75 km the les
Molaises signpost indicates a route forestière. Turn left and park under
the beech trees for a shaded picnic, then return to road.*
On entering Les Tainières, stop to admire an unrestored timbered
farmhouse on the right.

⑧ *Beyond village take right fork* and in 90 metres park on the verge below statue for panoramic view of Lyons-la-Forêt.

Lyons-la-Forêt The tourist tradition of dining too well in France may have started with King Henry I of England, who died here of a surfeit of lampreys which he had eaten at Mortemer Abbey. The central 18thC covered marketplace offers a choice of food for picnics. The rest of the village is self-conscious and commercialized. *Turn left on to the D6, signposted Gisors, then after 3.5 km ⑨ turn right, signposted Abbaye de Mortemer.* Drive past the sources of Fouillebroc and St Catherine, unless actively seeking a husband (according to local legend).

Abbaye de Mortemer Ignore guided tour, and stroll through 12thC ruins to lake. Children will enjoy wandering among miniature deer, sheep and hungry ducks. At weekends there are train rides around the park. *Open 10-12, 2-6.*

Ecouis The 16thC twin-towered church is remarkable both for its wealth of carved wooden panels and its superb statuary, of which the most unusual is Sainte Marie l'Egyptien or St Agnes - her identity is uncertain. She is shown swathed in her hair,which ripples to her feet.

Ecouis - Approaching Les Andelys, Château Gaillard is silhouetted against the
Château sky. *In the town turn left on to the main road and follow signposts for*
Gaillard *Château Gaillard Autos (turn right opposite church).*

Château Gaillard You must stop in the car park as there is a one-way system, but if full there is an overflow car park further down the hill.

The remains of this important fortress are doubly impressive when one discovers that Richard Coeur-de-Lion, King of England and Duke of Normandy, built it in just one year (1196) to defend Rouen from the King of France. The moat was dug 14 metres deep and was not broached in his lifetime. It was Richard's brother, King John, who lost the castle, and thus Normandy, to France.

Walk along steep, rough and sometimes muddy paths to the ruins. Not worth paying for a guided tour of the fort, as access to most of the huge battlements is free, with panoramic views of the Seine in both directions. The faint-hearted may prefer the almost equally fine view from the hillside by the car park, which also makes a picnic site.
⑩ *At bottom of hill follow signpost* Autre Directions, *then at T-junction turn left, signposted Pont-St-Pierre.*

Pont-St-Pierre *After crossing the River Andelle in the middle of the village, turn right into avenue immediately before Auberge de l'Andelle* for magnificent view of a romantic château, and an ideal picnic spot on the river bank. If it is wet, the Auberge de l'Andelle makes a sound-value lunch stop. It is popular with locals, has a cheerful atmosphere and offers hearty cooking; *tel 31.49.70.18; price band B.*

Abbaye de Fontaine-Guérard
(detour)

(11) For a worthwhile detour, *continue 0.5 km, then at church take tiny road signposted Abbaye de Fontaine-Guérard.* Drive through overhanging beeches and past an ivy-clad 20thC medieval ruin, reminiscent of some horror movie set. The abbey itself, founded by the Earl of Leicester in the 12thC, is a genuine ruin and several rooms in the 13thC chapter house can be visited. *Open every afternoon except Mon in season.*
Return to Pont-St-Pierre.
(12) *Just beyond the village turn right on to the D138, signposted Rouen.*
(13) *At Boos, turn left on to the N14.*

Hotel St-Léonard
(Le Mesnil-Esnard)

After entering Le Mesnil-Esnard, turn right at third set of traffic lights and follow the hotel's own signposts. Situated next to the church, this is a typical, moderately-priced, family-run hotel in an extremely quiet setting; tel 35.80.16.88; closed 14-31 July.

Le Mesnil-Esnard - Rouen

(14) *This next turning is easily missed. Just before the N14 curves to the left to descend to Rouen (6.5 km after entering Le Mesnil-Esnard), take minor road to the right, signposted Corniche. Continue across roundabout,* and soon reach a spectacular viewpoint. Park in lay-by on left, crossing the road carefully to avoid traffic approaching round the blind corner. From here, the whole of Rouen lies below you. The view is best appreciated at sunset, perhaps with a bottle of wine. *Descend Corniche to Rouen.*

ROUTE TWO: 94 KM

The great clock tower gate, Rouen.

Rouen - La Bouille

Leaving Rouen along the right bank of the Seine, following signs to Duclair/Canteleu/Lillebonne. Take care not to enter Autoroute A15. At crest of the steep ascent from Rouen, where there are traffic lights with a church on the left, (15) *Turn left into minor road; the Sahurs signpost is only visible after turning.* Delightful wooded drive to Sahurs. *Go straight on at crossroads (signposted Bac de la Bouille).*

The Bac (small car ferry) will take you across the Seine to the romantic village of La Bouille for seven francs, every half hour, 6-10.

Hôtel le
St-Pierre
(La Bouille)

Eccentrically elegant, comfortable hotel with classy cooking (specialities are fish and game dishes). The cheaper menu is best value. *Booking advisable; tel 35.23.80.10; closed Tues evening and Wed, Nov-April; price bands C/D.* If booked up a pleasant alternative is the simple Hôtel de la Poste opposite; *tel 35.23.83.07.*

La Bouille -
Hauville

From La Bouille follow the Seine, with tiny farmsteads nestling between river and cliffs.
(16) *At La Ronce turn on to the D64a signposted Mauny, then immediately turn right on to the D265 signposted Yville.*
(17) *Turn left at junction with the D45 and in 90 metres pull on to verge for view of the 18thC Yville château and Seine. Continue to Barneville, then take the D101 to Hauville.*

Hauville -
St-Wandrille

(18) *After crossing the D313, a 15thC stone windmill soon comes into view. The car park has excellent information displays (in French only).*
(19) *From the village rejoin the D313, which continues through the edge of the forest of Brotonne. At Pont de Brotonne cross the spectacular suspension bridge (toll: ten francs).*
(20) *Immediately after the bridge turn right on to the D37, signposted St-Wandrille. Beneath bridge turn left on to the D982. NB: extremely dangerous crossing of main road - take great care. In 100 metres turn left to St-Wandrille; park against the abbey wall to the left of gate.*

St-
Wandrille

The ruins of the abbey, founded by the saint himself in the 7thC, are worth a visit but not a tour, especially for women, who are banned from the cloisters. The old church has almost disappeared but has been replaced by a medieval barn, transported 50 km and rebuilt by the monks. It is a remarkable experience to attend Mass or Vespers, listening to Gregorian chant as old as the abbey. Mass 9.15 (Sun and Feastdays 9.45); Vespers 5.30 (Sun and Feastdays 5).
Leave on the D22, then (21) *take the right fork (D263) through a wooded valley.* (22) *At next crossroads turn sharp right, signposted Duclair. Follow D20 back to main road,* descending through beech woods where grassy verges provide cool picnic places.
(23) *Turn left on to the D982; shortly after turn right on to the D143 signposted Jumièges.*

Jumièges

The towering ruins of the Benedictine abbey are among the finest in France. The church was built by Abbot Robert, later Archbishop of Canterbury, and William the Conqueror attended its consecration in 1067. There are no guides to hurry you along. *Open 9-12, 2-6 May-Sept; 10-12, 2-4 Oct-Apr; closed Tues.*
Most abbey visitors ignore the church up the hill, but if you penetrate the Ministry of Works rubble (and go through the temporary internal partition), you will be well rewarded by the 11th and 12thC stonework and the naive painted wooden statues.

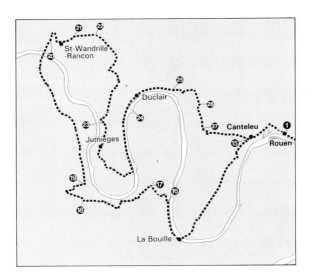

Restaurant du Bac
(Jumièges)

Take road signposted Bac de Jumièges to this old riverside inn. Friendly, informal (goat living in car park) and popular with locals, its amazing value four-course menu gives good Norman cooking in generous quantity. Particularly delicious pheasant pâté, and *escalope de veau vallée d'Auge.* In mid-meal, try the sorbet drenched in Calvados. *Booking advisable; closed Wed and Tues evening (and Mon evening out of season); tel 35.37.24.16; price band A.*

Jumièges - St-Martin-de-Boscher-villea

Follow the D65, passing through an archetypal Normandy scene of timbered farmsteads, each surrounded by its orchard, contentedly shared by grazing sheep, cows, hens and ducks. Just before Mesnil-sous-Jumièges, on the left, a farmhouse incorporates the remains of the manor where Agnès Sorel, mistress of Charles VII, died. Beyond the Bac at Mesnil the road runs between the river and orchards, where many of the farmers sell fruit, and possibly Calvados, at their gates. The local speciality is the Benedictine apple, once grown by the monks, which eats well but does not store (avoid M. Sellier who is wholesale only).
㉔ *Turn right on to the D982.* After Duclair, you stay beside the Seine, while on your left the base of the cliff provides cellars and garages.
㉕ *At La Fontaine take the D86 to Henouville, then immediately fork right.*
㉖ *At far end of Henouville turn right at crossroads;* about 300 metres downhill pause opposite a wooden gateway for a superb view across river and plain; in another 200 metres, a picnic site on verge.

St-Martin-de-Boscherville

㉗ *Turn left on to the D982 and immediately take right fork (D67).* It is well worth entering this Romanesque church, whose white interior has hardly changed since the 11thC. *Return to D982; continue to Rouen.*

From the tall, slate-fronted buildings around the harbour of Normandy's most picturesque fishing port, Honfleur, and the *planches* and casino of fashionable Deauville, it is only half an hour's drive to the rolling hills, green pastures, gentle valleys and romantic manor houses of this lovely part of Normandy.

The tour steers a careful course around the commercial and industrial city of Lisieux. Auge manors are a feature of the route; they vary considerably - from moated, timber-framed farmhouses, patterned with tiles or ornate brickwork, to minor châteaux built in the classical style. Most can be viewed from the outside only, but a few are open to the public.

The Pays d'Auge is also cider and cheese country. Regimented orchards cover large areas of the countryside, and there are many places where you can watch the cider-making process and buy flagons of liquid apple in various strengths - from juice to cider to the potent Calvados brandy. Normandy cheese is soft and luxurious, just like the scenery; along the route there are plenty of places where you can buy direct from the churn.

Those who require high standards of creature comfort need to search quite hard in the Pays d'Auge. The Hôtel de France in Orbec (see below) is much more than adequate, but for something special try the Auberge de Vieux Puits in Pont-Audemer, about 36 km north-east of Lisieux, *tel 32.41.01.48*. Timber-framed and complete with a cobbled courtyard, its reasonably priced bedrooms (though simple and a touch cramped) have plenty of rustic character, and the food (*price band C*) is among the best in Normandy.

▬▬▬ ROUTE: 146 KM

Orbec

In contrast to Lisieux, which is big and dull and exploits its pilgrimage factor to the full, the small country town of Orbec seems unconcerned about the tourist potential of its old buildings and its lazy, rustic atmosphere.

Hôtel de France
(hotel-rest-aurant, Orbec)

This may not be the oldest building in Orbec, but it is certainly one of the grandest. Bedrooms are comfortable and not expensive. The food cannot compete with that served at the town's most highly regarded restaurant, but it is good enough, and you can have *escargots* and *Saumon au Sauce Normande* for less than half the price you will pay for the cheapest meal at the quaint Au Caneton down the road.
Tel 31.32.74.02; closed mid-Dec to mid-Jan, Sun evening from mid-Nov to mid-Mar; price band B.

Orbec - Bellou

① *Take the D4, the Livarot road, out of Orbec. After about 8 km, turn left along the D161. Pass through Préaux, then turn right at the crossroads (the road is unsignposted and is not marked on the map). The D4 is far from dull, but the narrow minor road you turn on to is much more*

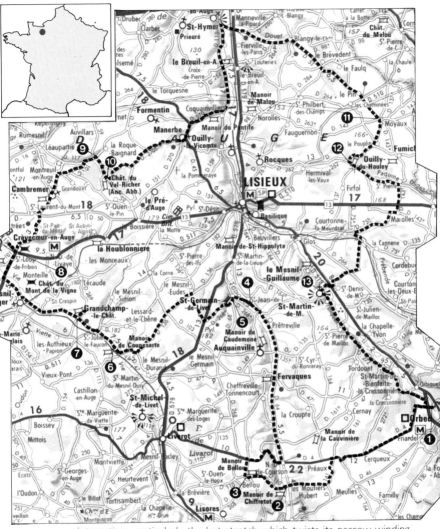

interesting, particularly the last stretch which twists its narrow winding way through woodland down to the Touques valley.

② *At the junction with the D64, at Les Moutiers-Hubert, turn left on to the D110 signposted Bellou.* The road crosses the river then winds up to the flat, tree-covered land at the top of the valley. Past the apple orchards, look out for a huddle of old farm buildings on your right, and pull over to admire the unostentatious, timbered perfection of 16thC Bellou, the first Auge manor on the tour.

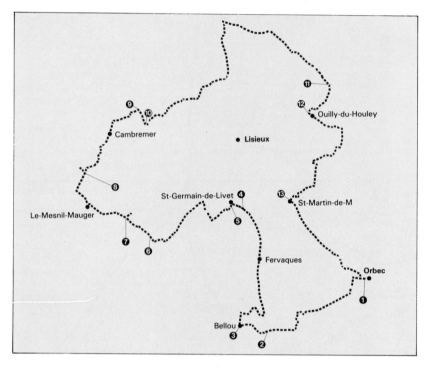

Bellou - St-Germain-de-Livet

③ *Take the next turning to the right, then turn right again at the main road. At the D64, turn left.* The undemanding nature of this road, which follows the meandering course of the wide valley of the Touques, allows drivers plenty of time to enjoy the gentle peace of the scenery. At Fervaques you pass a grand, sprawling château, now a music institution for the handicapped.

④ *At St-Jean-de-Livet, follow the signs - first left, then right - to St-Germain.*

St-Germain-de-Livet

This 15th-16thC château is one of the high points of the tour. Turrets, towers and timbers, and cleverly patterned bricks and stonework are reflected in the waters of the moat, while inside there are Renaissance frescoes, oak furniture and thick, creaking floorboards. The tiny car-park is the first encouraging sign that St-Germain-de-Livet is not on a well-trodden tourist track, but the fact that you have to pull the bell cord to call the *gardien* to gain entrance is what really makes you feel you are entering a privileged and private world. *Open 10-12 and 2-7 (2-5 Oct-Mar); closed Tues and mid-Dec to Jan.*

St-Germain - Coupesarte

⑤ *Return along the road leading to the château, then take the first right.* The narrow road climbs up, providing splendid views over the château and its estate; it continues along a ridge, drops down to a river and then rises up into the hills on its way to the D579. *Go straight across the main road*, and prepare yourself for a short stretch of narrow, badly surfaced, bumpy and extremely twisting lanes where grass pokes through the asphalt. You have to drive slowly here, and follow the directions carefully; the road is not marked on the map. *Where the signs indicate a cider farm to your left, bear right; at a T-junction opposite an old farm, turn left; and, at the next T-junction, turn left along the D136.* Beyond the crossroads this becomes a fine drive, past one very grand (and another less imposing but still stylish) stud farm; the views stretch into the distance. *At the junction with the D47 fork right.*

Manoir de Coupe-sarte

A short track leads to the most romantic of all the Auge manors. You cannot go inside the timbered farmhouse and you are not allowed to picnic beside it, but you can stand by the moat and admire this masterpiece of medieval domestic architecture.

⑥ *Continue to St-Julien-le-Faucon and turn left along the D511.*

De la Levrette
(restaurant, St-Julien)

The young owners of this modest, old roadside hotel are enthusiastic and welcoming, and understand the needs of those with young children. The country-style cooking is in the tradition of the area. *Price band A.*

⑦ *Opposite the hotel, take the D269, signposted Grandchamp-le-Château.*

St-Julien - Crève-coeur-en-Auge

When you reach the war memorial, turn right. The sight of the old timbered house here, with its grand, classical-style addition, is well worth this short detour. Fine old gatehouses stand at the corners of the manicured, moated gardens.

Return to the D269E. At Le Mesnil-Mauger, turn right, then right again on to the main road. At Crèvecoeur-en-Auge turn left on to the N13, and then right at the signpost to the Manoir de Crèvecoeur.

Manor, Bellou.

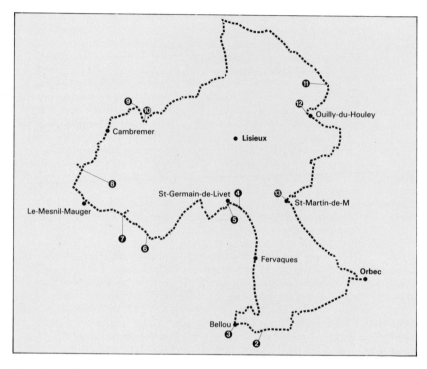

Manoir de Crèvecoeur

The main road is a little too near and the restored buildings are almost too perfect, but this is a museum rather than a home - and it does offer you the chance to look inside an Auge manor and to explore its outbuildings. Curiously, much of the museum is devoted to petroleum engineering and research, but there is a collection of old agricultural implements in the gatehouse and an audio-visual presentation on Norman architecture in the chapel. *Open 12-8, daily in July and Aug but closed Tues in June and Sept; closed Dec-Jan; weekends only rest of year.*

Crèvecoeur - La RoqueBaignard

⑧ *Return along the main road to the crossroads and turn left. At the junction with the D50 turn right then immediately left on to the D101, following the signs to La Roque-Baignard. The drive to Cambremer, and particularly beyond this cheerful village, is one of the most appealing sections of the tour. The road climbs past cider farms to wind its way along lush valleys and up, over and around rolling green hills, passing old farms and smallholdings. The sloping, grassy fields are ideal for picnics.*

La RoqueBaignard - Moyaux

⑨ *At the junction with the D59, turn right (or continue straight on for a short detour to a picturesque old cottage where you can buy delicious home-made chèvre). Slow down to enjoy the isolated leafy setting of* the château of La Roque-Baignard, and not far beyond, look up and to the right for a brief glimpse of a more formal and grand château, the abbey of Val-Richer.

(10) Fork left along the D270B. At Manerbe, turn left along the main road, then turn right on to the D270. At the T-junction turn left, then after about 5 km turn right on to the D280A, signposted (but the signpost faces away from you) Blangy-le-Château. From Blangy follow the signs to Moyaux. There is no shortage of interesting scenery along this section of the route; woodland is followed by the wide Touques valley, then the more intimate valley of the Chaussey and more woodland. At Le Brévedent there are evocative old farmbuildings; and on the final stretch, the leaning spire of Moyaux church provides comic relief.

Moyaux -
Orbec
(11) Just past the church, turn right for Ouilly-du-Houley. The thick woodland before Ouilly offers picnic possibilities, and as the road descends to the tiny village, look up and left to the massive château. *(12) At the stop sign past the Auberge de la Paquine, turn left along the D262, then turn right at the crossroads, signposted Marolles. Soon after crossing the N13, turn right along the D75B, signposted Courtonne-la-Mac (Courtonne-la-Meurdrac). At the D75 turn left, then first right, signposted La Gare. At the minor crossroads, go straight over, signposted St-Denis-de-Mailloc.* This is the most complicated section of the tour, so follow the directions carefully. Some of the roads are narrow and badly surfaced, but that - given the scenery - is part of the charm. *(13) At the main road (D519), turn right. After about 100 metres, turn left along the D149, then left again on to the D272.* Much of this road is single-track and there are several blind corners where you need to sound your horn; but it would be difficult to contrive a more unspoilt sequence of backroads for the closing stretch. *At the junction with the D519, turn right to Orbec.*

The area covered in the first loop of this tour is called the Suisse Normande, though there are no Matterhorns or alpine lakes here, not even any particularly high ground.

On its winding north-westerly course the River Orne has cut through the *massif*, creating steep banks and the occasional severe peak. The scenery along the valley is amongst Normandy's prettiest and most interesting, and although in terms of mere metres the heights may not be impressive, they certainly provide some dizzying views. The area is popular for a variety of other reasons. Many come for the canoeing, walking, fishing or rock-climbing; others come simply to throw themselves off the Pain de Sucre - firmly attached to their hang-gliders, of course.

The second loop of the tour takes you into the Parc Naturel Régional Normandie Maine, where bands of thick forest cover high ridges. There are few sights here but no shortage of marvellous views, and there is great scope for getting away from it all - something that is not always easy to do in the Suisse Normande.

If possible, allow two or three days for this tour - to attempt it in a day would mean missing too much. Clécy and Mortain are the best places for overnight stops; if you prefer to have just one base, choose Clécy.

Opposite: the church, Lonlay-l'Abbaye, Route Two.

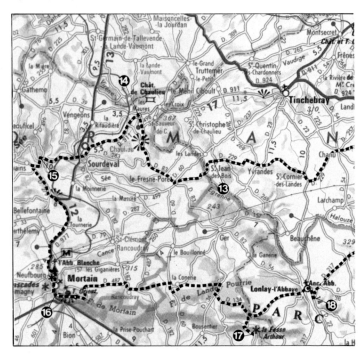

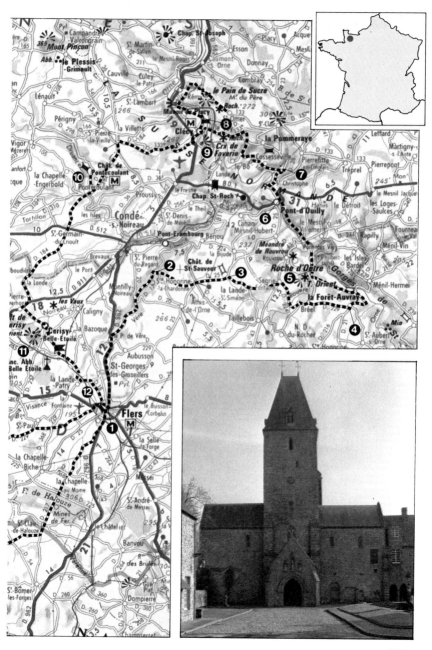

▉▉▉▉ **ROUTE ONE: 90 KM**

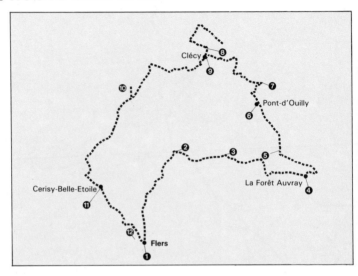

Flers -
Château de
St-Sauveur

There is little to keep you in Flers, so stop at the filling station, stock up with picnic provisions, take a quick look at the château on the east side of town, then head out of town.

① *Take the Caen road for about 4 km, then turn right along the D17, signposted Pont-Erambourg, and follow the river for about 7 km.* This is an evocative drive along a lush, steep-sided valley past a succession of moody, dark old mills which long since ceased turning out textiles.

② *Take the hairpin right turn on to the C10 (not on map) signposted Ste-Honorine.* The almost single-track road winds steeply up through forest to the heights. Just past a crossroads, look out for the château (La Pompelière) to your left. *At the junction with the D15 turn right, then turn left on to the D25, signposted Château de St-Sauveur.*

Château
de St-
Sauveur

The Renaissance was a time for decorative skills, extravagance and flights of fancy. The controlled, classical style of architecture that followed can seem cold in comparison, but this small, moated Louis XIII château retains some fine original panelling and is elegantly furnished. *Open 2.30-4.30; closed Tues, Wed and Feb; Oct-May open weekends and national holidays only.*

Château de
St-Sauveur -
La Forêt-
Auvray

③ *Turn left on to the D25, then turn right along the C3. At La Lande-St-Siméon turn right, signposted Segrie-Fontaine. At Segrie take the D224 to Bréel, then the D229 to La Forêt-Auvray.* These are beautiful, sleepy backroads through unspoilt villages of mellow old houses. Take your time and stop to explore either Bréel or La Forêt.

La Forêt-Auvray - Roche d'Oëtre

④ *From La Forêt take the D21, signposted Ménil* The views over the Orne valley from the road out of the village are a breathtaking taste of the scenery that is to come later on the tour. *At the valley bottom, just before the road crosses the river, turn left, signposted Roche d'Oëtre.* Soon after you turn off to the Roche, just after a double bend, stop at one of the gaps in the wall for a glimpse of an ancient fortified manor.

Roche d'Oëtre

The signs warn you to take care, and so you should. There are no guard rails at this magnificent viewpoint over the wild and wooded Rouvre Gorges, just a sheer 119-metre drop - the Suisse Normande at its most dramatic. There is a café at the top, with tables outside; unfortunately, but understandably, the notices put up by the *patron* make it clear that these are not for picnickers. There are, however, other places nearby where you can unleash your hamper.

Roche d'Oëtre - Pont-d'Ouilly

⑤ *Follow the D329 through St-Philbert to Pont des Vers.* From the deceptively high ground around the Roche, you wind down to the Orne to pass under the high arches of the 'pont'. *At the D18 turn left, then turn right on to the D167.*

Pont-d'Ouilly

Just before the sign announcing Pont-d'Ouilly, pull into the lay-by on the right and cross the road. A track to your left or steps to your right take you down to the river bank, where you can enjoy the Orne in one of its tranquil moods. There is plenty of space for a picnic; you can even hire a pedal boat to appreciate the river from a different perspective. Pont-d'Ouilly itself is one of the biggest villages (but not the most charming) in the Suisse Normande.
⑥ *Take the Thury-Harcourt road out of the village, then turn left along the D23, to St-Christophe.*

Auberge St-Christophe *(hotel-restaurant)*

This creeper-clad restaurant with nine well-equipped and newly decorated rooms is run with great care by the youthful M. and Mme Lecoeur. During the day you may have to pick your way through the toys of Lecoeur junior on your way to the dining room, but whether you are looking for a not-too-expensive lunch or a more extravagant evening treat, you are unlikely to be disappointed. *Tel 31.69.81.23; closed Sun evening (and Mon out of season); price band B.*

St-Christophe - Clécy

⑦ *Continue along the D23, then turn left on to the D168 and follow the signs to Clécy.* It is a gentle, wooded and winding route to this village in the heart of the Suisse Normande. At several points (but best from Le Bô) there are views of the steep rocky escarpment of the Pain de Sucre. The drive is easy, but take it slowly, stopping along the way at Le Vey; here you can picnic by the river, relax in a waterside café, or if you are energetic - hire a boat. You might even stay longer, at the comfortable riverside Moulin du Vey, *tel 31.69.71.08,* although rooms are about twice the price of those at Le Site Normand in Clécy.

Clécy   Clécy's tidy charm is appropriate for the main tourist spot of the Suisse
             Normande. There is not much to see here - just the church and the
             16thC Manoir de Placy, which houses a museum *(open 2-6 Sun and daily
             in July-Aug; closed Nov-Mar)* - but there are hotels and restaurants.

Le Site   Both the accommodation and the food at this half-timbered hotel and
Normand   restaurant, right in the middle of Clécy, represent good value.
(hotel-rest- Bedrooms are prettily decorated and comfortable, and the meals in the
aurant,   traditionally decorated restaurant are reliable. *Tel 31.69.71.05; closed
Clécy)*   mid-Jan to Feb and Mon mid-Sept to Mar; price band B.*

Route des ⑧ *For a detour to the top of the Pain de Sucre, take the D133C from
Crêtes,   Clécy, past the Auberge de Chalet de Cantepie, and just as you reach St
Pain de   Rémy, take the sharp right turn, signposted Route des Crêtes.* There are
Sucre   many rewarding trips you can take from Clécy, but this is one you
(detour)   should not miss. Follow the road until you reach a large grassy area
             which has been set aside for parking, and walk across to the edge of
             the ridge. The views over the meandering Orne are stunning. Less than
             one km further on, on the edge of the escarpment, is a hang-glider's
             launching ramp. *Return to Clécy the way you came.*

Clécy -   ⑨ *Go straight down the hill from the church in Clécy, cross the main
Ponté-   road, then follow the D133A and the signs to the château.* You may be
coulant   leaving the Suisse Normande, but the first 5 km of this drive, along a
             green valley, are particularly attractive. *The last sign to the château (as
             you come into the village of Pontécoulant) faces away from you and is
             difficult to see.*

Château   Sadly, but luckily for us, this is no longer a family home; old and
de Ponté- heirless, the owner of this charming lakeside château transferred it into
coulant   the hands of the local *département.* Long, formal lawns front the
             16th-18thC house, and behind there is woodland. The interior is
             somewhat musty but still very homely, and the ground and first-floor
             rooms shown on the guided tour contain many fine pieces of furniture
             from different periods and countries. *Open 10-12 and 2.30-6 (4.30 in
             winter); closed Tues and Oct.*
             ⑩ *Return to Pontécoulant village and take the D184, through St-
             Germaine-du-Crioult to St-Pierre d'Entremont. Turn right along the main
             D911, then turn left to Cerisy.*

Cerisy   The high, wooded hill of Mont de Cerisy, which overlooks this little
             village, is a popular spot. A toll road curves up through rhododendrons
             to the summit, where the surprising array of facilities includes tennis
             courts and a boating lake. Other attractions are the views across to the
             Suisse Normande from the rather spooky ruined château, and the
             chance to stroll or picnic among the woods.
             ⑪ *From Cerisy, follow the signs back to Flers.*

ROUTE TWO: 75 KM

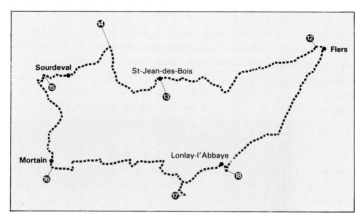

Flers -
Mortain

⑫ *Take the D25 out of Flers for about 1.5 km, then turn right along the D268, signposted St-Paul.* Beyond Chanu, the rural character of this route takes an increasingly firm hold, and once you are across the D22 the views over the Normandy countryside become more and more extensive.

⑬ *At St-Jean-des-Bois turn left along the D237 to Le Fresne-Poret, then turn right along the D83 to Les Maures.* There are some fine views from these minor roads, particularly around St-Martin-de-Chaulieu (not marked on map). *At Les Maures a short detour to the right, along the D911 for 100-200 metres, and then left along a bumpy track, brings you to a derelict château* - a quiet and atmospheric place for a picnic.

⑭ *Return to Les Maures and head west along the D911. At Sourdeval continue on the D911, signposted Vallée de Brouains.* Twisting and turning, the road descends through the fertile valley; steep slopes, dotted with remote farms, open out to more mellow countryside.

⑮ *After about 5 km, and just before a double bend and a tall chimney, turn left on to the D279, then follow the signs to Mortain.* Excitement follows the easy charm of the valley, as you negotiate this steep, narrow backroad up to the security of the D977, at a point which entirely justifies its name of Bellevue.

Mortain

One of the decisive, last battles of the Normandy campaign of World War II took place in the Mortain region, and this small unpretentious town which nestles high up on the edge of the Lower Normandy hills, looking out over the great expanse of the Sélune basin, has been largely rebuilt since that week of fighting and devastation. Mortain is a place to spend some time. Apart from the church of St-Evroult, which has a fine Romanesque doorway, most of the sights lie around the edge of the town. On the D977, to the north, is the Abbaye Blanche, an old monastery which is now a seminary and cultural centre. On the guided tour you are shown the chapter house, chapel and part of the cloister, all of which are 12thC. There is also an exhibition of African art, *open July to Mid-Sept, 10-12 and 2-6.* Above the town, to the east, there are wide views across the wooded countryside of the Parc Naturel Régional from the Petite Chapelle, and below the town there are two pretty waterfalls. If you find the leafy setting of the Grande Cascade too shaded (or too crowded) for a picnic, walk past the Petite Cascade to the wooded hillocks near the tiny chapel of St-Vital, built in the rocks.

The Grande Cascade, Mortain.

Cascades *(restaurant, Mortain)* Mortain does not lack hotels, only stylish accommodation. Similarly it is not short of restaurants, only places serving outstanding food. For a good-value lunch, however, the restaurant of this small hotel in the middle of the town is more than adequate. *Tel 33.59.00.51; closed Sun evening and Mon, early Mar and end-Sept to mid-Oct; price band A.*

Mortain -
La Fosse
Arthour

⑯ *Take the Domfront road out of Mortain, then turn left along the D487.*
Follow the Barenton signs (D182) from Rancoudray, pass the left turn back
on to the D487, and take the next turning to the left (unsignposted and
not marked on map). Turn right on to the D60, then first left, signposted
Le Breuil. At the D36 turn right, then turn left along the D134, signposted
La Fosse Arthour. This section of the tour may seem rather complicated
but it is about the most direct route to La Fosse and, with the
exception of the short stretch along the D36, the countryside you pass
through is completely off the beaten track. Even farms and houses are

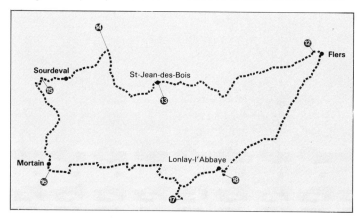

few and far between on these backroads which follow a high ridge,
partly forested and partly open, before dropping down to the floor of
a valley. Then comes the delectable approach through trees to La
Fosse, along the narrow and winding D134.

La Fosse
Arthour

After the totally unspoilt countryside of the drive from Mortain, La
Fosse Arthour brings you back to earth. Signs tell you where to park
and how to behave, and there is a modern restaurant. From the road
past the restaurant there are views of the River Sonce as it cuts its way
through steep banks to enter a large pool, and then departs in a
succession of little waterfalls. You should not expect anything quite as
splendid as the scenery along the Orne valley in the Suisse Normande,
but La Fosse offers the chance to picnic among restful scenery.
⑰ *Retrace a short way, then turn right to Lonlay-l'Abbaye.* Enchanting
roads led you to La Fosse; enchanting roads take you away.

Lonlay-
l'Abbaye

Dignity, beauty and tranquility - the church at Lonlay-l'Abbaye has all
three - from the outside, at least. It was part of an 11thC abbey, and
its presence dominates this village which nestles among wooded hills.
⑱ *Fork left by the war memorial in the village; turn left at T-junction,*
then follow the signs to Flers.

Southern Normandy:

HARAS DU PIN AND THE PERCHE

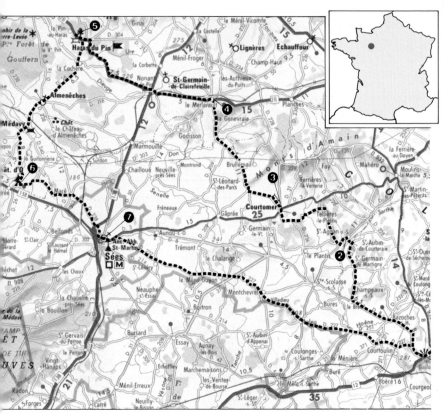

This tour is exceptionally full of interest and variety. The longer, northern loop takes in the equine elegance of the national stud at Haras du Pin, the extremely romantic Château d'O, and the cathedral town of Sées. The southern loop explores the more intimate countryside of the Normandy Perche, an area famous for its powerful Percheron horses (this is one of only three areas in France where the sturdy dray horses are bred) and its manor houses. Perche manors are quite different to the cosy, half-timbered farmhouses of the Pays d'Auge (see the tour in that area); they are much more defensive-looking structures, built of stone and embellished with turrets and towers. Unfortunately, only La Vove opens its doors to the public, but the route also takes you past several of the area's most noble *gentilhommeries*.

The scenery of the Perche is gentle and picturesque rolling hills, in part clothed by dense forest, and lush valleys. Grazing Percherons add an air of serenity; and throughout the region there are numerous seductive villages and small towns. Chief among these are Mortagne, the old capital of the Perche, and Bellême, the present capital, with its fine houses and splendid decorated church.

Mortagne is also the hub of the tour, and makes a convenient base. If you want to make an overnight stop *en route*, Sées would be a sound choice: it has several inexpensive, simple hotels. The driving on both loops presents no problems, and the route is far from complicated. Bear in mind that although the southern circuit is the shorter of the two, you will probably want to linger more along the way.

ROUTE ONE: 104 KM

Mort-
agne-au-
Perche

Although it is no longer the capital of the region, Mortagne is still the main tourist magnet of the Normandy Perche. The Porte-St-Denis, which houses a small local museum, is the only significant remaining part of the original 15thC fortifications, but numerous fine old houses survive in the streets, alleys and squares of this thriving hilltop town. The church dates from the late 15thC, and contains a huge carved altarpiece which came from a monastery in the nearby Réno Forest. There is an attractive though somewhat shabby arcaded market building, at one end of which is the tourist office, at the other a cinema.

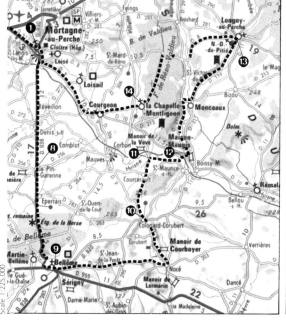

The sturdy Percheron.

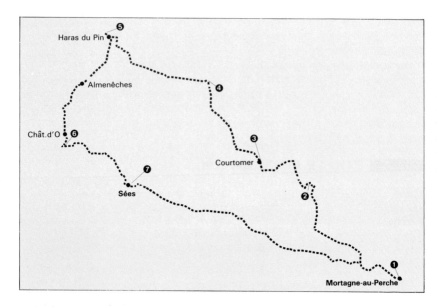

Hôtel Tribunal
(hotel-restaurant, Mortagne)

A quick look at the visitors' book will be reassurance enough: from the British who have made an overnight stop on their way to the beaches of the South of France, to the French, Germans, Dutch and other Europeans who have used it as a base for touring the Normandy Perche, all are generous in their comments about the food and the accommodation. The hotel occupies lovely old buildings on a quiet square near the church. The entrance hall, which is also the breakfast room and sitting room, is homely and welcoming - just as a country *auberge* should be. The restaurant is equally atmospheric, although slightly more formal. Bedrooms are inexpensive and perfectly adequate for a stay of one or two nights. For lunch, you will probably be happy to settle for the basic three-course menu, which includes a dish of the day; for dinner it is worth splashing out on one of the more extravagant menus. *4 Place du Palais; tel 33.25.04.77; closed Christmas-New Year; price band A.*

Mortagne-au-Perche - Haras du Pin

① *Take the Alençon road out of Mortagne, then turn right along the D8. Beyond Bazoches, and about 10 km from Mortagne, turn right on to the C5, signposted Champeaux-sur-Sartre. At the crossroads, where there is a calvary, bear left along the D271, signposted St-Agnan. Once you have turned off the fast D8, this becomes an appealing backroads drive. First, you pass an imposing château painted brilliant white; then you wind through sleepy, undulating countryside.*

② *At the junction with the D6, turn left, then turn right to rejoin the D271. After about 3 km turn left along the C2, signposted Tellières. Go straight on (not right) over the narrow river at the bottom of the hill, then turn right on to the D236 at the T-junction.* The D271 twists its way up a steep hill, through forest, with occasional fine views, while the C2 takes you past a small fortified manor and on through delightful stretches of woodland.

③ *At the D3 turn right, then left immediately along the D4.* On leaving Courtomer, note the large, privately owned château on the right. *Continue along the D4 to Le Merlerault.*

④ *At Le Merlerault turn left on to the N26 and follow the signs to Haras du Pin.* This is a fast main road which becomes increasingly attractive beyond Nonant-le-Pin.

Haras du Pin

Even those who don't love horses will be impressed by the style, indeed the majesty of the national stud. Uniformed stable lads (for no more than a gratuity) blind you with statistics about the size, speed and fecundity of the immaculately groomed stallions; the guided tour also includes a tack room full of finery and a collection of carriages. The stud was founded by Colbert, Louis XIV's minister; the small but imposing château (not open) was designed by Mansart, and the gardens by Le Nôtre, although both men are better known for their contributions to Versailles. From the château you can look out over lush countryside, or back through the main gate up a long and wide woodland ride. Even if you miss the spectacle of the horses setting off for or returning from their daily exercise, don't forgo a stroll along this grand, green avenue - and take your picnic things with you. The stables have most visitors mid-July to mid-Feb; horse races and carriage processions take place *the first Sun in Sept and the second Sun in Oct; guided tours 9-12 and 2-6.*

National stud, Haras du Pin.

Haras du *Pin -* *Chât. d'O*	⑤ *Go back a short way along the N26, then turn right along the D26 and follow the signs to Château d'O. At Médavy pull off the road to admire the 18thC château and the domed gate towers in the grounds.*
Château **d'O**	This place is as enchanting as the family name is curious. Elaborate and moated, its turrets, steeples and steep-sloping roofs are straight from a fairy tale. The original east wing is 15thC, the south wing is 16thC, and the west wing (the living quarters) is 18thC. The guided tour is brief. There are some fine statues in the rooms you are shown. One of the farm buildings has been converted into a restaurant (*de la Fèrme; menus start at price band B*); *open 2.30-6, 2.30-5 out of season, closed Tues.*
Château *d'O - Sées*	⑥ *Take the lane opposite the main gate of the château. Turn left at the T-junction, then turn right on to the C12. At Macé turn left, then turn right along the D238 to Sées.*
Sées	Sées has been an ecclesiastical centre since it became a bishopric in the 4thC, and its cathedral, whose magnificent spires can be seen from afar, is a fine example of Norman Gothic. The interior contains some fine 13thC stained glass, and is beautifully proportioned. However, the same cannot be said for the exterior, which is marred by the addition of ugly, unwieldy buttresses dating from the 16thC when the building was in danger of falling down due to subsidence. Although this act of constructive vandalism may have saved the cathedral, there is no denying that Sées has declined in importance over the years. More than a lick of paint is needed to restore the town to its former glory, but for all that it is an agreeable, unpretentious place. The numerous monasteries and seminaries combine to create an atmosphere of serenity around the cathedral; and it is worth looking at the former Bishops' Palace, the 18thC abbey and the old market building.
Nor- **mandy** *(restaurant,* *Sées)*	Its position, just across the road from the cathedral, no doubt brings this modest and popular restaurant a large share of the tourist trade. Marie Antoinette would not have approved (for herself, at least) of the workmanlike surroundings and plain cooking, but for holidaymakers on a budget there is much to be said for easily affordable prices. *Pl Gén-de-Gaulle; tel 33.27.80.67; closed mid-Sept to early Oct; price band A.*
Chéval **Blanc** *(hotel-* *restaurant,* *Sées)*	Sées is not the home of sophistication, and the rooms at the Chéval Blanc are unequivocably simple. However, the restaurant is slightly smarter than the Normandy, and the cooking is a touch more adventurous. *1 Pl St Pierre; tel 33.27.80.48; closed early Mar and mid-Oct to early Nov, and Sat out of season; price band B.*
Sées - *Mortagne-* *au-Perche*	⑦ *Take the D3 out of Sées, then turn right along the D227. At the junction with the D31 turn right, then almost immediately turn left to rejoin the D227. Join the D8 and follow the signs to Mortagne.*

ROUTE TWO 82 KM

Local farmhouse architecture.

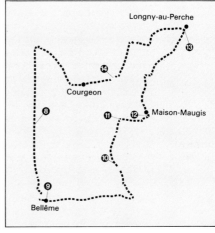

Mortagne-au-Perche - Le Pin-la-Garenne

From Mortagne take the D938, signposted Bellême. Typically French (but for the switchbacks), this road leaves Mortagne via an avenue of tall plane trees, and then heads, straight as an arrow, for Le Pin-la-Garenne, with some long views over the gentle scenery of the Perche. At Le Pin, tarmacadam smoothness gives way to ruts and the occasional pothole, as the road winds its way through the village. At the right-angle bend by the Hôtel des Voyageurs (see below) another avenue of trees leads up to a fine château. Although it is not open to the public, there is nothing to stop you driving up to the gates of the château; the avenue makes a pleasant walk, too.

Hôtel des Voyageurs *(restaurant, Le Pin-la-Garenne)*

Close your ears to the noise from the main road, and enjoy the creeper-clad exterior, cosy interior and low prices of this country inn. As the yellow and green sign indicates, it is a member of the generally reliable Logis and Auberges de France. *Tel 33.25.25.46; closed late Dec to early Jan, Sun evening and Mon; price band A.*

⑧ *Continue along the D938.* There are a few bends and bumps before the road recovers its sheen and lunges straight ahead into the distance on its roller-coaster route. Soon you enter the dense woodland of the Forest of Bellême. Look out on your left for a lake (Etang de la Herse); there are plenty of paths and delightful picnic places in the vicinity.

Bellême

The name is apt: Bellême has a turbulent past. It was the fortress of the Counts of Alençon, and was the site of many battles during the Middle Ages. Its position, on a spur, exemplifies its strategic importance, and the remaining fortifications are a powerful reminder of those brutal times.

Bellême is best appreciated if approached as follows. *When you reach the roundabout at the top of the hill (there are a couple of restaurants on your left) go straight over, continuing on the main road. Soon after, just by the war memorial, turn left, following the signs to the car park.* Before you enter the main gate to the town, wander along the narrow Rue Ville-Close to your right; here are some of Bellême's finest houses - stately 17thC and 18thC buildings, somewhat faded and peeling but still elegant. Through the gate is the town's spacious and steeply sloping main square, the focal point of which is the church. St-Saveur is no Gothic masterpiece, merely a squat 17thC local church, but its elaborately carved and richly painted interior is memorable.

Bellême -
La Vove

⑨ *Follow the signs towards Rémalard, then turn right on to the D203, through St-Jean-de-la-Fôret. At Nocé, head towards the church and take the D9, signposted Mortagne.* This is a route which gradually seduces you into the charms of the Normandy Perche. Pleasing until you reach St-Jean, undeniably pretty from St-Jean to Nocé, then uplifting (in all senses of the word) along the D9. But don't get carried away; look out on your right for the Manoir de Courboyer, and stop for a glimpse of this prince of Perche manors, with its round turrets and towers - both homely and dignified.
⑩ *At Colonard-Corubert turn left, then turn right along the D9 and follow the signs to Courcerault.* This is a marvellous stretch along twisting roads, through woodland, with views. *At Courcerault, go straight on; just after a mill house* (antiques enthusiasts should stop to browse) *turn left at the T-junction, for a short detour along the D256 to the Manoir de la Vove.*

Manoir
de la
Vove

La Vove is unique among Perche manors. It is not a particularly stunning example of local domestic architecture (although you will not be disappointed); but it is the only manor in this area that you can visit. *Open 10-5; closed Nov-Apr.*

Manoir de
la Vove -
Maison-
Maugis

⑪ *Head east along the D256; at the junction with the D10, turn right. Before you reach Boissy Maugis, turn left along the narrow C2, signposted Maison-Maugis,* and prepare yourself for a manorial feast. Keep looking right along this tree-lined lane so as not to miss first the medieval warmth of the Manoir de Moussetière, across the fields; then, the classical grandeur of the château of Maison-Mougis.

Maison-
Maugis -
Longny

⑫ *At the junction with the D291, head straight on, following the signs to Monceaux.* This is a lovely rural backroad, with several farms advertising bed-and-breakfast. *At Monceaux, turn left to Longny-au-Perche.*

Longny-
au-Perche

In many ways, Longny is Mortagne's poor relation; it is a less vivacious place, and its accommodation and tourist facilities cannot match Mortagne's. Geography may partly explain this state of affairs; after all, from its hilltop position Mortagne can look down on the countryside of

La Chapelle-Montligeon.

the Perche, whereas Longny is set in a bowl of the wooded Jambée valley. The tourist potential is there but, no doubt, the burghers of Longny have quite sensibly decided that the lazy appeal of the town's spacious main square and surrounding streets should not be spoiled. There is not much to see in the town, but on your way out you should take in the views from the chapel of Notre-Dame-de-Pitié.

Longny-au-Perche - La Chapelle-Montligeon

⑬ *Take the D8 out of Longny, signposted Mortagne. After entering the forest, and beyond the turning to Monceaux, turn left, signposted La Chapelle-Montligeon.* The narrow road cuts a rather eerie corridor through the dense, regimented forest, and is crossed by occasional wide paths which double as fire breaks.

La Chapelle-Montligeon

Pilgrims come in their thousands to this huge elaborate chapel to pray for the disabled. It completely dominates the tiny industrial village, and though awesome and incongruous, it has a grotesque fascination.

La Chapelle-Montligeon - Mortagne au Perche

⑭ *From the chapel go down the hill and cross the D5.* A quick backward glance will enable you to appreciate fully how out of proportion the chapel is, compared to the size of the village. *At the junction with the main road, turn right and follow the signs to Mortagne.*

Brittany:

THE NORTHERN COAST

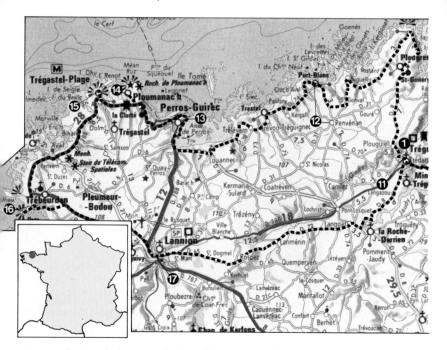

Sweeping sandy bays, rocky headlands, secret inlets and meandering estuaries: the Brittany coast is over 1,500 km long and has many moods. Nature has been more than generous here, for there is yet another dimension to the scenery: the mystery, even magic, of countless offshore islands, islets and rocks.

This tour gives you the chance to see the coast at its most intricate and complicated. The route takes in a few popular resorts along the pink granite coast to the west, but the high spots are in the less commercialized east. Around the Pointe de l'Arcouest, on Route One, the shore is dramatic and the sea a pattern of islands. Along the Côte des Ajoncs, on Route Two, the scenery is gentler, but even more intriguing: it is almost impossible to determine what is mainland and what lies offshore, and at low tide great stretches of sand and rock make wonderful beachcombing.

To give a chance to linger along the Côte des Ajoncs and fit in a trip to the island of Bréhat from the Pointe de l'Arcouest, the tour is best tackled over two or more days. The tour's midpoint is Tréguier, an excellent base if you want to be near the coast but away from the hurly-burly of Brittany's summer tourist trade. If you would prefer to stay outside the town, head 2 km west on the Lannion road, and take advantage of the good value offered by Kastell d'Inec, a converted farmhouse (tel 96.92.49.39).

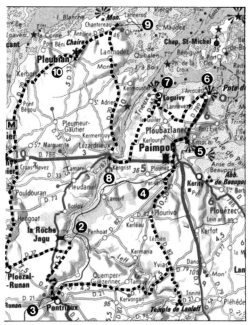

La Roche Jagu, Route One.

ROUTE ONE: 85 KM

Tréguier This mellow and dignified town was established in the 6thC by one of Brittany's founding fathers, St Tugdual. Legend has it that before he made Tréguier the seat of the diocese, St Tugdual rid the region of a dragon - and that he later went on to become Pope. Tréguier's history may be a subject for scholarly scepticism but its appeal to the present-day tourist is undoubted. Set at the confluence of two rivers, its sheltered, deep waters are a popular anchorage for yachts; the narrow streets are full of half-timbered buildings; and the spacious main square is dominated by one of Brittany's finest cathedrals. To avoid the steep walk from the marina, try to park by this magnificent building. It dates from the 13thC and contains some beautiful stained-glass windows. Make sure you don't leave this 'masterpice of airiness', as the philosopher Ernest Renan (a resident of Tréguier) described it, without visiting the serene Gothic cloisters. Near the cathedral, the 17thC house where Renan lived has been converted into a museum. *Open 10-12, 2-6, and 2-5, Oct-Mar.*

Tréguier - ① *Head east on the D786 and 1.5 km after crossing the bridge over the*
La Roche *river (and just after picnic site) turn right on to the D20. At the junction*
Jagu *with the D6 turn left then left again, signposted La Roche Jagu.*

La Roche Jagu   Restored about 20 years ago, La Roche Jagu lies buried in woodland above the River Trieux. Behind the homely château there are paths through the forest down to the river, where there are picnic places. *Open 1 April-15 Sept, 10-12.30, 2-7, rest of year Sun and hols only, 2-7.* ② *Turn left out of the castle entrance.*

Pontrieux   Once the road starts to wind steeply down, you soon reach this large and animated riverside village - a useful place to stop, wander, relax and enjoy the colour and bustle of Breton rural life. Pontrieux can also be reached by boat from Pointe de l'Arcouest (see below).

Pontrieux - Paimpol   ③ *Take the D6, signposted St-Brieuc, then turn left on to the D15. At Quemper-Guézennec turn right along the D79 to Yvias. At Yvias turn right for a detour to Lanleff.* The scenery along the road to Yvias is green and lush. Near the church and behind a tiny cottage in the backwater village of Lanleff are the curious ruins of a small, circular 12thC temple. *Return to Yvias and take the D82 to Plourivo to rejoin the D15.*

Paimpol   Paimpol is more a working port than a tourist resort, but the harbour is interesting and active, and there is quite a range of restaurants and modest hotels. *Follow the signs to the port*; park, then walk along the front for the best views of the river making its way out to the bay. ④ *Leave Paimpol on the D789, signposted Pointe de l'Arcouest.*

Château de Coat-guélen *(hotel-rest., Pléhédel)*   Some way out of Paimpol to the South-east, this beautifully positioned little 19thC château could provide a whole day's relaxation. The food is excellent - light and imaginative; there is a swimming pool, tennis and a nine-hole golf course. The atmosphere is relaxed, and the bedrooms are spacious. *Tel 96.22.31.24; Pléhédel is about 10 km SSE of Paimpol on the D79; closed Nov-Mar and Tues out of season; price band B.*

Kerroc'h Tower   *About one km from Paimpol, at a bend in the road, turn right along a signposted track.* It is only a minute's walk up to the squat, three-storeyed tower, and if you find that you have the place to yourself the promontory is fine for a picnic. From here you can see back to Paimpol and the low surrounding countryside, and out to the islands in the bay. The views are no better from the tower, but if you do climb it, don't go beyond the first floor - there is no viewing platform at the top and the balustrade is dangerously low. ⑤ *Continue on the D789.*

Pointe de l'Arcou-est   Providing you can tolerate the crowds of other visitors, there is no better place than this to stand and admire the extraordinary island seascape of Brittany's Côtes-du-Nord; quite close by, the island of Bréhat is surrounded by a mass of rocky islets.

Ile-de-Bréhat   The hour-long boat trip around the island is not to be missed, and it is well worth while spending a couple of hours actually on Bréhat. A mild

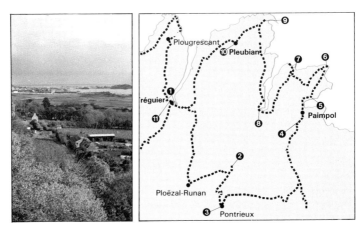

The coast near Paimpol.

climate has given this mass of pink granite a sub-tropical vegetation. There are no cars on Bréhat; it is an ideal place for getting away from it all. *Boat services depend on the weather; trips also go along the River Trieux to Pontrieux (see above). Tel 96.20.00.06 or 96.20.82.30.*
⑥ *Return along the D789 for a short distance, then turn right, following the signs to Loguivy. At the main road - the D15 - turn right (not signposted at time of going to press).*

Loguivy   From the promontory by the harbour mouth you can look across to Bréhat and the other islands. Although the views are less striking than from the Pointe de l'Arcouest, fewer people will be sharing them.

Loguivy -   ⑦ *Leave Loguivy on the D15; go past the turning to Ploubazlanec on left,*
Lézardrieux *and take the next turning to the right to Kergoff (not on map) - the signpost faces away from you. Carry straight on over two crossroads and turn left at the T-junction, signposted Lézardrieux. At the main D786 turn right.* This is a thoroughly rural alternative to taking the main road via Paimpol. *Approaching Lézardrieux, just before the graceful suspension bridge, turn right in front of the Bar du Pont.* A short track takes you to a river viewpoint under the bridge, another useful picnic place.

Lézardrieux ⑧ *Cross the bridge, turn right into Lézardrieux, and follow the D20.* The
- Sillon de glimpses of the estuary from this road are encouragement enough to
Talbert   take one of the two or three side roads to the right, signposted 'panorama', which lead to the river bank - and more picnic possibilities. One of these lanes offers the bonus of taking you to the Phare de Bodic, a strange building which looks more like a small castle or folly than a lighthouse.

   At Armor de Pleubian (not on map) turn right and then left to Sillon de Talbert.

53

Sillon de Talbert
The views from here are nowhere near as magnificent as those from Pointe de l'Arcouest, but this low-lying area of mudflats, marsh, sandbanks and seaweed has a charm of its own. The 3-km Talbert sand spit, a curious and unusual feature, makes an interesting walk - provided that the local motorbike boys are not using it for scrambling practice.
⑨ *From Sillon de Talbert take the D20, signposted Tréguier.*

Pleubian
The ornately carved calvaries - granite monuments depicting religious scenes, found in many of the province's churchyards - are one of the most notable features of Breton art. The Côtes-du-Nord is not in general the best area to see them, but near the church in this village is one of the finest calvary-pulpits in Brittany.

Pleubian - Tréguier
⑩ *Follow the signs to Tréguier.* For those who want still more seaside driving, detours along the coast are well signposted.

The sand spit of Sillon de Talbert.

◼ ROUTE TWO: 93 KM

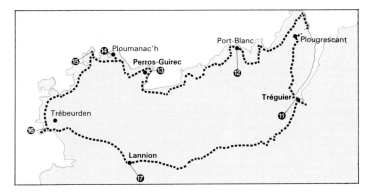

Tréguier -
Plougre-
scant

⑪ *Leave Tréguier on the D8. Ignore signs to the Circuit de la Côte des Ajoncs until you reach Plougrescant, then pick up the signposted route at the right turning just past the church with a wonderfully crooked spire.*

La Côte
des
Ajoncs

The route makes a winding tour of some superbly unspoilt coast, while inland the scenery is hilly, varied and intimate. There are countless picnic places from which to choose; there are coastal paths, some of which are waymarked; and at low tide you can walk out over the vast expanses of sand to clamber over rocks, examine rock pools, and watch the local fishermen collecting seaweed or digging for bait.

The route takes you through several sleepy hamlets but only one fishing village of any size, Buguelès. Make a point of stopping at Pointe du Château and Le Gouffre (not on map). At the Pointe there is a charming cluster of houses set behind a small beach and slipway and by a giant granite outcrop, and the views stretch right across the wide estuary mouth, dotted with rocky islets, many of which are crowned with small lighthouses. And at Le Gouffre there is a much-photographed cottage wedged unbelievably between huge granite boulders. The route is generally well-signposted; when in doubt turn right.

Port-
Blanc

After the simplicity of the previous stretch of coast, where even camping is forbidden, it comes as a surprise to arrive at a village where there are hotels. However, the concessions Port-Blanc has made to tourism are few: at heart it remains an unspoilt, peaceful fishing port. On the front, on top of Sentinel Rock, there is a small granite shrine to the Virgin Mary. Even more unusual is the chapel with a roof that slopes right down to the ground.

Port-Blanc -
Perros-
Guirec

⑫ *Follow the Circuit route through pretty Les Dunes (not on map); at the junction with the D38 turn right (do not follow the Circuit signs straight on). This is a fast road that passes through the resort area of Trévou-*

Tréguignec. At Trélévern, turn right on to the D73, left on to the D38, then turn right immediately and fork left (passing a boulangerie *on the left)*. Once you are through a short stretch of suburbia, this becomes a fine coastal drive as the road winds down then up through vivid countryside and cool woodland. In the distance, across the bay, the views of the Perros-Guirec headland provide a taste of the rugged scenery to come. *Turn right at the junction with the D6 and follow signs to Perros-Guirec.*

**Perros-
Guirec**

This bustling resort has a large marina and a thriving fishing industry. Grand old houses enjoy secluded settings among the pines that cover the slopes of the north-eastern headland, and at the bottom of the cliffs are two excellent sandy beaches. In summer, boats leave from Trestraou beach for the Sept Iles nature reserve.

**Perros-
Guirec -
Plou-
manac'h**

⑬ *From the marina follow the road signposted Corniche and Trégastel (D786)*. The Corniche is only a short stretch, so make sure you stop at the viewpoint on a bend just past the Plage de Trestignel: it will make up for the few built-up kilometres which now follow. About one km before Ploumanac'h, you suddenly find yourself in exhilarating open countryside. There is a lay-by near a sharp bend, from which you can walk towards the cliffs for yet more views.

**Plou-
manac'h**

The jumbled piles of huge light pink boulders that can be seen all along the Côte de Granite Rose are one of the most bizarre features of the entire coast of Brittany. When you leave the main road to drive into this small and cheerful family resort and working port, *follow signs for the* phare *(lighthouse)*. This will bring you to a big expanse of rugged parkland, the best starting point for striding off to explore the rocky shore: turn left for St-Guirec beach, or right to a striking headland. ⑭ *Return to the main road and turn right*. Just after crossing a creek, drive slowly so as not to miss the views of Ploumanac'h harbour. *Turn right into Trégastel-Plage and follow the signs to the Plage de Coz-Pors.*

**Tréga-
stel-Plage**

Trégastel-Plage lacks the vitality and appeal of Ploumanac'h, but pink granite boulders along the shore of this scattered resort make it worth a visit. The two main areas to explore are the Ile Renot, a long peninsula of rocks and secluded beaches, and the Grève Blanche. Near Coz-Pors beach an aquarium and museum have been built in the caves under a huge pile of rocks, on top of which stands an awful statue. ⑮ *Return to the main road and turn right.*

**Tré-
beurden**

Turn right as soon as you enter Trébeurden and follow the signs to the port. The green beauty of the wooded promontories which separate Trébeurden's sheltered sandy beaches is particularly striking after the rose-tinted strangeness of Ploumanac'h and Trégastel-Plage. Park by the headland on the front and climb up for views.

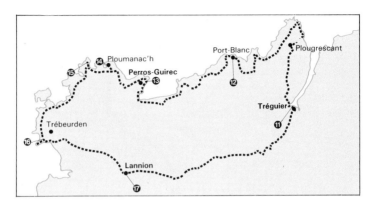

Manoir de Lan Kerrelac
(hotel-rest. Trébeurden)

If you feel like going for broke, this stylish, comfortable hotel is a good place to do so. Book a table by the window, and take your time over the seafood specialities. *Tel 96.23.50.09; closed mid-Nov to mid-Mar, and Mon (except mid-June to mid-Sept); price band C.*
⑯ *From the middle of Trébeurden follow the signs to Pointe de Bihit. The winding road leads to a viewpoint. Return and follow signs to Lannion.*

Lannion

Try to park by the Centre du Communications in Lannion; it is convenient, and is the easiest place from which to pick up the road to Tréguier when you leave. If you cannot park here, carry on following the Tréguier signs, then head for the Hotel de Ville (signposted); this will bring you to the main square where there are more parking places. Lannion is very much a working town, but its compact old quarter, on the left bank of the River Léguer, has character.

Kan an Dour
(restaurant, Lannion)

This rustic-style first-floor restaurant in a modern building is conveniently sited in the old town, and M. Guyon's *nouvelle cuisine* makes a change from the rich cooking that is more typical of Brittany. *7 Rue de Kériavily; tel 96.37.14.23; closed 1-10 Sept and Mon, Sept-June; price band B.*

Lannion - Tréguier

⑰ *Follow the signs to Tréguier, then turn right on to the D65 to Rospez. From here take the D72. At the junction with the D6 turn right, then left on to the D8. This is a much more rural (and not much slower) alternative to the main road back to Tréguier.*

North-west Brittany:

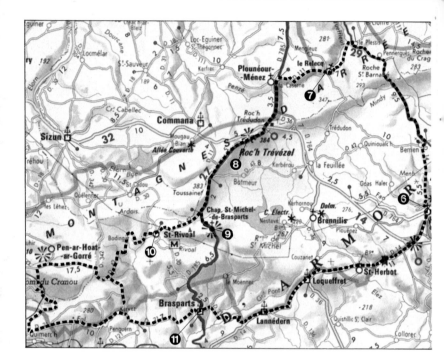

When you drive up into the Montagnes d'Arrée from the surrounding lowland it is hard to believe that their highest peak is not much more than 50 metres higher than the Eiffel Tower in Paris. But these are Brittany's biggest mountains and this area is one of the most beautiful parts of the interior of the province. In the east great swathes of woodland cover the hills, and sparkling rivers and streams cut winding paths through the cool forest. In summer the green is overpowering. But the mountains also have a severe and lonely side to their character; in the west, around Roc'h Trévézel, there are bare, jutting peaks, surrounded by gorse and heather, with hardly a tree in sight.

Since the creation of the Parc Naturel Régional d'Armorique in 1969, this whole area has enjoyed protected status, although one wonders whether things would have changed a great deal even without this act of conservation. Rural life continues much as it has for centuries and tourism seems to be no more than a sideline - accommodation is thin on the ground and modest in style, while restaurants are almost without exception simple.

The Montagnes d'Arrée are for those who enjoy peaceful villages and sweeping views. The tour takes you through the whole range of scenery that the mountains have to offer and includes stops at several interesting

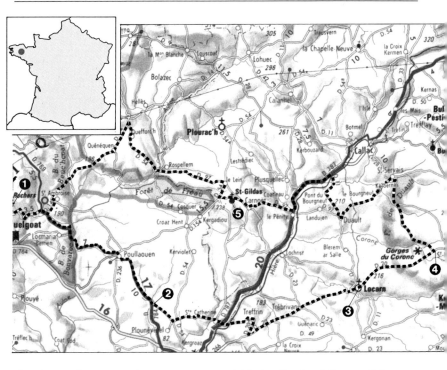

churches and an open-air museum; you might also like to visit one of the craft workshops signposted along the route. Many of the roads are narrow and you need to follow the directions carefully, but driving is not difficult.

ROUTE ONE: 93 KM

Huelgoat   Not only is the lakeside village of Huelgoat the best start for exploring the Montagnes d'Arrée, it is also almost the only place in the area that has much in the way of tourist facilities. Around its spacious main square and in the surrounding streets are four small hotels (the An Triskell, *tel 98.99.71.85*, is good value) and several restaurants.

    The name Huelgoat means 'high wood', and the great forests surrounding the village offer plenty of opportunities for walks along woodland paths. North of the village, giant granite rocks lie hidden among the trees; one, known as 'la Roche Tremblante', pivots on its base if pushed correctly; other rocks have been weathered into interesting shapes. South and west, the walks include one along the River Argent to a plunging chasm, and another along the canal that was built in the 18thC to serve the silver mining industry. Before leaving, fill your tank - filling stations are scarce on backroads of both loops.

**Huelgoat -
Locmaria-
Berrien**

① *Take the Carhaix-Plouguer road out of Huelgoat.* This is a winding road which cuts a narrow corridor through the forest before entering a wide valley.

**Auberge
de la
Truite**
*(restaurant,
Locmaria)*

This traditionally furnished restaurant on the Huelgoat-Carhaix road is reckoned to serve the best food in the area. Specialities include lobster and, not surprisingly, *truite de l'auberge*. Mme Le Guillous's cosy hostelry also has six bedrooms. *Tel 98.99.73.05; closed mid-Jan to early Mar, Sun evening and Mon (except July and Aug); price band C.*

**Locmaria-
Berrien -
Locarn**

② *About 4 km beyond Poullaouen, take the left turn signposted Plounévézel; soon turn left and cross the D54, signposted Ste-Catherine. At the junction with the D787 go straight across, signposted Treffrin. At the T-junction turn right along the D20A.* Once you have crossed the D54 there is the first of many long views over the undulating Breton countryside. Because traditional farming methods are still employed here, hedgerows have not been bulldozed, nor trees uprooted or cut down; the patchwork pattern of small fields and clumps of woodland

Opposite: Huelgoat's lake.

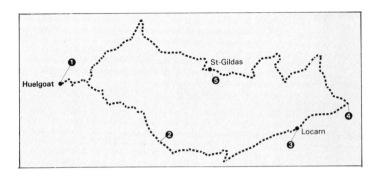

remains more or less as intimate and restful as it has been for hundreds of years. *At the junction with the D20, turn left to Locarn.*

Locarn

A break from driving is in order after the invigorating descent through a leafy valley before the road rises up to reach the quiet hillside village of Locarn. The views over a tributary of the Hière merit more than momentary contemplation; the church contains some fine stained glass; and the silver reliquary of St Hernin, the 16thC cross and 17thC chalice, which are kept in the presbytery, are well worth seeing.

③ *From Locarn take the D20, signposted St-Nicodème, turn left (the signpost to the Gorges faces away from you) then, after about 2 km, turn left once more.*

Gorges du Coronc

From the small parking area, a 15-minute walk through woodland, alongside a narrow river and past big granite outcrops, brings you to the spot where the river passes under a great pile of boulders in a series of small waterfalls. The path continues, but children (and adults, no doubt) will be happy enough to stop here to clamber over the rocks. On a hot day the shade of the forest and the sound of the river are a welcome tonic for those who are starting to feel weary. You need to search around for picnic places; alternatively, the Ty-Pikouz, a small, simple *auberge*, just along from the car park, is an adequate place to stop for a meal or a snack.

Gorges du Coronc St-Gildas

④ *Return along the short no through road to the Gorges, then turn left and follow the signs to St-Servais (there is one unsignposted T-junction where you should turn left). At St-Servais turn left (not signposted but opposite the church) and as you climb up out of the village take the left turn to Duault.* In contrast to the route from the Gorges to St-Servais, the road follows a high ridge from which you can look out over great expanses of utterly rural countryside. *At Duault bear right on to the D11; drive on for a short while then turn left along the D787. The D11 winds gently down to the main road and the Hière valley. Opposite a trout farm, turn right, signposted Carnouët and Chapelle St-Gildas.*

St-Gildas   The chapel, which stands at the end of an unsignposted track lined by an avenue of trees, is visible from the road. Around the roof at the rear of the 16thC building are some fearsome grotesques (one of which is enjoyably crude). Opposite the main door to the chapel and across a stile, a 5-minute walk takes you to the top of a hill from which you can enjoy the most extensive views on this loop of the tour - winds permitting, this is an ideal place to reflect on the charm of the Breton countryside.

St-Gildas -   ⑤ *Return along the tree-lined track and turn left. At the T-junction turn*
Huelgoat   *right, then turn left at the crossroads, signposted Morlaix. At the junction just past Quefforc'h, follow the signs to Huelgoat.* The scenery varies almost as much as the road twists and turns; eventually you rejoin the road which leads through the dark forest back to Huelgoat.

ROUTE TWO: 87 KM or 102 KM

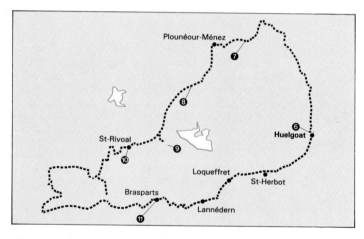

Huelgoat -   ⑥ *Take the D14 north to join the D769 at Berrien. At Le Plessis turn left*
Le Relecq   *along the D111 to Le Relecq.* From Huelgoat the road climbs up to run through high open countryside, part moorland and part grazing land. The D111 is through woodland.

Le Relecq   Time seems to have stood still in this village; the only indication that tourists ever pass is the sign advertising the local potter. Driving between the pillars of an old gateway on the right-hand side of the road, you enter a large rustic square. On your left is a small L-shaped cluster of stone houses. Opposite, a couple of somewhat shabby, more substantial houses stand in delightfully natural gardens, and on your right

View from above the chapel of St-Gildas.

is the church of the old Cistercian abbey. Dating from the 12thC (although the façade is 18thC), the church has a dilapidated charm which is entirely in keeping with the rest of the village.

Le Relecq -
Roc'h
Trévézel

⑦ *Continue on the D111. At Plounéour-Ménez turn left on to the D785.* For the most part the Montagnes d'Arrée can only be described as impressively hilly; the Roc'h, however, is definitely a mountain. Its jutting peaks, which rise out of a high moorland plateau, can be seen in the distance even before you reach Plounéour, although the nearby communications mast is likely to be the first thing that catches your eye. Not far beyond the D764-D785 crossroads is a signposted footpath to the Roc'h (there is no special car park, just pull in by the roadside). It is only a few minutes' walk to the top, and the views from here are among the most memorable on the tour: to the west you can see as far as Brest; to the north the Baie de Lannion is visible, while to the south you can see the St-Michel mountain (your next stop) and beyond to the Montagnes Noires, Brittany's other principal mountain chain. The view to the south-east, over the St-Michel reservoir, is unfortunately marred by the nuclear power plant buildings. A leisurely picnic will give you time to absorb it all; however, if you prefer not to carry your *baguettes, cheese* and *vin de table* quite so far, the next stop offers another agreeable picnic spot.

Roc'h
Trévézel -
St-Michel-
de-
Brasparts

⑧ *Continue on the D785, then either turn right to St-Rivoal along the D42, or, for a short detour to the Montagne St-Michel, keep on the D785, past a small crêperie, then turn right to St-Michel.* A flight of steps from the car park leads to the tiny chapel of St-Michel-de-Brasparts, which crowns this great rounded mountain; the views from here are stunning, although not quite in the same class as those to be seen from Roc'h Trévézel.

St-Michel -
St-Rivoal

⑨ *Return to the D785 and turn left. After about 2 km turn left again along the D42 to St-Rivoal.*

St-Rivoal

After so many viewpoints the open-air museum at this sleepy village makes an interesting change. Nowhere else is the conservationist spirit of those who run the Parc Régional more evident. Here you can see a variety of well-preserved Breton buildings; other exhibits include agricultural implements and machinery. *Open May-Oct; closed Tues.*

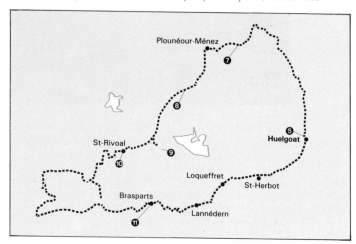

St-Rivoal -
Brasparts

⑩ *From St-Rivoal, take the D42 in the direction of Le Faou.* This winding road provides just the right contrast to the bleakness of the peaks around Roc'h Trévézel, as it makes its way up and down through woods and farmland. Those who are pressed for time should take the short route to Brasparts. However, the scenery on the longer route makes it well worth driving the extra 15 km.

Short route: turn left after about 7 km, signposted Lopérec, then after 3 km turn left on to the D21 to Brasparts.

Longer route: continue following the signs to Le Faou until you reach the turning to the left signposted Quimerc'h; at the junction with the D21 turn left, signposted Brasparts. After a stretch of open countryside, the road descends into Le Forêt du Cranou and the mood of the tour changes yet again as you pass through a great band of oak and beech woods. There are several places where you can pull off the road to walk into the depths of the forest, and almost next to the turning to Quimerc'h there is a picnic site, with tables. Soon after this the road emerges from the woods, becoming quite narrow for a while. From the D21, which follows the line of a high ridge, you can look out over what seems to be the whole of southern Britanny. Near Kervez the road leaves the high ground of the ridge.

Brasparts	During the 16th and 17th centuries the parish closes of Brittany became a focus for creative energy, and they are now one of the special features of the villages of the region. Partly as a result of the spiritual vigour of the times and partly because of inter-village rivalry, increasingly elaborate graveyard sculptures (calvaries) were crafted, while in the churches themselves it was woodcarvers who made their mark. Brittany's two most famous parish closes are at St-Thégonnec and Guimiliau, some 20 km north of Roc'h Trévézel (see earlier on this tour), but the one in Brasparts is a good example; the calvary is particularly fine and the church one of the most interesting on the tour.

Brasparts -	⑪ *Continue along the D21, signposted Huelgoat. At the junction with the*
Lannédern	*D14, turn left to Lennédern*. Both this village and its neighbour,
and	Loqueffret, have small parish closes that are worth pausing to see. The
Loqueffret	church at Lannédern is tucked away on a hillside to the left of the main road, and is easily missed.

Roc'h	After leaving Loqueffret look out on the right for the brown sign to this
Bégheor	*'magnifique pointe de vue'*. A short walk from the tiny area where you can your car brings you to the edge of an escarpment and a large rock (not marked on map). You are unlikely to disagree with the sign's description of the panorama; it is worth climbing on to the rock to get above the few trees which impede your view.

St-Herbot	The big Gothic church in this tiny village has a finely carved porch beside which is a small charnel house. The interior of the church is dank, dark, but atmospheric and worth a visit for its carved oak screen. Opposite the church there is a café which is also an *épicerie* and bread shop; a *digestif* or a cup of excellent coffee in these friendly surroundings would be a perfect way of rounding off the drive.
	Continue along the D14 to Huelgoat.

South-West Brittany:

CORNOUAILLE

The ancient kingdom of Cornouaille, which was given its name by early British settlers from Cornwall, is a region of marked contrasts. The north is majestically hilly; the south-west is flat - except for the rugged Pointe du Raz; and the south is an intricate maze of rivers, inlets and bays. As the landscape has its widely differing moods, so too do the resorts: Audierne is animated, Bénodet sophisticated, Concarneau bustles, while pretty La Forêt Fouesnant goes about its business in a more restrained way.

Not all these places are featured on this tour, which as far as possible steers clear of the most crowded areas, where the summer traffic can be nightmarish; but the route is within easy reach of all the major south-western resorts. The northern loop includes one of Brittany's most picturesque villages, a quiet stretch of coast and some extensive views. The southern loop starts with the restful River Odet, then becomes much more coastal, taking in fishing villages, seaside resorts and some beautiful scenery.

Fishing is such a key industry in this area that you are overwhelmed when it comes to seafood. The same is not quite so true of hotels. If money is no object you could opt for the Manoir du Stang, *tel 98.56.97.37*, a grand mansion set in noble grounds just outside La Forêt Fouesnant. Less formal and considerably cheaper is Le Goyen in Audierne, *tel 98.70.08.88*; the harbour-front building has been attractively renovated and the food is excellent. And there are, in addition, the hotels mentioned *en route*.

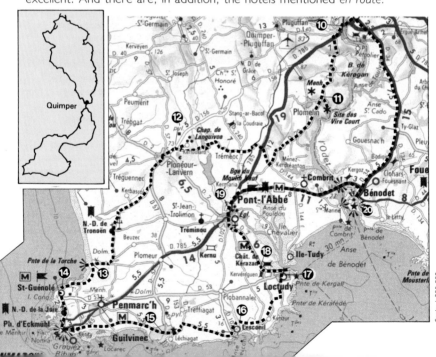

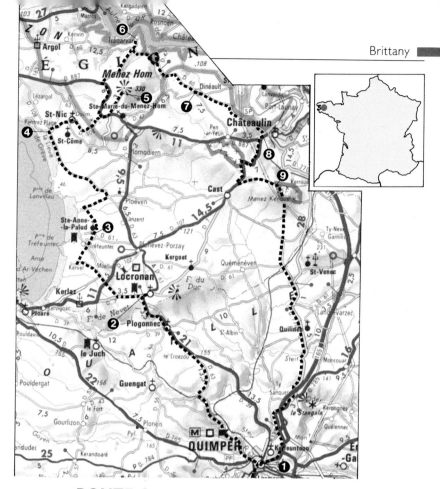

ROUTE ONE: 104 KM

Quimper This big, thriving and stylish town, set in a beautiful wooded valley, was the capital of Cornouaille. If you explore no more than its old quarter of cobbled streets and half-timbered buildings, your visit will have been worthwhile. Within this compact area there are chic shops, a mouth-watering covered market and Quimper's main sights: the imposing Gothic cathedral with its 19thC spires; the Musée des Beaux Arts, which contains works by Rubens, Boucher, Boudin and Fragonard, as well as interesting paintings of old Brittany; and the Musée Départemental Breton (adjacent to the cathedral in the old Bishop's Palace), the perfect place to get a feel for Breton history and culture.

Next door to the Brittany museum is the tourist office; ask here about boat trips along the River Odet.

Quimper is an excellent start for this tour, but a word of warning: be prepared for busy traffic and exasperating one-way systems; it is best

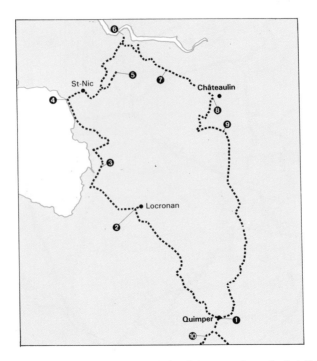

to park on the north bank of the river, near the cathedral; if this proves impossible, follow the signs to the large *centre ville* car park.

Quimper -   ① *Take the Douarnenez road out of Quimper. On the outskirts of the*
Locronan   *town fork right on to the D63, then follow the signs to Locronan.*

Locronan   A worthy contender for the prize of 'most picturesque village in Brittany', Locronan used to make its money from the manufacture of cloth; today its prosperity comes from the crowds of tourists who come to admire the grey granite beauty of the Renaissance buildings around the main square. In the chapel adjacent to the church, do not miss the magnificent black granite tomb of St-Ronan.

Near the church, a small local museum has exhibits which range from Breton furniture and costumes to contemporary art. Other buildings house antique shops, tea shops and craft *ateliers*.

Overlooking the village is the Mountain of Locronan; from here you can look west to the Baie de Douarnenez, north to Menez Hom (see below) and north-east to the Monts d'Arrée. Every July a pilgrims' procession makes its way to the mountain-top. These *pardons* (but here called *troménies*) are a feature of Breton life, and if you get the chance to see one, you should.

Au Fer à Cheval, Locronan.

Au Fer à Cheval
(restaurant, Locronan)

Conveniently situated on the main square opposite the church, this comfortable restaurant offers sound value. From the lowest-priced menu, the *limande meunière* is recommended, if available. *Tel 98.91.70.74; closed mid-Nov to mid-Dec; price band A.*

Manoir le Moëllien
(hotel-rest-aurant, near Locronan)

If you would prefer to eat (or sleep) in more gracious surroundings, *leave Locronan on the D7, signposted to Douarnenez, then turn right, not far from the village, at the signpost to the Manoir.* A few minutes' drive brings you to this large and lovely 17thC country house set in splendid rural isolation. Beams, antiques and good food await you inside. Bedrooms (all on the ground floor) are comfortable, although fairly expensive; you can eat quite cheaply. *Tel 98.92.50.40; closed mid-Nov to mid-Dec, Jan to mid-Mar, and Tues Oct-Apr; price band B.*

Locronan - Ste-Anne-la-Palud

② *Take the Douarnenez road out of Locronan. After about 2 km, turn right on to the V3 (beyond the turning to the Manoir), then follow the signs to Kervel, Tréfuntec and Ste-Anne-la-Palud.*

Ste-Anne-la-Palud

In July and August this rural backwater is forced out of hibernation. Not only do campers, attracted by the sweeping sandy beaches, colonise the empty fields, but great hordes of pilgrims descend on the lonely church to take part in one of Britanny's biggest *pardons*.

Plage
(hotel-rest., Ste-Anne-la-Palud)

The setting is out of this world, but there are other qualities which combine to make Mme La Coz's beachside hotel an absolute gem and an ideal place to recharge your batteries. It is comfortable, well-equipped (there is a heated swimming pool) and the cooking, particularly the seafood, merits superlatives. There is a price to pay for such high standards, but you get value for money. *Tel 98.92.50.12; closed Oct-Mar; price band D.*

Ste-Anne-la-Palud - Pentrez ③ *At the crossroads by the church, head for the sea and follow the signs to Ploéven until you reach another crossroads; turn left here, signposted Lestrevet (but signpost difficult to see).* Between Ste-Anne and Ty-Anquer and from Lestrevet to Pentrez, the road hugs the coast, and there are fine views across the Baie de Douarnenez to Cap de la Chèvre. There are plenty of places where you can pull off the road for a picnic, a dip in the sea or a walk along the beach.

Pentrez - Menez Hom ④ *From Pentrez follow the signs first to St-Nic, and then towards Châteaulin. At the junction with the D887, turn right, then turn left to Menez Hom.* Once the road begins to climb after St-Nic the views become increasingly better, culminating with the magnificent panorama that is spread out before you when you reach the top of Menez Hom, on the western edge of the Montagnes Noires. From this viewpoint the long peninsulas and huge bays of the complicated west coast are as clear as a map; and the Monts d'Arrée are visible in the distance to the north-east.
⑤ *Return to the D887, turn right and after about 2 km turn right again, following the signs to Trégarvan.*

Trégar-van The wooded slopes of the north bank of the meandering Aulne are a delightful contrast to the vast scale of the view from Menez Hom. Down in the valley, this small village is one of only two places on the tour where you can get to the river's edge.

Trégarvan - Quimper ⑥ *Return to the D60 and turn left.* For a more rustic view of the river than from Trégarvan (and better picnic places) *detour left, signposted L'Aulne, after about 2 km.*
⑦ *At Dinéault follow the signs to the left of the church to Châteaulin de Gare (do not take the D60, signposted Châteaulin).* The route follows a high ridge, affording occasional glimpses of the Aulne.
⑧ *By an industrial building called Ets Kerbrat, just before the suburban approaches to Châteaulin* (a fairly ordinary town with a pleasant riverside setting), *fork right; at the main road turn right, then left along the D7, signposted Douarnenez. After about 3 km, turn left, signposted Chapelle de St-Gildas, then left again at the crossroads (unsignposted).* The short stretch on the pretty, winding D7 is partly through forest; the minor road you turn on to (not marked on map) takes you first through a leafy backwater, then up through open, rugged countryside.
⑨ *At the crossroads before the communications mast, turn right.* The road, as straight as a Roman road, descends from the high ground, providing the last big vistas on this loop of the tour. *At the junction with the D770, turn right for Quimper.*

ROUTE TWO: 96 KM

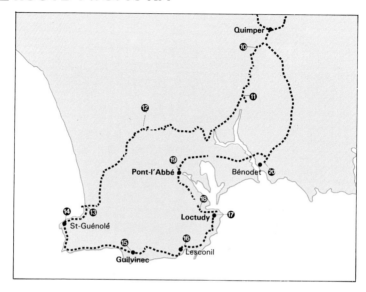

Quimper -   ⑩ *Follow the signs to Pont l'Abbé out of Quimper, then turn left along the*
Vire Court   *D20, signposted Plomelin. After about 4 km turn left to Vire Court.*

Vire   The approach to Vire Court is irresistible. A tunnel of trees leads to a
Court   parking area, from which it is only a short walk, past a ruined house, to
the wooded banks of the Odet. By the slipway, take the path above
you on your left until you come to a small picnic area (there is just one
table) on a small headland overlooking the river.

Vire Court -   ⑪ *Rejoin the D20 and turn left, signposted Ile-Tudy. After about 5 km,*
Chapelle de   *turn right along the D144, signposted Quimper; cross the main road and*
Languivoa   *follow the signs first to Tréméoc, and then to Plonéour-Lanvern. Just before*
you reach Plonéour, turn right to Chapelle de Languivoa.

Chapelle   This short detour brings you to an utterly rural backwater of farms,
de   cottages and barns and one very quaint outbuilding with moss-covered
Langui-   thatch. Above the road and dominating the village is a big church with a
voa   curiously-shaped tower. East of the village are the ruins of the Chapel
of our Lady of Languivoa, where young mothers used to pray to be
given enough milk to suckle their children.

⑫ *At the junction with the D156, turn left into Plonéour, then take the*
D57, signposted Penmarc'h. After about 2 km turn right, signposted Mejou,
then follow the signs to Pointe de la Torche.

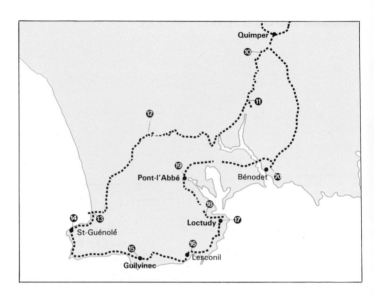

Pointe de la Torche   The sign recording the number of people who have drowned off the Pointe makes it abundantly clear that this is not a safe place to swim. However, the island-like promontory, surrounded by rocks, is a pleasant spot for a picnic.
⑬ *A short way from the Pointe, turn right to St-Guénolé* (road not marked on map).

St-Guénolé   First impressions of St-Guénolé are not encouraging - grey houses spread about a flat, bleak peninsula. But you soon warm to the salty character of this quiet holiday resort and important fishing port. There is a long sandy beach, a lighthouse and a museum of prehistory, but these are minor attractions compared with the extraordinary rocky plateau that extends from the shore. Rough seas breaking against these fiercesome, jagged rocks are an exhilarating sight.

La Mer *(hotel-restaurant, St-Guénolé)*   This small hotel and restaurant serves the best seafood in St-Guénolé. *Tel 98.58.62.22; closed mid-Oct to late Nov, Mon out of season, and Sun evening in early Feb; price band B.*
⑭ *Leave St-Guénolé via the lighthouse, then take the road signposted Kérity.* A ridge of dunes lies between the road and the sea, so pull off the road and find a sheltered, sandy nook from which to view the intricate, rocky seascape. *On entering Guilvinec, follow the signs to the port.*

Guilvinec   Gaily painted trawlers add vivid dashes of colour to the monochrome granite buildings surrounding Guilvinec's harbour.
⑮ *Drive right round the port and follow the signs to Lesconil.*

Lesconil Lesconil is another agreeable, small fishing port, prettier and more charming than Guilvinec. As you reach the outskirts of the village, there is a short track which leads to one of the best beaches along this southern coast: golden sand, interesting rocks and big boulders providing shelter from the wind make it an ideal picnic place.
⑯ *From Lesconil follow the signs to Loctudy.*

Loctudy The views from Loctudy's port are among the prettiest on this tour: across the mouth of the estuary to Ile-Tudy; along the estuary to the thickly wooded island of Garo, and beyond to Ile Chevalier. From the harbour you can take a boat trip up the Odet to Quimper, or out to sea to the Iles de Glénan (a rocky archipelago with interesting birdlife). There is also a passenger ferry service to Ile-Tudy, where there is a lovely long beach. If lack of time rules out a boat trip, do not miss Loctudy's Romanesque church; don't be put off by the 18thC façade.
⑰ *Follow the signs to Pont l'Abbé until the right turn to Ch. de Kérazan.*

Château de Kérazan Look for the scenes of old Brittany in the art collection housed in this gracious château with lovely gardens. The house was given to the Institut de France in 1929; it dates from the 16thC. *Open 10-12 and 2-6; closed mid-Sept to May.*
⑱ *Continue to Pont l'Abbé and follow the signs to the middle of town.*

Pont-l'Abbé *Turn right by the Hôtel de Ville and park by the river, or (except on market day, Thurs) turn left and follow the signs to the car park in the market square.* Pont l'Abbé is the capital of the Bigouden district and its inhabitants stick firmly by their traditions. The museum by the Hôtel de Ville has a large collection, but just wandering the streets you are likely to see people in traditional dress.

Pont-l'Abbé - Benodet ⑲ *From Pont-l'Abbé follow the signs to Bénodet. On reaching the Odet, you will have to pay a toll to cross the river; drive slowly over the bridge, taking in the views over the estuary.*

Bénodet Bénodet may not have architectural panache, but it is slick, smart and very popular, and enjoys a splendid setting among pine trees at the mouth of the Odet. Various boat trips are available (the options are much the same as from Loctudy) and there is also a passenger ferry to Ste-Marine on the opposite bank of the river.

Le Jeanne d'Arc
(hotel-rest., Ste-Marine) If you decide to cross to Ste-Marine, don't be misled by the outside of Le Jeanne d'Arc, a small hotel and restaurant not far from the beach. Within what appears to be a simple road-house is a fairly smart and highly regarded restaurant which serves delicious seafood. *Tel 98.56.32.70; closed Nov-Mar, Tues and (except July and Aug) Mon evening; price band C.*
⑳ *From Bénodet take the main road back to Quimper.*

Ile de France:

THE GATINAIS AND FONTAINEBLEAU

A thousand years ago, the Ile de France *was* France. Outside a radius of about 80 km from Paris nothing important happened and the French kings exerted no real authority. The Ile was then a land of rich meadows and broad, slow-paced rivers and a good deal of it was taken up by the royal hunting forests of Fontainebleau, Rambouillet and St-Germain-en-Laye. In the middle ages, on the foundations of the hunting lodges, great monumental palaces arose, with satellite châteaux around them.

Today, Paris and its suburbs occupy much of the Ile; industry has made famous abroad the names of places which once consisted only of a manor house and a couple of farms; highways and railways from all corners of France converge on it; and the broad rivers carry many commercial barges. Shops, hotels and restaurants tend to proclaim a Parisian *chic*, and to charge Parisian prices.

The tour sets out to explore the rivers and countryside south of Paris where some flavour of the bygone Ile still lingers. The centre is Nemours, a Roman town, and ancient capital of the Gâtinais, a tract of marshy woodland and wild heath, noted for its honey. On the southern loop you follow Nemours' river, the Loing, and go westward among villages which few strangers seek out and no trains stop at. The northern loop covers well-trodden ground in the forest of Fontainebleau, but tries to avoid the crowds, and also takes a look at the forest's less-frequented outposts.

Church with twisted spire, Puiseaux.

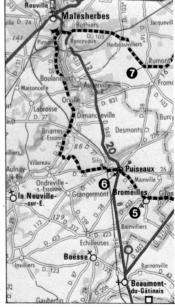

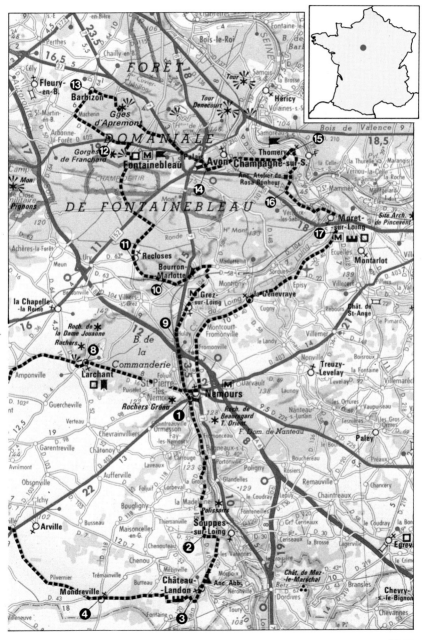

ROUTE ONE: 75 KM

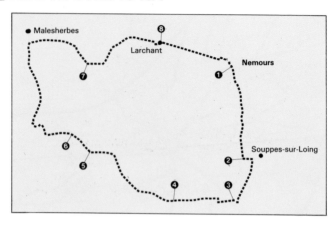

Nemours

For most foreign tourists, Nemours is a town you see from the motorway. The Autoroute du Soleil, Paris to Marseille, which is also the E1 international highway from Le Havre to Palermo, sweeps round it. There is a motel - (Euromotel: *tel 64.28.10.32*) - 2 km along it, going south, but like all European motels it is costly to stay or eat at. As an important river crossing of Roman Gaul, the town was a military station and it preserves the rectilinear Roman layout which was once enclosed in perimeter ramparts. The stern old château on the river bank, just south of the Grand Pont, is steeped in memories of the Agincourt and Joan of Arc era, when it was briefly in English hands. The restored section incorporates the civic museum - a collection overshadowed by the Ile-de-France prehistorical museum across the river in Avenue Stalingrad (where you will find two large car-parks).

On either side of the main thoroughfare, most streets are one-way. This makes town-centre driving confusing, despite the geometrical plan of the 'urban nucleus'. Some fine old buildings survive, and round them are some smart expensive shops, but the farther you go from the centre the less there is to catch the eye. The exception to that is the park on the right of the main exit to Orléans, just beyond the bridges: strange stony pinnacles, the Rochers Gréau, rise from the sandy soil.

Les Roches *(restaurant, Nemours)*

It is close to the church of St-Pierre and a short walk from the Rochers Gréau. This is probably the best restaurant in Nemours and by no means the most expensive. Duck, guinea-fowl and beef are cleverly dealt with and service is brisk. *Avenue d'Ormesson; closed two weeks Feb, and Sun evening, Mon midday; tel 64.28.01.43; price band C.*

Nemours - Baigneaux-

① *Keeping château and Loing close on left, follow one-way system round Place Victor-Hugo and go straight across at traffic lights, signposted*

sur-Loing *Baigneaux.* If you have come from the rarified atmosphere of the Vosges tour, you may find this route claustrophobic. Factory chimneys obstruct the view, industrial sites have replaced the workshops of humble craftsmen. (The most celebrated local entrepreneur emigrated to Delaware, USA, and started a chemicals factory. It expanded into the multinational which bears his family name: Du Pont.) To this valley the Bohemians of the Latin Quarter brought their mistresses on spring flower-gathering expeditions. Among the river meadows and singing birds Mimi's friend, in *La Bohème*, pouted: ''But in the country you never meet anyone.'' She would make no such complaint today.

Baigneaux - Smooth and relatively quiet, the road enters rural scenes and cuts
Ch.Landon through maize plantations and attractive woodland with far-ranging views across the Loing to the Champagne country.
② *Turn left at crossroads, signposted Souppes, right at sugar factory and straight on at crossroads (no signpost).* The sturdy old tower of Château-Landon's parish church is visible ahead - and more factory chimneys.

Château- One of the venerable fortified hill-top towns which ring the Paris basin,
Landon Château-Landon exacts a toll from visiting motorists: narrow streets and a labyrinthine one-way system. Park on the outskirts, near the abbey - it is not far to walk. The site indicates a prehistoric settlement; the Romans were here, and so was the wandering monk who brought Christianity to the Gaulish princes - St Gâtian. Foulques le Réchin, born here in 1043, offspring of a local brigand chieftain, was the first of the Plantagenets, England's longest dynasty. Remnants of fortifications from those distant days are best seen as a group from the terrace adjoining the market square. And do not forget to look into Notre-Dame church with its fine open-work belfry - medieval, but quite modern compared with some of the hoary stones around it.
③ *Leave by the D43, signposted Beaumont.*

Château- The scene is a foretaste of typical Gâtinais landscapes on which a 20thC
Landon - agriculture, with strips of woodland for windbreaks, has been imposed.
Puiseaux ④ *Just after Mondreville turn sharp right, signposted Pilvernier. Near an antiquated church, cross the main road - the D403.* Bromeilles church is seen ahead; around it huddles the small town. These insignificant byways are smooth and straight and a pleasure to drive on. Don't hurry; don't let the variegated flora of the verges become a blur.
⑤ *Follow signs to Puiseaux: narrow road, sharp bend.*

Puiseaux The church's architectural features, including a curiously twisted spire, attract students of ecclesiastical building.
⑥ *Cross the main road and bear left, signposted Pithiviers. After 2 km turn right, signposted Francorville, and cross the Essonne river in two stages. This is an insignificant little road, but soon you turn right to a better one (the D25, no signpost) and enter Briarres.*

Briarres-sur-Essonne

If it were a place on one of the *grandes routes*, you would hardly notice it as you hurtled through. Here, in the sleepy Essonne valley, it is one more of those Gâtinais villages which seem to have sprouted naturally and harmoniously out of the roots of their churches. In such places rustic trades once thrived. Their shops are shops such as you can only find in the country and in them you may discover evidence of occupations now forgotten: the gathering of saffron, madder, wild honey, coriander and chicory, fungi and other useful plants.

Males-herbes

The château, uphill beyond the church, not well signposted, is another kind of time-capsule: the world of Marcel Proust. Although his 'Combray' (now Illiers-Combray) is 64 km away near Chartres, the disdainful château suggests the life-style of the landed *noblesse* that Proust describes in *A La Recherche du Temps Perdu*. Malesherbes is on the route of the *Hauts Dignitaires* - historical personages who did the state great service and built mansions in the Ile de France on the proceeds. The first Malesherbes was a courtier of Louis XVI; his descendants have been in possession ever since: worth visiting. *Open summer months only, pm daily except Mon and Tues.*

Males-herbes - Larchant

⑦ *Follow signs to Rumont, there take second left and after 0.75 km turn right, no signpost. Turn left, signposted Amponville. After that hamlet turn right, signposted Larchant.*

Larchant

Larchant has only 500 inhabitants (charmingly known as Liricantois) but the abbey church of St-Mathurin could hold thousands, even though it is obstructed by long-term restoration works. It is sometimes fairly crowded for evening concerts and recitals of sacred music. There are sand-dunes all round the village, which for centuries has exported the sand to glass factories. Numerous walks and picnic spots.
⑧ *Return by the D16 to Nemours.*

The Rochers, a short walk from Larchant, are big outcrops, some forming weird shapes.

ROUTE TWO: 74 KM

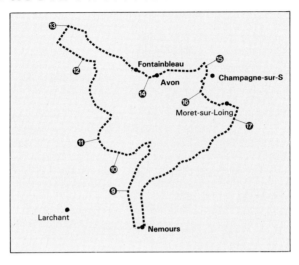

Nemours -
Bourron-
Marlotte

⑨ *Leave Nemours on main road north and just beyond motorway turn right, signposted Grez-sur-Loing.* Delius, the English composer, lived here for the last 37 years of his life and Robert Louis Stevenson parked his canoe at the jetty when writing *An Inland Voyage. Continue straight on, signposted Bourron-Marlotte.*

Bourron-
Marlotte

The château is a mini-Fontainebleau. Moat and canal emphasise its serene formality. The whole makes a superb picture. *Open Sat and holidays, Mar to Oct.*
⑩ *Bear left towards railway, then across main road (no signpost).* The road goes in among the aged oaks of the Fontainebleau forest, mercifully shady in summer heat. *Bear right to Recloses.*

Casa del
Sol
(restaurant,
Recloses)

Parisians beat a path every evening to Mme Colette's oak-beamed dining-room. (In warm weather meals are served on the terrace.) You plunge in through a thicket of auto-club, credit-card and Logis de France plaques. Exceptional dishes *à la mode du pays* and wines far from *ordinaires.* Delicious crab. The *patronne,* herself a vegetarian, strikes a neat balance between the wholesome and the fancy cuisines. *63 Rue des Canches, Recloses; tel 64.24.20.35; closed Mon evening and Tue, also all winter; price band C.*

Recloses -
Franchard

⑪ *Turn right from Recloses on to the D63e and after two intersections (not marked on map) turn left into the forest. Follow signposts for Franchard. Be prepared to miss a turning or two: forest roads and trackways are confusing. At monument turn left.*

Franchard The monument commemorates half a million beeches, oaks and pines destroyed in the severe winter of 1878-9. The area is a nature reserve, but picnicking is encouraged. Fine sandy topsoil on eroded rock, a feature of the forest topography, makes walking a pleasure. At the Hermitage, 1.5 km ahead, you are within strolling distance of a famous rocky ravine, the Franchard gorges.
⑫ *Join the major road - the D409 - westbound and in 1.5 km turn right, signposted Macherin. Here turn right again for Barbizon.*

Barbizon The 'cradle of Impressionism', enthusiastically prettified for tourists, ceases to have meaning for those in search of the rustic seclusion and soft light which attracted Millet, Corot, Rousseau, Daubigny and other painters. They came, not intentionally to create a new movement, but to lead a landscape-painting renaissance; and the English artist Constable and the Dutch masters Hobbema and Ruysdael were their inspiration. The early Impressionists met in a great barn at Barbizon to criticise each other's works. Rousseau and Millet became residents and you can visit their houses; also their favourite pub, the Auberge Ganne. The present-day 'studios' of Barbizon do a roaring trade in Impressionist reproductions.

Auberge de l'Empereur At Chailly-en-Biére (where Millet and Rousseau are buried and where Monet, Renoir and Sisley painted), this restaurant earns a red 'R' in the Red Michelin guide for its superior cuisine at reasonable prices. *About two km north of Barbizon on the D7; tel 60.66.43.38; closed in winter; price band B.*
(Barbizon)

Barbizon- ⑬ *From Barbizon, take the Fontainebleau road and bear right, no*
Fontaine- *signpost.* In 0.75 km park the car and inspect the Apremont gorges on
bleau the left. Along with those of Franchard, they are the outstanding natural curiosity of the forest. You walk on fine crystalline sand and view fantastically contorted sandstone pillars. *Continue on Route du Château to Fontainebleau.*

Fontaine-bleau Perhaps you have seen the palace before; everyone must, at some time in their lives. You will certainly have seen pictures of its regal frontage with the famous double flight of steps and in front of it the cobbles of the Cour des Adieux, as it was called after 1814, when Napoleon said farewell to his Old Guard there and everyone broke down and wept. So celebrated is this 'true abode of kings' that one forgets it is attached to a sizeable town which has its own life, history and antiquities.

Here the saintly Louis XI, around 1260, sat under an oak tree and dispensed justice; here the Mona Lisa was first exhibited in France; here the renowned landscape artist Le Nôtre planned his most ambitious gardens; here Napoleon imprisoned a Pope and here he signed away his own imperial powers; here in World War II, at different times, both German and Allied commanders-in-chief were established (soldiers

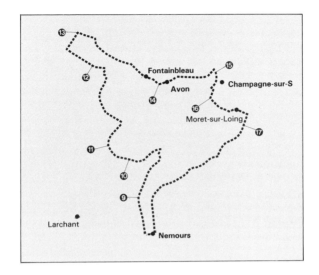

drained the carp pond and ate all the fish, so tales of the longevity of Fontainebleau carp may be treated with scepticism); and here, when NATO set up its first headquarters at the palace, former enemies came together as colleagues.

(14) *Follow signposts to Avon. Turn left at traffic lights on Rue des Cascades and follow signposts to Thomery, which lies in an arm of the Seine.*

Thomery (15) *Turn right, signposted Champagne. Instead of crossing river, turn right and right again into street named for the painter Rosa Bonheur.* Visit the charming Château de By, where Rosa lived, a tremendous celebrity in her 19thC heyday. Part of the building is a museum, a reconstruction of the scenes which inspired her paintings.

(16) *Under a canopy of trees turn left (no signpost) for Moret-sur-Loing.*

Moret-sur-Loing An old-fashioned town, approached through noble gatehouses. Impressionists Sisley and Pissarro lived and worked here, and those who know and like their work will have a sense of *déjà-vu* in the shimmering riverscape and its weeping willows. Three rivers and a canal converge at Moret, an interchange of long-haul barge traffic.

(17) *Cross the Loing and turn right, signposted Ecuelles; right again for Nemours.*

Moret-sur-Loing - Nemours The quiet road hugs the canal bank all the way. There are footpaths and parking places all along it and the level countryside gives no hint of imminent factory chimneys.

There is more to the Alsatian provinces than shepherd dogs, white wines and memories of Franco-German confrontations. There are big towns standing guard on the Rhine: Strasbourg, Colmar, Mulhouse. There is a turbulent chaos of highlands, the domed and crinkled peaks of the Vosges. There is plenty of folklore - in places the main occupation seems to be getting into fancy dress and slapping the thighs to a brass band. (Both the *Marseillaise* and the greatest of all march tunes, the *Marche Lorraine*, were composed here.) Alsace was German for 800 years, then given to France, then taken back, then bitterly fought over ... all that is history, but it explains the prevalence of German names and dialects (and German tourists) and a somewhat heavy pork-and-goosefat sort of cuisine.

The loop is based on the mountain resort of Gérardmer and it encircles the high hills, where places prominently marked on the map turn out to be tiny hamlets. At the Grand Ballon (1,426 metres) it touches the summit of the Vosges. There you can trace your circuit without the map, squirming among torrent valleys and forests and small glacial lakes. *Ballon* is a corruption of *bois long*, a reference to the evergreens which once softened the outlines of the high escarpments.

The road touches at many a ski-ing centre and passes under many a chair-lift: this is the winter playground of various Rhine cities. Outside the short winter season, accommodation at hotels, *gîtes* and *fermes auberges* (farm guest houses) is no problem. There are few foreign tourists.

▬▬▬▬ ROUTE: 142 KM

Gérard-mer   Tourism is highly developed here, which is as it should be because the tourist office at the railway station proclaims itself the oldest in France, established 1875. Discos and night-clubs make for a lively night-life. Outdoor activities are centred on the lake which washes Gérardmer's doorsteps only 400 metres from the town centre. Charlemagne was here - if you doubt it you will be shown the rocky outcrop which bears the hoofprint of his horse. Early this century Gérardmer must have been a lovely old town, a scene from Grimms' fairy-tales. It escaped all the medieval wars, all the turmoil of Revolution and Empire, even the Franco-Prussian war of 1870 and the First World War. But it was almost obliterated in the last days of 1944 when the German army withdrew across the Rhine and now there is scarcely a building older than that date. The streets are clean and colourful, with many floral displays and gift shops. Local products include pine honey, Vosges *charcuterie* (smoked hams and sausages, chiefly) and a cheese called Le Gérôme. The wines come from French vineyards on the Rhine and are stronger and less flowery than German Rhine wines.

Ⓘ *Leave town by the main street, Boulevard d'Alsace, and bear right on to the D147, signposted Col de la Schlucht. Turn right on to the C12, signposted Xonrupt, then left, signposted Lac de Longemer.*

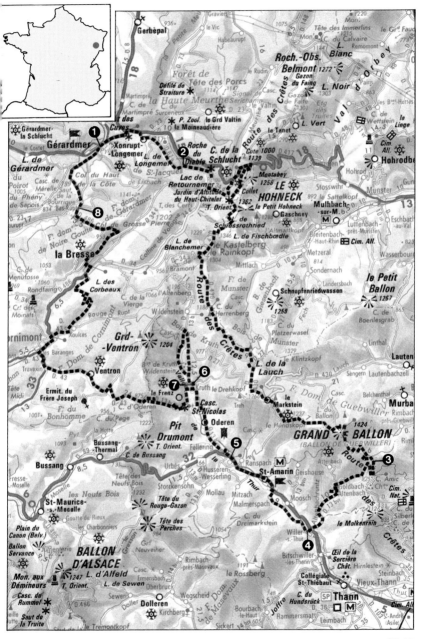

Xonrupt-Longemer
Summer pastimes and winter sports occupy adjacent sites in many Vosges resorts; consequently, scenes of activity alternate with scenes of near desolation. At Xonrupt, in summer, you tour a corridor of boarded-up chalets for skiers. Five minutes later you roll past the Longemer lake, which is almost invisible behind tents, caravans and the coloured sails of boats on its surface. In winter, all the action shifts to the chalets and to *aprés-ski* diversions.

The village houses Expo Faune Lorraine, a collection of the wildlife of the Vosges *en tableau* in mini-landscapes of growing vegetation. The exhibition is more educational than entertaining, promoting the ideals of a conservation-conscious community in a serious but quite endearing way. *Open daily, pm only, June-Sept.*

La Moineaudiére, just across the main road, takes all the stock-in-trade of a typically musty provincial museum - butterflies, eggs, wild flowers, minerals - and displays them with imaginative presentation and skilful lighting effects. Well worth a quick tour of inspection. *Open daily, all year round.*

Xonrupt-Longemer - Le Collet
② *At the end of the lake turn right, signposted Retournemer.* Here the road curves round a smaller lake, another hectic aquatic playground. *Turn left, signposted Le Collet.* Energetic passengers can get out of the car at this point and climb the well-marked short cut to Le Collet, where you will meet them half an hour later after some low-gear work in the car. *Turn right, signposted Le Collet, and right again on to the D430.* More slow climbing and more hairpin bends are in front of you: this is the start of the Route des Crêtes.

Le Collet - Le Markstein
The Alpine garden of Haut-Chitelet, on the right at 1,228 metres should not be missed. Here, amid kaleidoscopic rockeries, the University of Nancy cultivates species of high-altitude plants, some quite rare, from all over Europe and also from North America, China and Japan. Admission is free. If you want a scientific tour, a resident botanist will conduct you round. Delightful surroundings, but you must not picnic here. *Open daily July-Oct.*

On the left, a stone's throw farther on, you come to a roadside parking area where you may picnic; tables and benches are provided. (Note: the Alsatians are sensitive about litter.) There is a panoramic indicator at which you have wide and spectacular views over a comprehensive tract of the Vosges and the provinces of Haut Rhin and Bas Rhin. This summit is called the Petit Hohneck. The '*petit*' must be ironic - at 1,362 metres it is higher than any other point on the Hohneck massif. Pray for a high cloud base on this section. For many who travel it, swirling mist blots out the true grandeur of the scene.

Route des Crêtes
You have now reached the high ground and for the next 35 km will follow the crests from which the Vosges mountains sweep down among jumbled foothills to the west and drop abruptly to the Rhine valley in

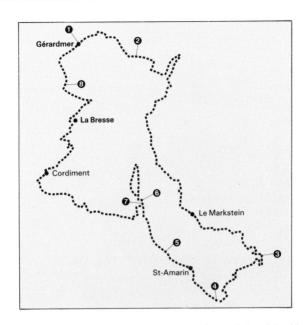

the east. At times you will see the southern chain of the Vosges at the Ballon d'Alsace; then the Belfort Gap, and beyond it the Jura mountains. Eastwards, in clear weather, the Black Forest in Germany is plainly visible. To the south-east you may catch a glimpse of Mont Blanc. These highlands were once remote from the world, known only to shepherds and smugglers (they were the historical frontier between Germany and France). In the First World War the heights marked the extreme right of the Allied line. Your road, the Highway of the Crests, was built by French military engineers towards the end of that war. It could not have been a communications link of any significance, nor was it strategically important; but it makes a wonderful skyline drive.

The kilometre stones give distances and altitudes, the latter ranging from 1,200 to 1,300 metres. The road is mostly unfenced, with near-vertical drops of several hundred metres.

Le Markstein

Not a village, merely a ski station. Neighbouring slopes are etched with ski-tows. Just before arriving at Le Markstein you may see people hang-gliding in the direction of Lac de la Lauch, another of the little melt-water lakes which are embedded like precious stones in the forested and heather-clad foothills. Hereabouts the road itself enters pine forests, but they do not obstruct the tremendous panoramas. There are marked nature trails here and there. Chalets and cafés are springing up, and at the latter you may buy bilberry tart, the local speciality, for your picnic at one of the numerous sites.

Highlands of Alsace, with the Haut-Koenigsbourg fortress seen left of centre.

Grand Ballon

Here the Route des Crêtes reaches its greatest altitude, 1,424 metres. The summit is a scattered community of hotels, bars and ski terminals. From it, your descent on the south side is moderately severe in places. The zigzags are well banked, but treat the slippery cobbles on the bends with respect if the surface is wet.

Guebwiller
(detour)

To the left, just beside the Goldbach turning, an enticing but very minor road goes off to Guebwiller, the so-called Pearl of the Florival. (Many small Alsatian towns are 'pearls' of something or other.) Guebwiller's vineyards and wine caves, Friday evening folkloristic spectacles and wide range of leisure opportunities attract many people to the Florival, which in spring and summer is indeed a floral valley. This detour would add about 30 km to the tour.

Alsace
(restaurant, Guebwiller)

This is the restaurant of one of Guebwiller's three hotels. The atmosphere is a trifle bleak but the food is meticulously prepared and served and lavish portions are offered. You are clearly in an establishment which is used to catering for strong hungry people in a bracing climate. The rabbit terrine is a meal in itself. Smoked Strasbourg sausage and smoked leg of pork are among the meats served in the regional *sauerkraut* platter. Memorable baking, including bilberry tart. *140, Rue de la République; tel 89.87.83.02; closed Fri evening and Sat lunch; price band B.*
③ *Turn right, off the Route des Crêtes, signposted Goldbach.*

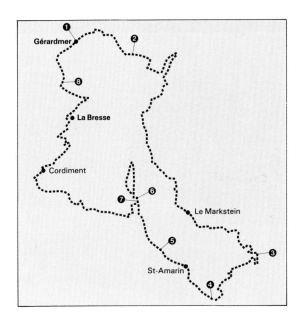

Goldbach - Willer-sur-Thur

The road drops alarmingly, the hairpins seem to go on for ever ... and all at once you are on the Bâle-Nancy highway.

④ *At Willer-sur-Thur (observe the attractive church with its eccentrically coiffeured spire) turn right on to the main road, left across the river and bend sharp right at the station yard.* On this minor road a few hamlets cower away from the thunder of traffic on the N66. *Keep left and turn left again into St-Amarin.*

St-Amarin

Formerly a stopover on the old-time *diligence* routes, St-Amarin is trying hard to become a tourist centre by exploiting its hilly surroundings and the attractions of the Thur valley in which it sits. A gridiron of footpaths is marked with the signs of the Club Vosgien; the most popular route is upstream to Ranspach and Wesserling, notable for wild flowers and spring blossom. Escorted walks to the Vosges highlands, including the Route des Crêtes, along which you have just driven, are organized by the Club. (*They take place on Wed every week, July to mid-Sept, one whole day, not too strenuous*). Another possible guided excursion is to the Sée d'Urbés (actually a peatbog) and the source of the Moselle river about 10 km west on the N66.

⑤ *In 3 km turn off the main road, signposted Kruth.* The road is narrow, and carries local tourist and forestry traffic, but the surface is good.

Kruth

The restaurant Perring often has local river trout on its menu.

⑥ *Turn right in the village and bear left, signposted Barrage.*

Lac de Kruth-Wildenstein

Above the dam is one of those little smudges of turquoise which you saw far below as you passed along the Route des Crêtes. *Take the serpentine road round it, preferably anti-clockwise.* It turns out to be an impressive sheet of water - artificial, but serene in its setting. At the top end the stream which feeds the lake tumbles headlong in cascades; picnic spots on both sides of the water - consult the information board at the Barrage, which also gives details of short walks.
⑦ *Turn right in Kruth, signposted Ventron.*

St-Nicholas

In 1.5 km you arrive at the toy chapel of St-Nicholas, hexagon-shaped with modern stained-glass windows. Alongside it, more powerful cascades, a whole mile of them, come racing into the Thur. Paths follow the rapids on both sides and you can picnic beside them.

Auberge des Cascades de St-Nicholas
(restaurant, near Kruth)

It stands on the right, close to the cascades, a rather fussy-looking chalet-hotel backing on to the pine forest. André Schwoob runs a clean inexpensive establishment. The *auberge* is not grand, nor is it unpopular with visitors, so book ahead for a bed or a meal. Typical Alsatian cuisine, *quiche Lorraine* (the authentic kind, without cheese), smoked ham, sauerkraut and appetising fruit tarts. Herr Schwoob is justifiably proud of his command of languages. You may already have seen the plaque on the door. It portrays a hand balancing a steaming saucepan on a tray, with the legend 'Plat du Terroir': a low-budget regional menu. *Route du Ventron, Kruth; tel 89.82.28.26; price band B.*

St-Nicholas - Ventron With many windings and a threat now and again to give it all up and turn back, the road sets itself to surmount the last ridge of the highlands. At the summit, the Col d'Oderen (875 metres) you leave the Haut-Rhin province and return to that of Vosges. A tortuous descent on the west side threads round-topped wooded hills.

Ventron Inhabitants of this modern village seem to choose to live as far from each other as possible, consistent with the narrow confines of the valley. They would seem to have a lonely life in winter, and here the snow lies late. But of course it is not at all lonely - winter is when Ventron really comes to life. The centre of winter-sports activity is the Hermitage of Frère Joseph overlooking the village. *(Turn left at crossroads just before entering Ventron.)* Besides ski-schools and chair-lifts there are two hotels, one big enough to host conferences. Their restaurants offer a sophisticated Alsatian cuisine - at a price. Summer visitors to Ventron energetically explore the woodland, fish in the trout streams and gather rustic fruits, including the wild raspberries and strawberries from which liqueurs are distilled. The countryside round about offers some strenuous rock-climbing, but nature really designed the whole scene for picnicking and sipping your *vin fin d'Alsace* and dozing in the sunshine.

Travexin On the left, before you turn right to the main road - the D486 - is a permanent exhibition of wood sculpture, a demonstration of the Vosges craftsman's inherited skills in taking cold timber and breathing life into it again.

Cornimont - Xoulces Cornimont is a small industrial town, much knocked about in 1944. *Drive through without stopping and bear right, signposted Xoulces,* along the torrent valley; *at Xoulces turn left.*

La Bresse To anyone coming from the upland hamlets, La Bresse is like a city, especially when it is humming with winter-sports visitors. Clean and colourful, almost entirely rebuilt since 1944, it attracts summer visitors who like to see a bit of life around them in the streets, bars and cafés.

Auberge du Pecheur *(La Bresse)* This offers the best of venison, trout in Riesling and other Alsatian delicacies; also a classy wine-list with excellent house wine by the carafe. *On the D34d, 6.5 km north of La Bresse; tel 29.25.43.86; closed two weeks in June and Dec, Tues and Wed out of season; price bands B/C.*

La Bresse - Gérard-mer Much holiday traffic negotiates the awkward hairpin bends on this road. At wayside houses local produce is sold, including goats' cheese and pottery - but you may find better bargains in Gérardmer.
⑧ *At Bas-Rupt, turn right before the river bridge to a minor road.* On the right, a rock-painting of Notre-Dame de la Cruse draws attention to her rustic shrine. *Re-enter Gérardmer.*

In the geological upheavals of pre-history, water in this locality south of Orléans was trapped on clay beds and settled into stagnant ponds. The resulting lakeland, now known as the Sologne, is a cartographer's nightmare, and to the hurrying motorist on the N20 a featureless land; and to those who explore it a dreamy country of silent pools and heather and abundant wildlife. This route, one continuous circuit, goes through the Sologne; then, by way of the great châteaux of Cheverny and Chambord, it crosses the valley of the Loire to the fertile plain of Beauce. This is not a conventionally beautiful drive; more of a voyage into a mysterious twilit world. Foreigners to France look blank when you mention the Sologne. French tourists have heard of it, but few have been there. In a few years maybe all that will change. There are plans to create wildlife parks and ecological reserves and to offer shooting, fishing and boating expeditions among the jigsaw puzzle of the meres. Meantime, the network of backroads does not spoil the simplicity and soft colours of a countryside which guidebooks too often dismiss as mournful and melancholy. There are no towns apart from the tour centre, Beaugency. It can be a fair distance between filling stations. Hotels are tiny, so do not count on rooms or meals at short notice. In secluded areas like this, touring families should consider accommodation at camping parks, pre-booked through a reliable operator.

▬▬▬▬ ROUTE: 140 KM

Beau-gency

Everything in Beaugency slides downhill to the Loire. Even the lateral streets have a slight tilt. Many travellers have slid through this cosy, genteel little town - it used to have the only bridge on 60 km of river. One who knew the place well was Dunois, Bastard of Orléans, faithful warrior of France and comrade-in-arms of Joan of Arc. His modest château is wedged under the town walls, beside the gate facing the square keep called Caesar's Tower. (You are in a district of Roman memories: the Orléanais is named after Marcus Aurelius.) The château is now the Orléanais museum, not very interesting. Time is better spent roaming the alleyways and, at night, strolling under old-fashioned street-lamps. Hardy walkers should look out for the *Sentier de Grande Randonnée* signs marking a fine long-distance footpath, which starts at Beaugency, goes along the south bank of the Loire and ends at Chinon in Touraine, 140 km away.

(Accommo-dation and eating, Beaugency)

A reasonable, above-average hotel is the Ecu de Bretagne; it has plenty of parking space, always a consideration at Beaugency; *Place Martroi; tel 38.44.67.60.* An acceptable restaurant, if you do not insist on gourmet fireworks, is the Auberge des Trois Cheminées; *Route Blois; tel 38. 44.74.20, price band B; the Auberge also has a car-park and a few rooms.* ① *Leave the town by the Route d'Orléans and turn right at the traffic lights in Baule.*

Beaule   A narrow little lane with a fine view of the Loire as you enter Meung.

Meung   Do not be put off by the fact that it lies on a busy highway. Easy to
                park in, this is a pleasant town of solid houses, semi-subterranean
                waterways and woodland walks. Its pale château and ruined *donjon*
                recall the adventures of two French poets, Jean de Meung (responsible
                for most of the medieval poem-cycle, the *Roman de la Rose*) and
                François Villon. Villon came to Meung under sentence of death - twice.
                And twice he benefited from an unexpected general amnesty.

Auberge   There are better places than Meung to eat or sleep in, but if you are
St-   doing either, an out-of-the-ordinary establishment is the Auberge St-
Jacques   Jacques close to the château. It is mentioned in Dumas' *Three*
(restaurant, *Musketeers* as the hostelry where the prickly d'Artagnan fights a duel
Meung)   and is wounded, all because another guest has smiled at the colour of
                his horse. M. and Mme Le Gall, chef and proprietress, keep a neat
                house and serve idiosyncratic fish dishes; *tel 38.44.30.39; closed two
                weeks Oct, Jan-Feb and Mon; price band B.*
                ② *Cross the Loire.*

Cléry-St-   Guidebooks call it dull, but many visitors are charmed by the half-
André   timbering of the gaunt old houses. Centuries ago it was an important
                stopover on the pilgrim route to Santiago de Compostela in Spain and
                when farm labourers ploughed up a primitive statue of the Virgin and
                Child the place attracted pilgrims on its own account, especially when
                the statue started working miracles. To house it, Charles VII and
                Dunois began the large church of Nôtre-Dame (1430) and Louis XI
                completed it - to the satisfaction of generations of martins which peer
                inquisitively at you from cracks in doorways and arches as you enter.
                The statue is on the altar, the bodies of Louis XI and his queen are in
                the crypt. Their skulls are displayed in a glass case.

Cléry -   The road is wide with ragged-edged tarmac and an undulating surface,
Ligny-le-   best taken at moderate speed. It is the gateway to the Sologne and for
Ribault   the next 40 km you may expect to see pheasant, hare, deer and
                possibly wild boar. In the season (late autumn, winter) you will hear
                shotguns and see sportsmen emerging from the undergrowth.
                ③ *Turn right, signposted Ligny-le-Ribault.*

Ligny-le-   Pause for a glance at the illuminated windows of the church, with
Ribault   leaded glass in unconventionally abstract designs.

St-   At Ligny, in the middle of what is generally considered a gastronomic
Jacques,   desert, another Auberge St-Jacques rates an entry in Michelin. *Tel 38.*
Ste-Anne   *45.41.54; closed throughout Sept; price band B.*
(restaur-   Freshwater fish and game dishes and snacks, from both homely and
ants, Ligny) cordon bleu recipes, are nicely presented at the Auberge Ste-Anne, M.

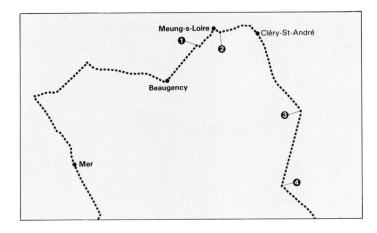

Lelait's bar-restaurant; *opposite the church in Place de l'Eglise; tel 38.45.42.19; closed Mon evening and Tue; price bands A upwards* - the broad price range reflects the cosmopolitan clientèle. This backwater is always thronged; it is a mystery where all the people come from.
④ *Turn left on to the road signposted Lamotte-Beuvron.*

Ligny - Yvoy-le-Marron
Woodland, boggy heath and lonely farmsteads on this road. Some farms sell goats' cheese, a Sologne speciality. Within a few minutes' walk of the road you might discover hidden pools and a rich, strange botany. But in autumn excitable wildfowlers deter you from straying and the most interesting looking meres are protected with chain-link fences and No Entry signs.

Yvoy-le-Marron
This small metropolis has curious houses, some red-bricked and pantiled, others faced with tiles stuck in cement. Such communities support carpenters, coopers and wheelwrights, all the old trades; and you may see a spire of blue smoke rising from the trees, indicating that charcoal-burners are at work somewhere not far off.
⑤ *Turn right, signposted La Marolle.*

Monté-vran (detour)
Turn left in Yvoy-le-Marron. Both roads going east skirt the zoological park of Montévran. The entrance is on the N20, Orléans-Vierzon road. Rare fauna of the region is Montévran's speciality but, like so many zoos, the place gives the impression of being short of cash.

La Marolle - Vernou
Characteristic Solognais cottages at Montrieux - squat bricks and half-timber, flat tiles or thatch or 'cob' (timber in-filled with a mortar of clay and straw) for the older buildings; an education in rural domestic architecture. Deer may be a hazard on this stretch. Tales are told of fatal collisions between motorists and bucks in the rutting season.

93

Typical Sologne timber-frame cottage at Courmemin.

Vernou   Visit the dried-flower workshops. You follow signs *Fleurs Séchées* to the farm meadow where everlasting flowers grow in many colours. The workshop turns out decorative items of various kinds, including ceramic heads adorned with dried blossoms. Sounds awful, but the results are sometimes artistic and Gil, Patricia and friends offer a cheerful, not heavily commercial, welcome. A small bouquet at ten francs makes a souvenir of a possibly unique cottage craft.

Cour-memin   It is set in its own little lakeland where duck and water-lilies abound and is among the most venerable of Sologne communities. On the left, as you leave, you have a close-up view of the Etang de l'Oie, an exceptionally pretty pool. Nearby and all along the well-surfaced but corrugated road you will find parking spaces and woodland clearings which make useful picnic places.

Fontaines -en- Sologne   At this rather down-at-heel village (the main-street bar/café totters alarmingly) you make your exit from the Sologne.
⓺ *At the village crossroads turn left, signposted Selles, then bear right, signposted Cheverny.*

Cheverny   Entering the trophy room at the château, confronted by 2,000-odd stags' heads, you understand why the wildlife of the Sologne was not quite as prolific as you had hoped to find it. Cheverny also has its cultural side - the guidebooks rhapsodise over tapestries, paintings and furniture. Such places breed shops and stalls the way the Sologne meres breed tadpoles. Here you can buy local wines, honey, glassware, pottery, wood carvings, leather, jewellery and stuffed animals. Souvenir

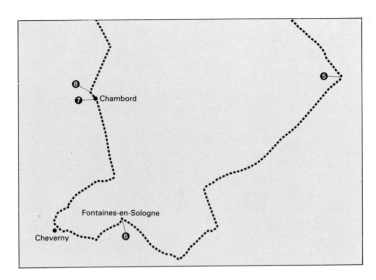

items are certainly of superior quality and the general layout is spacious - the orangery, a separate heated building, is itself capable of accommodating 500 visitors. But the whole operation is geared to mass tourism and one's heart sinks at the sight of all those coaches in the car-park. *Open am and pm in tourist season.*

Cour-Cheverny Centre of 24 wine communes, some in business for 450 years. They grow the white Romorantin, Sauvignon, Pineau and Pinot grapes and the red and rosé Gamay, Pinot Noir and Cabernet. The tourist office, tel *54.79.95.63*, will tell you which cellars and vineyards are receiving visitors and selling wine on which day. From here the road to Bracieux is excellent, through open country with wide horizons.

Villesavin *(detour)* On the left, approaching Bracieux, take the minor road to the Château de Villesavin ($\frac{1}{2}$ km), a lovely mellow old building of monastic and manor-house origins. It was never 'improved' by the extravagances of monarchs and their mistresses, but always remained in private hands. A stroll round the exterior is enough - there is nothing memorable inside.

Le Relais *(restaurant, Bracieux)* Here is a pleasant uncluttered dining-room and genuine local cuisine in the otherwise unremarkable village of Bracieux. You will appreciate the finesse which goes with the unassuming friendliness of M. Robin. A la carte prices for such dishes as quail with cabbage salad and river-fish-and-oyster *blanquette* are out of this world. But there is no shortage of customers for them, or for the humbler *plats du jour*; best to reserve a table. *1, Avenue Chambord; tel 54.46.41.22; closed Tues evening and Wed; price band D.*

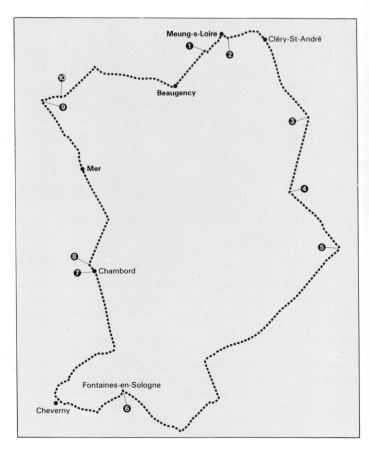

Meung-s-Loire
❶
❷
Cléry-St-André
❿
❾
Beaugency
❸
Mer
❹
❺
❽
❼ Chambord
Fontaines-en-Sologne
Cheverny
❻

Bracieux -
Chambord

Enter the conifer plantations of the Forest of Boulogne. Although straight, wide and well-shod, the road is intersected by ramps which you may find the hard way, by hitting them. There are no warning signs. When you pass through the boundary wall of the Chambord estate you still have 7 km to go to the château - which gives an idea of the scale on which this biggest of Loire residences is conceived. The park's boundary wall, enclosing a sanctuary for deer and wild boar, is 35 km in circumference.

Cham-
bord

The strange agglomeration of towers, belfries and chimneys, like a mushroom growth in stone, will be familiar to readers of books about Loire châteaux - it is usually the jacket illustration. Few of the 400 apartments are furnished, but all are redolent of court history and intrigue. Molière presented his plays here. Having bought your parking

ticket and paid your entrance fee you are free to roam unescorted - a rare privilege in Loire châteaux. Ascend the famous double-spiral staircase: those going up are invisible to those coming down. Walk among the chimneys on the roof - it is like walking through a fantastic stage set, for a Kafka dramatisation perhaps. *Closed Tues.*
⑦ *From the car-park follow the signs for Orléans.*

Chambord - Mer For 8 km you are still in the park of Chambord where game is under protection. On your left is the area open to the public, with some rectilinear paths for pedestrians. At the roadside on the right is an observation post, one of three 'hides' for studying the wildlife. But you really need binoculars. There is a helpful interpretative display in words and pictures.
⑧ *At the perimeter pavilion turn left, signposted Mer, then bear right on the D112.* Beyond the crossroads the Loire smiles up like an old friend. For views of an exceptional stretch of the river, park your car close to the bridge and go over and back on foot.

Mer The stained-glass windows in the church are worth more than a glance in passing.

Mer - Talcy These are the fringes of Beauce: the landscape is flat, the sightlines along the roads run straight to the horizon. You feel that if you could climb a tree you would have a view of Chartres cathedral, 80 km away - but there is not a tree in the landscape. An old-fashioned windmill on the right and then the prospect of Talcy château ahead remind you that you have come into another sort of country and that the Loire divides two cultures and two different styles of life and character.

Talcy Modest by Chambord standards, with no river running by, Talcy is impressive in its own way and good value for its relatively homely period furnishings. *Closed Tues.* It has fine Renaissance gardens which were laid out by horticulturists who had also to be skilled mathematicians and sergeant-majors too, one suspects, to keep the plants growing to order and preserve the uniform patterns of the gravelled walks and parterres. The shade of the 16thC poet Ronsard hangs over Talcy. He loved the owner's daughter and she inspired him to write the favourite recitation piece: *Mignonne, allons voir si le rose...*
⑨ *Return to the D70 and turn left, signposted Concriers.*

Concriers A well and its bucket and chain are a feature of many churchyards in this region, but have a look at the Concriers well - it must be one of the biggest ever constructed.
⑩ *Turn right and immediately left, signposted Josnes.*

Concriers - Beaugency In 7 km a fine avenue of poplar trees welcomes you back to Beaugency and the Loire.

The Middle Loire

In the Romance languages, many rivers are masculine, but not the Loire. Is this because she is wayward and unpredictable in her course? But *La Loire*, between Blois and Tours, is feminine in a different way. She is graceful and shy, hidden among low cliffs and vineyards in the flattish landscape, scarcely visible until you reach her banks. The tour is entitled the 'Middle Loire' but it is really an expedition to three rivers and three major riverside châteaux. It explores the Loire in the north, the serpentine Indre in the south-west, and, en route, it crosses and re-crosses the Cher, a waterway of modest charm and tranquility. The three principal châteaux - Amboise and Chaumont on the Loire and Chenonceau on the Cher - are among the most historic, photogenic and dramatically-poised in all France.

This is the 'garden of France', a great salad bowl with a timeless and refined air which proclaims the prodigality of nature and the Gallic countryman's genius for co-operating with the natural order of things. Such are among the themes of novels by Balzac, Zola and Alain-Fournier, set in this region.

Nor would a little preliminary reading of court and political history up to the *belle époque* be a bad thing on this tour. Much of that history was written around the châteaux and seigneurial demesnes through which you will pass. From Montrichard on the Cher, our northern loop offers lightly-trafficked alternatives to the main touring highways and achieves new perspectives on some famous sights. Southward you will penetrate the shallow valleys of the Indre and its tributary the Indrois, secret waterways unknown to many tourists.

▬▬▬ ROUTE ONE: 88 KM

Mont-richard

This township on the northern bank of the Cher is backed by the woodlands and deer-parks of the Montrichard and Amboise estates. Under a ruined keep like a block of concrete, atmospheric churches and half-timbered houses are crammed into an urban nucleus which has remained virtually intact since the Middle Ages. There are tourist roads through the forests - these forests actually have trees - and numerous picnic areas, cool on a hot day; also attractive riverside paths where the Cher loiters under pale *tuffeau* cliffs honeycombed with mushroom caves and wine cellars, some visitable. A few miles downstream the Cher becomes a canal. Of several small hotels, the Tête Noire in Rue de Tours is the biggest, the Bellevue at Quai de la République probably the most appealing to the visitor. You will find ample parking close to the principal sights between the Rue de Vierzon and the river bank. At quays on the sleepy river you may hire boats.

① *Following signs 'Autres Directions' from town centre, cross river and crossroads and turn left, signposted Loches. (Ignore the road on the left to the ancient abbey; it is strictly private.) After 5 km turn left on to the unsignposted road through the larchwoods.*

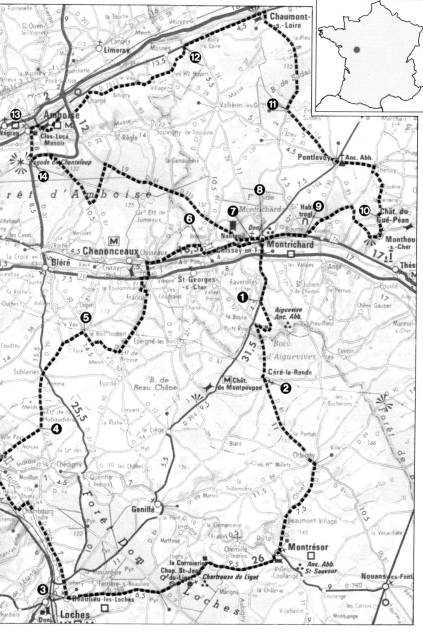

Entrance to the Charter-house of Liget.

Cère-la-Ronde
(detour)

The road on the right leads in 8 km to the château-museum of Montpoupon, via the fringes of a lake. This *gentilhommerie* has a history of 700 years devoted entirely, it seems, to field sports. The multifarious trophies of the chase, the saddlery and so forth will interest riding and hunting enthusiasts, not others. But the place is impressive, with a splendid *châtelet* (gatehouse) and you may picnic under its walls.
② *From Céré-la-Ronde follow signposts to Orbigny.*

Orbigny

No village in this part of France lacks interest for the ecclesiastical pilgrim, and Orbigny church with its iron-studded doors, pump in yard and colourful abstract stained-glass is particularly noteworthy. High up on an old house opposite the church you can make out a warning to horsemen of times past, *Défense de Trotter.*

Mon-trésor

Very narrow streets, single-file for donkeys in the old days: vertical expansion compensated for lack of horizontal space. From old houses to old church to old ivy-clad château, everything is tall and slim.

Le Liget

Beyond orchards, predominantly pear, the route crosses flat open country. At 8 km, just beyond the turning on the left to the Charterhouse, look out on the left for the 12thC chapel of Liget

standing all alone. It is locked, but you can get the key from the
Charterhouse. The medieval frescoes inside are a revelation. This
chapel was founded by Henry II in remorse for the murder of Thomas
à Becket at Canterbury. You can also visit the Charterhouse - on foot.
The car park is on the right of the road.

Le Liget -
Loches
Now you are traversing the old hunting forest of Loches, and also a
section of the tourist circuit called *Route des Dames de Touraine.*
Beware, therefore: stray deer and also motorists with eyes on maps.

Loches
The poet Alfred de Vigny (*'J'aime le son de cor, le soir au fond des bois'*)
was born here. Much earlier, the fortified town and its château were
the heart and homeland of war-ravaged Touraine. Avoid the lengthy
official tour of the fortress - it is enough to sit among the willows on
the Indre bank and reflect on the rough story of those honey-coloured
walls. King John of England sold them during Richard Coeur-de-Lion's
absence abroad. Richard was furious. On his return he repossessed
Loches in three hours - a feat which stupefied the medieval chroniclers.
In the dungeons Louis XII kept many noble prisoners, confining them for
greater security in small iron-bound cages. The Duke of Milan survived
eight years of crippling confinement and on release he stumbled and fell
dead, dazzled by the sunlight. The Loches skyline is impressively floodlit
on summer nights. For superior local products - dolls, glassware,
pottery - visit the art gallery Le Moulin at Flére la Rivière.

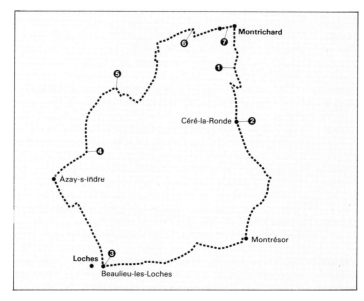

La France
*(restaurant,
Loches)*

The restaurant of the Hotel France at Loches is deservedly popular and prior booking is advisable. Michelin-recommended for value-for-money. The very reasonable fixed-price menu might include soup, river eels in Vouvray wine, a game pie and a creamy pudding. *Rue Piçois: tel 47.59.00.32; closed Sun evening and Mon lunch between Sept and June; price band A.*

③ *Take the D25 to Chambourg and continue on road signposted Azay-sur-Indre.*

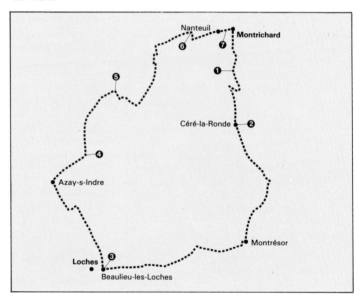

Azay-sur-Indre

The road uses two bridges and an *îlot* to cross the Indre. Before the first bridge, on the left, there is a children's playground; after it, a beautiful shady park with benches, ideal for a picnic. Watch a game of *boules* on the nearby court. You may park safely at the roadside and once you are among the greenery the picnic spot is quite secluded.

*Azay -
Sublaines*

Bid farewell to the pretty Indre where it receives an even prettier tributary, the Indrois, hedged in with willows, alders and fruit gardens. *Turning right, head for Sublaines, rejoining ④ the D25. It is a deceptively quiet little road. But in the harvest season tractors and combines take it over, and you cannot always hear them coming. On rural roads generally, the local farm traffic claims priority over city folk and tourists.*

*Sublaines -
Chenon-
ceaux*

⑤ *Bear right after Sublaines, signposted Villaines, right at crossroads signposted Luzillé, then left (no signpost). At subsequent crossroads (exercise care) follow the signs for Francueil. At the road junction after*

Francueil bear left then right, signposted Epeigné as far as the church; thereafter follow signs for Chenonceaux and glimpse the celebrated château on the left as you cross the bridge on the Cher.

Chenon-ceaux

Cottages smothered in ivy and vine, window-boxes and hanging baskets full of geraniums... this is an epitome of a 'garden of France' showplace. Proximity to the château, 1.5 km down the road, accounts for the many bars, hotels, antique and souvenir shops.

Bon Labou-reur
(restaurant, Chenon-ceaux)

Knowledgeable locals recommend the restaurant of this medium-sized Chenonceaux hotel for a taste of the regional cuisine at its most refined. River fish, including pike, imaginatively presented in *terrines* and *mousselines*. An exclusive *tournedos* called 'Vendôme'. Some of the great wines of Touraine are on the list, including Camay and Montlouis. *Tel 47.23.90.02; closed between Nov and Mar; price band C.*

Chenon-ceau

Note that the château of Chenonceau has dropped the 'x' - carelessness on the part of some old-time lawyer's clerk. Most delicately sited of Loire valley châteaux, most evocative of the loves and jealous rages of the grandest *dames de Touraine*, it has the added advantage of being visitable at one's own pace - none of the cattle-market regimentation which guides impose on visitors to some of the stately homes of France. Sumptuous as the interior is, nothing can surpass the view from the south bank of the Cher, upstream or down. Picnic among the trees, where you can fix in the memory the solemn beauty of Chenonceau and its reflection under seven supporting arches. (Each time you buy the well-known Menier chocolates you are contributing to Chenonceau's upkeep.) *Open all year.*

Chenon-ceaux - Nameuil

⑥ *Return through the village on the main road and at Chisseaux take the first left into Rue d'Eglise.* This road climbs and winds and once again a panorama of the valley opens out. *At crossroads follow the lane signposted La Touche, go straight on at next crossroads, turn right at the road junction and at the bottom of a steep hill turn left.*

Chissay
(detour)

If you turn right at the bottom of the hill and right again you come in one km to the intricately-wrought iron gates and railings of Château de la Menaudière, now an expensive restaurant, but a stylish building, perhaps worth shopping at for a drink. On this road, observe how naturally the cottages appear to grow out of their environment.

Nameuil - Montrichard

⑦ *At the main road turn right and almost immediately second left at a five-way junction.* On the left, note the cluster of antique farm buildings, with an even more antique *donjon* among them. Such buildings, originally the square central towers of châteaux, were safe deposits for family archives. The more ostentatious *donjon* of Montrichard, your destination, is now ahead.

ROUTE TWO: 80 KM

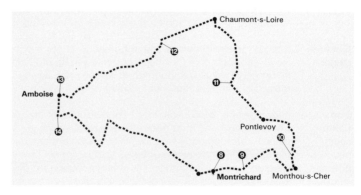

Mont-richard

⑧ *Follow 'Autres Directions' signs. Do not cross river bridge but go straight on, signposted Bourré.*

Bourré - Monthou-sur-Cher

⑨ *Turn left at Bourré, signposted Pontlevoy, then right at crossroads, signposted Thenay.* Monthou is a quaint little place to stretch one's legs in. Its rather lop-sided château, three towers conical and the other bell-shaped, offers an hour-long tour - a bit too much for what is mostly bric-à-brac. Mercifully there are no ice-cream kiosks or hucksters of trash and you are welcome to picnic in the park.

Le Gué-Péan

The château is a big four-square *gentilhommerie*, authentically furnished and lived in. It has come down in the world. Four centuries ago, as a powerful royal fortress, it helped write a pathetic page of English history. Young Mary Tudor, afterwards 'Bloody' Mary, came here with her lover Brandon. To reinforce a claim to the French throne she pretended to be pregnant by the deceased French king. But his widow outsmarted Mary and sent her packing. In frustration she married Brandon. A grandchild of the union was Lady Jane Grey, nine-day queen of England - beheaded in her teens by order of her grandmother 'Bloody' Mary. *Open all year.* ⑩ *Follow signs to Thenay, then Pontlevoy.*

Hôtel de l'Ecole *(restaurant, Pontlevoy)*

Elegant, creeper-covered, spotlessly clean, this hotel at Pontlevoy has only a few rooms and they are often booked weeks ahead, the price is so reasonable. Fine panelling indoors, wrought-iron furniture under a vine pergola outside. Families patronise the restaurant because children can eat for a ten-franc supplement on the adults' bill. Inexpensive but limited à la carte menu; the cellar contains only the best, so wines are inevitably pricey. *Tel 54.32.50.30; closed pm Mon and lunch Tue in low season; price band B.* If you lunch here, allow time for a stroll to the neighbouring 11thC abbey which incongruously houses a Heavyweights Museum - not prizefighters, but vintage commercial vehicles.

Pontlevoy - *Chaumont*	⑪ *Turn left to the main road in town centre then right, signposted* *Chaumont, at crossroads.* Sudais lake is on right. Picnic spots abound. On Sundays you will have company. This is a meandering, but suitably regal approach to the great château ahead.

Chau-mont
Cylindrical towers, battlements, drawbridge...a toy fort come to life-size. The pure Renaissance interior expresses the Valois dynasty's notorious obsession with exotica. The startling coolie-hatted structure in the corner of the stable yard has served in its time as dovecot, art workshop and children's riding school. *Closed Tues, Jan-May. Leave by the road past the church.* Here is the Loire, looking queenly.

Chaumont -
Amboise
⑫ *Approaching Mosnes, take the minor road on left, signposted Les Hauts Novers.* It is a narrow, uneven alternative to the main route, but worth it for quaint hamlets and some neat cameos of the Loire valley.

Amboise
This town is famous for fishing-tackle - and tourists. There are nooks and crannies to explore and some delightful ornate brick-and-stone houses, orange and white, among which you should not overlook Clos-Lucé and its rose garden on Rue Victor Hugo, five minutes' walk from the château. (Best to park at the château or on the riverfront tarmac.) Clos-Lucé, a Renaissance manor-house, is where Leonardo da Vinci lived and died, a guest in his old age of François I. A secret passage connects the house with Amboise château, 400 metres away. Now a museum, it has models and blueprints of Leonardo's inventions, including prototype gliders, parachutes and swing-bridges. His specifications are hard to decipher - he was left-handed and wrote backwards. The château, once the biggest in the Loire valley, was cut down in size after the French Revolution, but is still a grand sight on its walled cliff above the river. View it from Amboise bridge or from the Ile d'Or (accessible by road) in midstream. Inside, you may be deterred by the long academic discourse of the guide and the commercialisation. ⑬ *Leaving tourist office on right, take the first left, signposted Bléré, along a tree-lined avenue. Turn right at signpost for Pagode.*

Chante-loup
The Chanteloup park is highly recommended for picnics, walks and a snooze beside the lake, lulled by the humming of dragon-flies and the scuffle of lizards. The château has gone but the Pagoda remains. The view from the top tier (150 steps, no elevator) embraces the Loire valley and the Amboise forest.

Chanteloup -
Montrichard
Take the D31 going east, then the D81 on the right, signposted Chenonceaux. Later turn left, signposted St-Règle, and then right on to the D61. Another sizeable lake, the Grand Etang de Jumeaux, is on the right, just before you emerge from the forest and descend - with a final panorama of the Cher valley - on the red roofs of Montrichard.

Loire:

'Fair Touraine' has a magic sound: it calls to mind maids, knights and minstrels, affairs of the heart and indeed of Plantagenet power politics, played out in fairy-tale châteaux. Nowadays they call it more prosaically Indre-et-Loire, from two of the principal rivers. Heading south-west from Paris towards the Biscayan coast of France you must pass through this region. The châteaux are not all frivolous - some are menacing and steeped in blood, for around them, for more than two centuries, from Richard Coeur-de-Lion to Joan of Arc, the French struggled to throw off the English yoke. In riverbank towns and villages an amiable rusticity goes hand-in-hand with stormy memories.

It is a quiet, watered land, mostly agricultural with traces of royal hunting forests, not overburdened with tourists. The Indre, Cher and Vienne rivers make their way through it into France's longest river, the Loire. The first loop of the figure-of-eight explores the country south-west of Tours, the old capital of Touraine; it keeps south of the Vienne river and runs along the frontiers of Anjou, where England's Plantanaget dynasty originated and where some members of it returned to die. The other loop makes for the Loire valley and embraces several important châteaux. Much of the driving is through woodland and past grassy slopes, with no shortage of picnic spots; just as well - restaurants are rather thin on the ground.

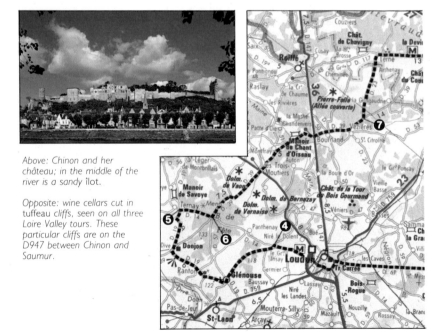

Above: Chinon and her château; in the middle of the river is a sandy îlot.

Opposite: wine cellars cut in tuffeau cliffs, seen on all three Loire Valley tours. These particular cliffs are on the D947 between Chinon and Saumur.

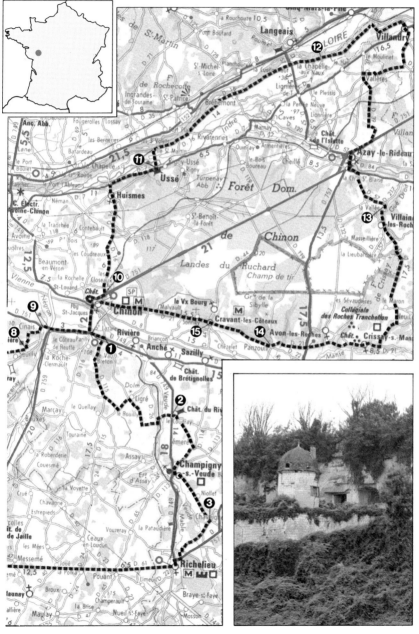

ROUTE ONE: 96 KM

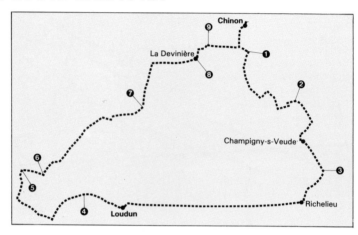

Chinon

A mixture of the quaint and the trendy, the town receives many tourists. The ruined château, more of a château-fort, sprawls over a ridge which stops short above the Vienne river and the town; and it has done so, in one form or another, since Roman times. '*Petite ville, grand renom*', wrote Rabelais - but after it came into the hands of the Plantagenet kings in 1154, Chinon's whole history was the history of its château. The kings' pride in it started the fashion for royal residences in the Loire country.

You can walk round the dilapidated ruins and enter chambers where the Dauphin, afterwards Charles VII of France, toyed with his beautiful but brazen mistress Agnès Sorel, the first woman in France to go topless. You can enter the great hall where in 1429 the Dauphin came under the spell of a very different woman, when one of history's most dramatic scenes was played: the royal prince, disguised among his courtiers, was instantly recognized by the innocent country girl Joan of Arc. *Open 9-12 and 2-7; closed Wed out of season, and Dec-Jan.*

Park off Rue J. J. Rousseau and walk through the Grand Carroi, the quarter of tight-packed, top-heavy medieval tenements. There, near the ascent to the château, you will find a couple of interesting museums, one devoted to the history of Chinon wines and cooperage, the other evoking the town's daily life in bygone ages.

Sainte-Maxime
(restaurant, Chinon)

Fresh country-style and *chasseur* food from the purest ingredients. The short *à la carte* menu offers river fish prepared to traditional recipes and sometimes truffles and *foie gras*. *31 Place du Général de Gaulle (behind town hall); tel 47.93.05.04; price band C.*

① *Leave Chinon by tree-lined avenue across the Vienne (two bridges) and turn left on to the D751; after 0.75 km turn right, signposted Ligré.*

Chinon -
Le Rivau
A steady ascent through tunnels of leaves and branches. Note the liana-like creepers on the ancient trees. The upland landscapes are like a tract of central Europe, all vines, sunflowers and maize.

Château
de
Marçay
(restaurant,
Marçay)
This famous hotel provides the gourmet experience of the region and the fresh-fruit-based desserts can be quite memorable. An atmosphere of restrained aristocratic elegance will suit some, and make others feel slightly uncomfortable. *At Marçay, 6.5 km from Ligré, 13 km from Chinon; tel 47.93.03.47; closed Jan and Feb; price band D.*

② *Just before entering Ligré, turn right, signposted La Mortière. Cross the railway and the Veude river and at the main road - the D749 - turn right, then immediately left, signposted Lémere.*

Le Rivau
On the left. This Gothic château is mentioned by Rabelais and it has powerful Joan of Arc associations (it is not alone in that). Pierre-Laurent Brenot, owner and painter, exhibits his works.

Champ-
igny-sur-
Veude
The florid Sainte-Chapelle, a pious work of Louis de Bourbon (1540), has some beautifully luminous stained glass. Tours are guided with reluctance and there is not much to see. Unfortunately, you have to go round before they will let you walk in the gardens.

③ *Having followed the Veude river upstream to Chaveignes, turn right signposted Richelieu. All the villages hereabouts delight students of architecture. For the lay visitor, the charm lies in the harmony of old cottages and farmsteadings and the endless vistas of rolling countryside.*

Richelieu
La Fontaine called it "the finest village in the universe." The great Cardinal was not satisfied with that: he decided that Richelieu should become capital of France (this was around 1630) and he pillaged the château of Chinon for masonry to create his 'new town'. It is now a strangely lifeless place, like an Olympic village when the Games are over. Take a stroll in the great park, a mathematical diagram of sycamores and chestnut avenues. Admission is free except during July, Aug and Sept. The most endearing bit about Richelieu is the resurrected steam train, vintage 1900, which trundles you to Chinon and back on summer weekends.

Richelieu -
Loudun
Tormenting lanes are behind you, but there are more to come, so make the most of this dead-straight and peaceful road.

Loudun
A hilly site: perimeter avenues round its base mark the lines of the old city walls. Inside them it is not easy to find parking space. Thanks to Cardinal Richelieu (he could not bear to see noble buildings in 'his' landscape unless he owned them himself), the former citadel is reduced to one square tower.

(Eating, Loudun)	Loudun is a convenient lunch stop. If you feel extravagant, try La Reine Blanche, *price band C*. If merely hungry, eat at the *crêperie* in Place de la Poulaillerie, *price band A*. The local speciality is *tuffeau du Loudunais*, a spicy rock-cake. (*Tuffeaux* are the low chalky cliffs of the Loire region which have been excavated in many places for storerooms, wine caves and even dwellings.)
④ *Leave Loudun by the Angers road, turn left on to the D14, signposted Insay, then left again on to a narrow road signposted Glénouse.*
Loudun - Ranton	This is the *Côte Loudunaise*, an attractive drive above the valley of the Dive with a chance of cool breezes on a hot day. There are magnificent views to the south-west just before Ranton and again on leaving it.
Ranton	The thin wooden racks scattered over the fields are for drying the maize-cobs. Note the unusual construction of the farmhouses, done with small irregularly-shaped cobbles. One farmhouse is the Musée Paysanne, exhibiting agricultural life of the past century, *open every afternoon in summer*.
Curçay	The donjon (a maximum security tower) on the right is a landmark from the middle ages, but not of much significance historically. On the left, from the fine viewpoint, a downhill footpath goes through the village and takes you to the bank of the Dive river canal - a pleasant 20-minute stroll, and an ideal spot for a picnic.
⑤ *Continue on the D19 to the right, then left, signposted Ternay.*
Ternay	The Manoir de Savoye is on the left as you leave the village. It is a family-owned château and, despite the misleading symbol on your map, it is open at all reasonable hours. In fact, the residents seem genuinely pleased to see visitors - which is rare enough in these parts.

⑥ *Follow road signposted Loudun, then turn left on to D39 for Chinon.* |
| **Ternay - Lerné** | ⑦ *Continue over two crossroads, Les Trois Moûtiers (an old word for monastery) and Bournand. At Vezières bear left, signposted Lerné.* You will see apricot orchards among the groves and woodlands of this serene and undulating landscape. Tiny picturesque cottages are a feature of all the villages, notably Lerné, where there is also a really elegant church. After Lerné the Château du Coudray on the right is not accessible. |
| **Fonte-vraud** *(detour)* | *Backtrack on the D17 to Fontevraud (16 km).* The glory of this huge 12thC abbey departed at the French Revolution, when it became a state prison. But it still contains the tombs of two English queens and two English kings (Henry II and Richard Coeur-de-Lion). There is no truth in the myth found in many guide books and travel books that the British royal family continually pleads for the bones to be removed to Westminster Abbey. |

▬▬ **ROUTE TWO: 84 KM**

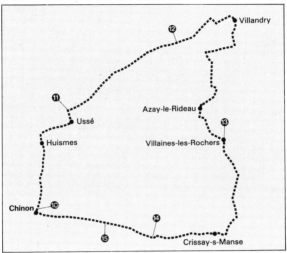

Lerné - La Devinière	⑧ *Bear left at the fork signposted Côteau, and enter Seuilly; then turn left at road junction, signposted Cinais.* Rabelais' *Gargantua and Pantagruel* is set in this countryside.
La Devinière	The Rabelais museum is best seen from outside: a simple 15thC cottage, steep-pitched with slender stone pillars and an outside staircase, *open daily except Wed.* ⑨ *After Cinais, follow the D751 to Chinon.*
Chinon - Huismes	⑩ *From Chinon take the Tours road past the château and turn left, signposted Huismes.*
(Eating, Huismes)	They sell apples and pears (*Bon Chrétien*, whose homeland this is) at the farm. A useful lunch stop is La Devinière (not to be confused with the village of Rabelais), close to Huismes church, with agreeable service rendered by *patron* Michel Martin; *price band B.* No embargo on children here, or at the perfectly adequate Auberge du Grillon, almost next door; *price band A.*
Ussé	The château tour is long and costly, the guides are incomprehensible, the leaflet is dull and entry to the formal gardens is prohibited. Best sit opposite, under the catalpa trees at the Café au Bois Dormant, gossip with the cheerful young proprietors and enjoy the view of this white-stone château, the scene of Perrault's *Sleeping Beauty* story. *Open daily, Easter-Oct.*
Ussé - Villandry	⑪ *Take the first left and, on three narrow bridges, cross the Indre,* a river which flirts a long time with the Loire before actually joining it;

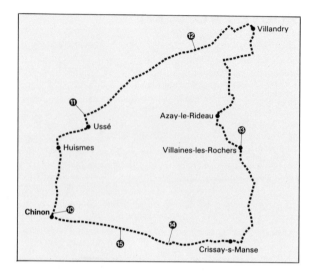

then turn right, signposted Azay. This riverside drive is delightful, partly wooded and offering plenty of shade. The Loire, the longest river in France and the most useless navigationally, rolls over shallows and past end-to-end *îlots* (sandbanks).

In 5 km there is an idyllic picnic spot, with parking and riverbank footpaths in both directions. Close to Bréhémont is another good picnic area on low dunes. After Bréhémont, look over your left shoulder for a view of the graceful *pont suspendu*.

La Chapelle Here you have access to several sandy *îlots*. On the right is the furniture workshop of M. Moral, who does chests, tables and so on in oak, mahogany and cherrywood with traditional carvings.
⑫ *Bear left, signposted Villandry, then right through a leafy glade (beyond the monument) into Villandry.*

Villandry You may park under the lime trees beside the main road. The château, pure Renaissance, was built in 1532 on earlier Gothic foundations called Colombiers. The three-tiered gardens (water, ornamental, kitchen), severely geometrical, are one of the mandatory sights of the Loire.

Azay-le-Rideau The babel of tongues in the queue for admission confirms the worldwide fame of this 'floating' château on a diverted loop of the Indre. Feminine taste inspired the interior décor - the royal treasurer's wife ran riot in 1510, until François I nailed her swindling husband and confiscated the place. *Open all year.* The *ridellois* (inhabitants of Azay) are carpenters and fruit-growers and their white wines, Côteaux de Touraine, have achieved the distinction of an *appellation contrôlée*.

Azay - Villaines

⑬ *Turn left, then right, signposted Villaines les Rochers.* This is a dreamy, winding route through vineyards. From the top of the steep hill you have a broad view of a well-clothed, well-watered landscape.

Villaines - les- Rochers

This is the 'troglodite' village, where cellars and garages are hollowed out of the *tuffeau* rock. The basket-making co-operative, flourishing since 1849, when a parish priest founded it, welcomes visitors and does not harass them.

Chrissay- sur-Manse

A charming, completely unspoiled village, almost wholly pre-16thC, Chrissay merits at least half an hour of your time. Park the car near the first old well and stroll the skein of alleyways. The tourist office, on the street which leads to an abbey (not open to visitors), occupies someone's kitchen, and that someone has developed a nice line in home baking and honey - so picnic ingredients are at hand, and so is the picnic site, down the hill beyond the church and second well, on the path signposted Vieux Moulin.

Chrissay - Cravant- les-Côteaux

⑭ *Continue on the D21, crossing main road and bearing right at Panzoult.* This is a fast, well-surfaced road with little traffic, but do not ignore the pleasant views which now open over the vale of the Vienne river. They are typical of the panoramic prospects of Touraine which have been a feature of this loop.

Cravant's big bottle.

Cravant- les- Côteaux

The gigantic wine bottle on a wall advertises the local vineyard, from whose cavernous cellars you can bring away a bottle or a half-case, together with some understanding of the mystique of the Chinon wine trade.

⑮ *Continue on the D21 to Chinon.*

Rivers of Jura

The Franche-Comté, the historic 'free country' which separates the upper Rhone valley from the Swiss border, is a region of flattish Alps and chalet-style dwellings inhabited by men and women of *montagnard* character, clean and industrious and moderate in all things. The Jura mountains, which form a crescent-shaped barrier to this ancient province, reach heights of around 1,500 metres, but they are not a chain of peaks - more a rippling banner of high pastures and folded hills, coloured dark green (the forests), bright green (the meadows) and grey (the limestone crags). The tinkle of the cow-bell emphasises the serenity of the uplands, traffic is light, and it gives way, morning and evening, to herds of milking cattle in the lanes.

The cuisine is largely based on dairy products and the fish (some species peculiar to the region) from beautiful clear rivers which have forced their way through the broken limestone to create, on a smaller scale, a landscape similar to the Belgian and Luxembourg Ardennes. Among culinary ingredients, the *Gruyère*-type cheese called *Comté* is pre-eminent; the tour touches at some points the so-called *Route du Comté* which connects the principal *fromageries* and the caves where the cheese is matured.

The centre of the figure-of-eight is Pontarlier. One loop follows the Swiss border and takes in stretches of the Doubs, which some consider the most impressive river in France. The second loop embraces the springs of Ain, another limpid torrent, and a variety of Jura scenery.

On backroads in these parts, fuel can be quite a rare commodity, possibly on account of the proximity to Switzerland, where it is cheaper.

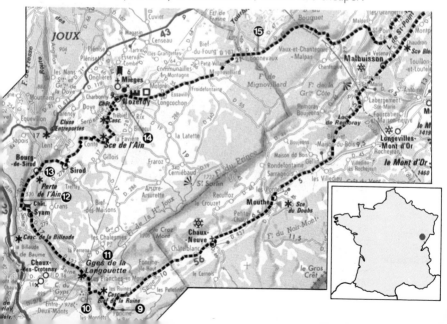

The Saut du
Doubs, close
to point ①

ROUTE ONE: 83 KM

**Pontar-
lier**

Pontarlier is the town everyone knows and no one stops at - it is the
last French town you pass through *en route* from the Channel ports to
Switzerland and Italy. There is really not much to stop for, unless you
are attracted by the grotesque little spruce-wood bottles in which the
local liqueur, an inferior kind of *retsina*, is sold. In the streets on either
side of the main street an awkward one-way system is in force.

Grand Hotel de la Poste *(restaurant, Pontarlier)*

On Pontarlier's main street, but by no means as grand as its name, this coaching-house of ancient repute offers an excellent introduction to the Jura cuisine. On the fixed-price menu you may be supplied with stuffed pike, crayfish *gratin* or kirsch-flavoured *fondue* as well as veal and poultry dishes. *55, Rue de la République; tel 81.39.18.12; closed mid Oct-mid Dec, Mon and Sun evening out of season; price band C.*
① *Cross the bridge over the Doubs river and turn left on Rue de Morteau; then follow signposts for Montbéliard, afterwards for Morteau.*

Pontarlier - Montbenoît

On the outskirts of Pontarlier, on the left, note the tall needle-like spire of the little church at Doubs. After you have crossed the river of that name at Arçon, you will perhaps rub your eyes at the first of the natural 'wonders' and *trompe-l'oeil* effects for which the river systems of the Jura are notorious: the Doubs appears to be flowing uphill.

Mont-benoît

The solemn old abbey church has been a beacon of the faith for 700 years and during that time some comical wood-carvings have made their appearance on the pulpit, the pews and the misericords. Observe the two peasant women pulling each other's hair out, and similar naïve examples of wood-sculptors' piety.

Auberge de l'Abbaye *(restaurant, Montbenoît)*

Like some other restaurants on this route, the Abbaye at Montbenoît bears the sign *Route du Comté'*, which means that it offers not only the famous cheeses of the region but also some local speciality on the fixed-price menu. It could be *coquelot-au-vin*, *féchuns* (stuffed cabbage), *potée* (sausage stew) or *pauchouse* (fish in white wine). A rather ambiguous proverb says of it that one glass is enough. *Tel 81.38.11.63; closed Wed and Sun evening, and mid Nov-mid Dec; price band B.*

Montbenoît - Morteau

The road squeezes through an impressive canyon called the Défilé d'Entre-Roches. You can park on the left and should really get out and walk a short way to appreciate the grandeur of the ravine. Five km on, with the dark forest fleece on your left growing ever more dense, you come to the statue of St Ferjeux at Remonot. This saint introduced Catholicism to the Franche-Comté. Near it is the grotto of La Chapelle, which has a church tucked inside it. Walk past the altar, if no service is in progress, and cross a bridge. Beyond the bridge a network of caverns runs deep into the rock. After the grotto you have to drive through another awesome defile, the Coin de la Roche, where the crystal-clear Doubs thrusts through high forested cliffs and emerges suddenly on an open plain.

Morteau

It would be a village in more populated parts of France, but here it is a sizeable town spread over green pastures at about 1,000 metres altitude. People come here for their holidays - there are fine walks in the neighbourhood and first-class fishing, bathing and canoeing on the Doubs, which is here a sedate, unhurried river. Local industry seems

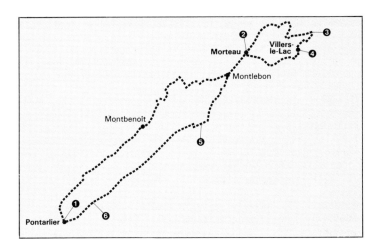

equally designed to attract the tourists: at Morteau they make clocks, bells and chocolate - and of course cheese. The restaurants Paris - *tel 81.67.06.70; price band B* - and Bel Air - *tel 81.67.00.98; price band C* - specialize in the Jura cuisine, which here comprises *Comté* and Emmental cheeses, mountain butter, smoked ham, fishy *croûtes* and the locally celebrated smoked sausage called *Jésus de Morteau*.

② *Continue through the town, an uphill road signposted Besançon. At Les Fins bear right, then turn sharp right on to the D215, signposted La Suisse. This is a steep road with many hairpin bends and good views of the last ripples of the Jura range in Switzerland. Follow signposts for Villers-le-Lac and after the steep descent to the crossroads go straight on.*

Saut du Doubs   The cascade, 27 metres high, would be impressive on most rivers, but the Doubs proceeds amid so many natural wonders that you take big waterfalls for granted. Ideally, one should take a two-hour walk along this stretch of the river as far as the Chatelot dam and the *Belvédère*. From the car park, where hotels, both Swiss and French, add nothing to the view, a ten-minute walk brings you to the *Saut* (cascade). There are scores of trinket stalls - even though one of them describes itself as the *Loup Solitaire*. The souvenirs are nasty without being particularly cheap. But this should not deter you from viewing the Saut, one of the *Grands Sites Régionaux* - of which there are only 15 in all France.

③ *Returning, keep left along the river, signposted Villers.*

Villers-le-Lac   It has an amphitheatrical site above the Doubs and from the quay near the bridge you can embark for a voyage downstream, where beech, pine and chestnut climb almost vertically from the glassy water's edge. There are lovely walks around Villers too, along which the local tourist board has provided belvederes. The Swiss frontier is only 8 km down the road - a crossing with minimal formalities. In fact, at times you find the gate open and unattended.

④ *Trace the windings of the Doubs upstream and re-enter Morteau. Follow the one-way system through the town. Turn right on to the D437, signposted Les Gras, and cross railway and river.*

Grand' Combe- Châteleu

Several venerable occupations are pursued here and in neighbouring hamlets: ham-curing in timber oast-houses called *fermes à tuyé*; taxidermy; and woodworking. On the right, signposted Ferme Atelier, is the 'Ecomuseum' of Beugnon, where rare old implements of blacksmiths, wheelwrights and foresters are displayed. This may sound boring, but the exhibition does give real insight into the harsh life of the *montagnard* people.

Les Gras - Pontarlier

⑤ *Keep right in Les Gras.* Hereabouts the road goes into the forest again, picks up a tributary of the Doubs and comes within inches of the Swiss frontier. Beware the occasional very sharp bend. There are up-and-coming ski centres on this road, notably Les Alliés. Just beyond Les Etraches, on the right and within one km of the road is another slender rocky gorge, the Défilé d'Entreportes. ⑥ *Straight on for Pontarlier.*

ROUTE TWO: 109 KM

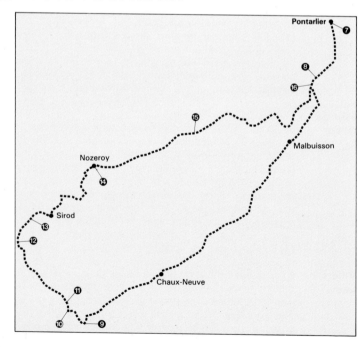

Pontar-lier   *Leave by the main road for Switzerland, signposted Lausanne, and*
⑦ *turn right, signposted Malbuisson.* Almost immediately you are in a
deep and eerie ravine.

Fort de Joux   The gloomy old fortress high above you seems to have come out of a
Gothic novel, and in its long history it has known some Gothic
moments. The young Mirabeau, some years before the French
Revolution, was imprisoned there at the instigation of his own father.
Another patriot, the Negro Toussaint-Louverture, died here in captivity
in 1803. You cannot reach the fortress from this road and in any case it
is an empty shell.

Oye-et-Pallet   As you leave this hamlet there is a splendid view of the Lac de St-
Point, whose 7-km length you are about to measure.
⑧ *Keep left at head of lake.*

Chaudron   On the left, a short footpath climbs to the source of the Bleue river -
not a very dramatic scene, but you could picnic here with the expanse
of the lake in front of you. It is the largest in the Jura.

Mal-buisson   An important water- and winter-sports area with numerous hotels and
open-air cafés.

Laberge-ment-Ste-Marie   If you have not yet inspected a Jura bell foundry, here is an
opportunity. The Obertino establishment has been making bells for
schools, chapels, hotels and especially for cattle since 1834. To some
extent, the casting, firing and stockpiling of the bells are still done
according to methods which were in use when Louis-Philippe was on
the throne. You may walk around freely. You can buy bells and bell-
shaped trinkets - paperweights and suchlike - of different sizes, in
bronze or steel. *Closed for holidays throughout Sept.*

Mouthe   To the left, a rough walk of about ten minutes takes you to the springs
of the Doubs - humble enough origin for a torrent which, as you saw
on the northern loop of this tour, soon becomes a majestic river.

Chaux-Neuve - Les Planches-en-Mone   After Chaux-Neuve you will pass through rocky canyons with many
acute curves. Most tiny hamlets along the route aspire to become ski
resorts; ski-ing is very much a growth industry in the Jura. Foncine-le-
Haut has restaurants, bars and a general *après-ski* atmosphere. It also
marks the start of a forest trail (on the right) which leads out to high
pastures and the Bulay viewpoint, with its panoramic indicator at 1,139
metres. At Foncine-le-Bas there is fuel at a price.

⑨ *Turn right, signposted Champagnole, and bear right to the D127.*
Hairpins continue coming thick and fast, and on this section of the route
they are all shrouded in woodland.

Les Planches-en-Mone

Just before you enter the village you will see on the left a car park for the use of those who walk to the Langoulette gorges 0.75 km away. ⑩ *Bear right at road junction.* The roughish track on the left leads to the smaller Langoulette parking area, close to the precipitous steps which lead along the side of the gorges past a series of spectacular waterfalls. This undisciplined river is the Saine. The Langoulette gorges are a really fine sight, especially after heavy rain. Not the least striking aspect of them is the row of houses close to the village, which teeter on the very brink of the chasm. (They say they chain their toddlers to the railings to prevent them from falling in.) At Les Planches honey is sold, said to be of epicurean quality.

⑪ *Bear right in village, then follow signs for Syam.* The road passes through a corridor of shining rocks.

Syam

The château is Italianate, not very old or distinguished. But it costs little to enter and it is one of the few accessible private houses in the region. *Open Sat, Sun and Mon only.* ⑫ *At road fork, bear right.*

Bourg-de-Sirod

On the right is a short footpath to the Pertes de l'Ain. *Pertes* are swallow-holes. The infant Ain river is supposed to disappear through fissures in its limestone bed. Whether this is a 'wonder' or not, it will be one if you actually see it happening. If you pass through Bourg-de-Sirod in dry weather following prolonged rain it may be worth while visiting the *pertes* on the off-chance of seeing the phenomenon.

Fortunately this pretty little river gradually recovers and reappears and becomes an attractive waterway, flowing into the Rhône near Lyon.

Those interested in idiosyncratic craft pottery should not miss the Pertes de l'Ain studio of Régina Le Moigne, opposite the road fork; a rustic creeper-covered building with huge tubs of fuchsias in front. The work is of a high standard, according to experts.

Pertes-de-l'Ain
(restaurant, Bourg-de-Sirod)

This restaurant offers a simple menu from the less adventurous side of the Jura cuisine - a sort of refined peasant diet. Prices are extremely reasonable and a smooth house wine is available by the carafe or half-carafe. *Tel 84.52.26.31; closed Mon; price band A.*

⑬ *The road bears right* and goes through the mountain in a tunnel. *From Sirod, follow signposts for Conte.*

Conte

The narrow streets of the hamlet can be hopelessly congested on Sat and Sun. One km onward, bear left for the source of the Ain. For once, this is a source worthy of a big beautiful river. Its emerald pool, astonishingly deep, is lost in woodland - you locate it from the sound of dripping water. A picnic area, admirably set up, is close by.

Nozeroy

Long ago this was the feudal capital of a well-populated district and it still has its old ramparts and fortifications, its medieval castle and important Gothic church, enclosed in decayed city walls.

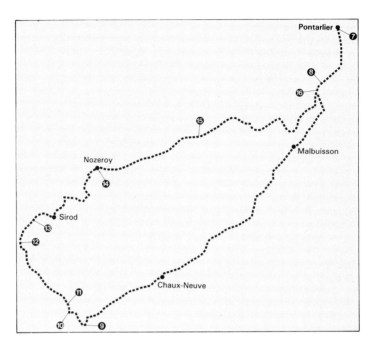

(14) *Bear right in Nozeroy and within 100 metres turn right again, signposted Longcochon. The road looks difficult and there are some formidable gradients, but it is good enough and it traverses rich pastureland, flowery in spring and summer. Watch out for sauntering cattle around milking time. Follow road signposted Pontarlier.*

Bonne-vaux
(15) *Next door to an attractive house fronted with lapped tiles, turn right, signposted Lac de St-Point; on arrival at the lake, turn left, signposted St-Point. On the right, at the bar, small craft are hired out.*

Les Grang-ettes
The arts-and-crafts gallery Du Mouton Noir on the right is among the most stylish and interesting in the whole of provincial France. About 25 artists have their studios here and display wrought-iron work, clothing, jewellery, ceramics, glassware and sculptures of a serious standard.

Le Bon Repos
(restaurant, Grangettes)
The restaurant of this two-star hotel is praised for its no-nonsense, thoroughly satisfying country cuisine. It is privately owned and family-run by people who clearly like their job and enjoy meeting strangers - especially children. *Tel 81.89.41.89; closed Nov and Dec; price band B.*

Grangettes - Pontarlier
(16) *At the end of the lake rejoin the route by which you travelled out, and at the main road turn left, signposted Pontarlier.*

121

South of Dijon on the Riviera route, or north of Lyon if you are heading for Paris, the motorway brushes aside a hilly territory of bracken, gorse and foxglove. It looks rather wild and inhospitable, more like the west of Ireland than the centre of France. It has been called, from the metallic glint of its rocky outcrops, the Land of Golden Stones. On the hottest day there may be a breeze sweeping across the moor and rattling the shutters of roadside cafés. "Do those windows have to be open?" asks a tourist. "Yes, madame," says the *patronne* sweetly, "we have arrangements with the Paris hairdressers."

The unlikely wilderness protects some of the famous vineyards of the Saône valley. For mile after mile on the main road the small red and white posts and the rows of stakes along the furrows mark the complicated classifications and sub-divisions of the Burgundy wine *communes*. They were the monks of Cluny, long ago, who put these lands under cultivation. Wherever you climb out of the valley, you find that all roads still lead to Cluny. It is one of the great names in the history of western civilization.

It is also this tour's centre. The two loops thread the wilderness, which of course is not a wilderness at all once you have come to grips with it. The northern loop proceeds by way of the Grosne valley to make a circuit of the Mont St-Romain ridge (579 m) and returns via the prehistoric caves of Azé on the slopes of the Mâconnais. The southern loop is short, almost a rally-driver's route with many zigzags and hairpin bends. It explores the spectacular uplands which look to the Beaujolais region in the south.

▰▰▰▰▰ ROUTE ONE: 81 KM

Cluny

No doubt the Mâcon wines helped provide the wealth and influence of Cluny - like other Burgundian convents and monasteries, Cluny's Benedictine abbey acquired much sunny alluvial soil and judiciously developed it. The ruins and restorations of that immensely rich foundation still overshadow the little town. It has been a major pilgrim venue for a thousand years - and still they come, as you may gather from the number of hotels and the latest pilgrim amenities, including hamburger joints. "We are on the American circuit," says a *restaurateur* - as though that explains everything. Cluny is thronged in summer and parking is not well organized. (Use the roadside parks on the way to the industrial zone, a ten-minute walk from the centre.) It lies on the TGV track, so you may see that high-speed train hurtle through; and an important trans-European highway, the Swiss-Atlantic, passes close by. For all that, an air of monastic calm pervades the scene. Twenty minutes suffice if you are merely walking round. If you are keen on Romanesque architecture you will need the whole day.

Cluny - Toury

① *Leave town by the Pont de la Levée and D15 road and turn left at rail crossing, signposted Varanges.* The road, disconcertingly cambered,

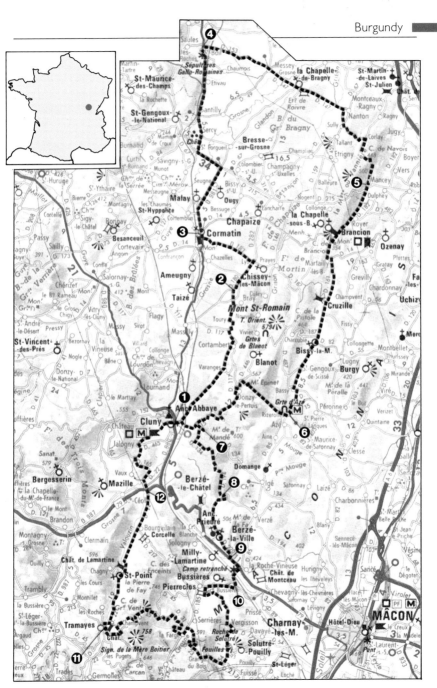

enters the parkland of the *forêt dominale*, an old-time game preserve of the monks. *Keep left, signposted Cortambert, turn left at road junction (no signpost) and follow signs to Toury.* In this little maze of forest trails there are roads unmarked on the IGN map and it is easy to go astray - but not far astray.

L'Orée du Bois
(detour to hotel-restaurant, Massily)

Turn left just before Toury and follow signposts for Massily to the hotel at the river bridge, 3 km on. Festooned in flowers (the ubiquitous geranium predominates) and floodlit at night, the place is smart, friendly, cheap and much frequented by local people. Few foreign visitors - though Mme Ginette Monamy remembers with pride the day the B.B.C. descended on her. They loved her chicken Benedictine with crayfish. *Tel 85.50.00.25; closed Feb and Mon; price band A; rooms at a reasonable price, but usually booked up.*
② *From Toury make for the D180 and turn right.*

Lys

This old-fashioned village has a cosy charm all its own. The bar, which doubles as a greengrocer's, is a haven for dedicated beer-drinkers: it sells real ale, something quite uncommon in rural France.

Cormatin

Rooms in the castle are distinguished by their mouldings and carvings. The entrance is on the right as you approach it. Park on the broad pavement, pay to enter the building but walk in the park for nothing. For craftwork and souvenirs, continue up the main street and look out on the left for signs to Galerie Artisanale. The work of about 20 local artists, photographers and woodworkers is on display.

Cormatin - Sercy

The route traverses the broad valley of the Grosnes and its tributaries. ③ *Turn left at the crossroads and continue north on the D981 - a 'red' road on the map, but a very quiet one.* Vineyards abound and some delicate wines are produced, eminently drinkable but lacking the *réclame* of the burgundies of the Sâone valley and Côte d'Or regions. To the rear, you have striking views of the Mont St-Romain ridges, the highest summits of the Mâconnais.

Sercy

Nothing to detain you here. The church is boringly modern and the medieval castle ruins, though picturesque, are fragmentary. The eye-catching château at the end of the lake is not open to visitors.

St-Gengoux

Just beyond Sercy turn sharp left and in 2 km enter St-Gengoux-le-National, a throw-back to the Middle Ages with a well-preserved 12thC church.

St-Boil

Burial chambers of Romans and Gauls, following some great battle unrecorded in history, have been excavated at about $1\frac{1}{2}$ km along the minor road west of the village. To visit them, apply to the *mairie* in St-Boil. There is not much to see, but the site is atmospheric.
④ *At the end of the village turn right, signposted Messey. A winding*

Famous names in Burgundy.

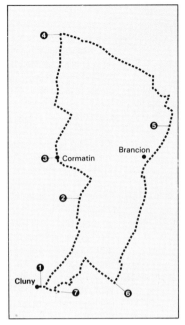

road, but well-surfaced; continue through the long sprawling village of Messey, road now signposted Nanton, and re-cross the Grosne river.

Le Moulin de la Chapelle
(rest., La Chapelle-de-Bragny)

The terrace of this restaurant, delightfully situated among lilyponds and lawns near the river bank before you enter La Chapelle-de-Bragny, is an ideal place for toying with *coq-au-vin* and sipping a glass or two of Mâcon wine. French touring organizations say that both food and drink are cheaper than they ought to be. Drop in unannounced, but be prepared for leisurely service. *Tel 85.44.00.58; price band A.*

La Chapelle-de-Bragny

It has the usual rustic equipment of a simple little church and a modest château (private, as so many in this region are). If you have come from more tourist-oriented places you will appreciate villages like La Chapelle, which seem to be locked in a time-warp. To sit and study an unpretentious château amid untrampled surroundings where no touring coach has penetrated can be a refreshing change from the dubious pleasures of being herded around some great showplace to the tedious accompaniment of a guide's monologue.

Nanton

The first of the hilly places on the route. Note some modification of architectural styles - cottages built of small bricks with red pantiled roofs. To the south you have the first of increasingly dramatic views.

Nanton -
Brancion

The road narrows as it climbs. After Sully it enters dense woodland. From Corly onward it is low-gear work, a narrow, tortuous and steeply-graded ascent. Above the tree line, on the rugged shoulders of Vannière, you have fine views to the north. There is a parking area at the summit of the road, Col des Chèvres, and a marked path goes off to the high point of the ridge (500 metres). The walk takes half an hour and not everyone will want to attempt it but, if you do, and always providing there is no mist, the summit panoramas are enough to take away such breath as you have left.

⑤ *Keep left in Mancey and right at next crossroads, signposted Brancion.* Here you are back among vineyards. *Turn sharp right, signposted Château, to Brancion.*

Brancion

It has been a little metropolis of the hills for 1,000 years and has the historic stones to prove it: a château-fort on 8thC foundations, embellished with 12thC towers, dungeon and gatehouses; a 12thC Romanesque church with faded frescoes, hardly discernible; an inn and a covered market of the 15thC and cottages to match. You buy picture postcards at the ancient communal bakehouse, which was in use as recently as 1930. You cannot always drive through Brancion - the closely-knit streets are pedestrianised on Sundays and holidays. For a first-rate picnic spot, go up the hill behind the village, park at the top (fine views of the Charollais and shaggy Morvan in the north-west) and take the short winding path into a grassy clearing.

Cruzille

As you enter the village, inspect the modern (1982) sundial, which is as inaccurate as most of the old ones. Drive up to the château - it is worth looking at, though you cannot enter despite the map's suggestion that you can. It is now a school for the mentally handicapped.

Sundial,
Cruzille.

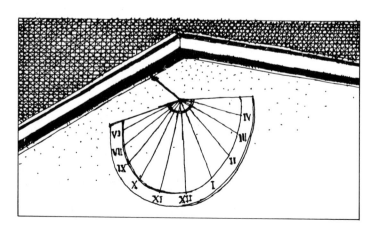

Lamp sculpture in the studio, Vignes du Maynes.

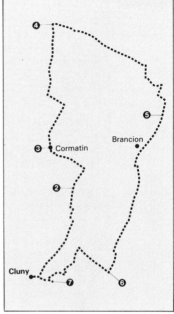

Vignes du Maynes This is the large white house on the outskirts of Cruzille. It claims to be the oldest wine *domaine* in France - *maynes* is dialect for 'monk' and the Maynes labels all bear the cherished crossed-keys symbol of the Cluny abbots. Since 1954 the vineyard has been organically cultivated. No anti-freeze. In fact, the wine is so free from additives that some French customers complain this Mâcon lacks the agreeable tang of insecticide. Three nice people run the business. Mme Guillot, having lived in London, speaks good English. You are not pressured to buy but, if you do, go for a half-case rather than a bottle or two. Part of the house is a museum of old trades.

⑥ *After 8 km turn right to the D15, signposted Cluny.*

Azé On the right, in 2½ km, are some large and exceptionally interesting caves on three levels. A subterranean river runs through and there is no dearth of stalactites. Science, aided perhaps by legend, peoples the caves with sub-humans from half a million years ago. The tour is well conducted, the leaflets are sensible and the admission fee is not extortionate. Near the entrance is a pottery, a restaurant punningly named *La Fortune de la Pot* and a swimming pool for children.

Azé - Cluny The road climbs steeply, then descends to Cluny.

127

ROUTE TWO: 56 KM

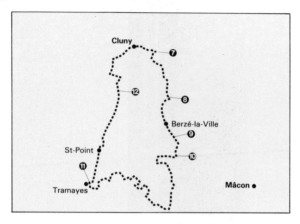

Cluny -
Berzé

⑦ *Leave Cluny by the D15 (on which you returned from the previous loop) and 1½ km beyond the level crossing turn right on to the D134, signposted Mâcon.* It is a well-engineered road, ascending fairly steeply into an evergreen forest. Near the junction is a picnic area.

⑧ *At next junction turn sharp right, signposted Berzé.* This is a single-track road between acres of vineyards.

Berzé-la-
Ville

There are 11th and 12thC Byzantine-style frescoes on the walls of the Chapelle des Moins; they merit at least a brief survey. The chapel is open daily between Easter and late Oct.

⑨ *Descend to major road; turn left and right, signposted Bussières.*

Bussières

Here they make and sell good goats' cheese. In the adjoining village (a five-minute walk) of Milly-Lamartine, the poet and patriot Alphonse de Lamartine spent his boyhood. The tomb and grottoes of Jocelyn, the subject of one of this poet's best works, can also be seen.

⑩ *Opposite the Milly-Lamartine turning, turn left; then right (no signpost) and left, signposted Vergisson. Entering Vergisson, turn sharp right to a narrow road signposted Solutré-Pouilly.*

Solutré-
Pouilly

Some years ago, under the towering Roche de Solutré, a cave full of bones and pots revealed a settlement of prehistoric horse-tamers. It justified setting up a museum in Solutré-Pouilly, but everything worthwhile was carted off to the Mâcon museum 16 km away. Solutré-Pouilly is a pretty little place with orange-pantiled roofs, huddled under the tremendous rock and successfully resisting the 20thC.

(restaurant,
Solutré)

There is nothing sensational about Pichet de Solutré, a country bar/hotel, but it is a useful halfway house for snacks and drinks.

Tasteful advertising, Solutré-Pouilly.

Solutré-Pouilly - Tramayes
Here you pass between the Mâcon and Beaujolais regions, close to the hamlets whose combined names, Pouilly and Fuissé, signify renowned white burgundies.

Mère Boitier *(detour)*
On the descent to Tremayes, look for the left turning signposted Signal de la Mère Boitier. It is 2 km to the car-park and picnic area under the 758-metre summit. If the weather is clear, take the steep path to the Signal viewpoint and panoramic indicator, about 20 minutes there and back. The view is wide and magnificently kaleidoscopic. In late afternoon the sun gives a rosy glow to the snows of the French Alps.

Tremayes
The château is not open to the public.
⑪ *Turn right in the village, signposted St-Point.*

St-Point
It is the principal resort and Sunday-afternoon-excursion destination of the inhabitants of this mini-mountainland: what used to be called a 'climatic station'. Here you have an opportunity to reward the children for their patience on the trip by showing them some amusements. There is an artificial lake with swimming, fishing, wind-surfing and pedal-boating amenities; also a dry-land playground and an open-air restaurant and snack bar. Picnic tables are strategically distributed and you will find privacy if that is what you want. On the left, just beyond the village, is the Château de Lamartine, chief of the poet's residences in this district, now the Lamartine museum. You may feel that the *memorabilia* assembled here are rather humdrum; but the official tour is, for a change, pleasantly informal.

St-Point - Cluny
⑫ *Continue north on the D22, crossing the railway and the Swiss-Atlantic highway. Follow signposts to Cluny.*

To think of summer in the Alps is to think of the clanging of cowbells in bright green meadows, geranium-laden chalets and snow-capped peaks rising above dark forests. Actually, this image has more to do with Austria and Switzerland than with France, but the French Alps can deliver the goods if you know where to look. Without doubt, the place to look first is the area covered by this tour, to the east of the glorious Lac d'Annecy. Throughout an intricate network of valleys, considerable mountains rear up behind pastoral scenes to rival almost anything in the Tirol or the Valais. Even the ski resorts here have mostly been developed with some regard for appearance and for traditional styles.

From fashionable Megève, at the south-east corner of the area, streams flow north to join the Arve and south-west to the Isère, separating the massif slightly from the Alps proper. Its backbone is the Chaîne des Aravis, a range which makes up in drama what it may lack in sheer altitude, and which offers fine views of neighbouring Mont Blanc.

Not surprisingly, the Alps don't offer the choice of roads that you find elsewhere in rural France, and this tour necessarily contains a larger-than-usual proportion of yellow roads, and even some red. The two loops start from close to the major resort of the area, La Clusaz. The northern one takes you through deep gorges and over the highest pass, the Col de la Colombière; the southern one offers less drama but plenty of other interest. The roads are not steep, but they are often narrow, and there are some exciting drops.

NOTE: the Col de la Forclaz (Route One) is cleared of snow, but not as a matter of high priority. If there has been recent snow, the Col will probably be closed. This applies from early October right through to early June. To check its condition ring the tourist office at La Clusaz (tel 50.02.60.92). The Col de la Colombière is not generally cleared of snow and is likely - but not certain - to be closed all winter and indeed through spring. Again, check with the La Clusaz tourist office. The rest of the roads used on both loops are likely to be clear, even in winter, within 24 hours of a heavy fall of snow: but it must again be emphasized that this is a rule of thumb. On-the-spot enquiry is the only way to avoid disappointment.

▆▆▆▆ ROUTE ONE: 103 KM

St-Jean-de-Sixt   The setting of St-Jean is its most interesting feature: two streams converge on the village from the east, but fail to meet - they come within a km of one another only to be forced apart again by the mass of Mont Lachat. The more northerly stream - the Borne - flows into the Arve at Bonneville, and its waters thus join the mighty Rhône as soon as it has left Lake Geneva. The southerly Nom becomes the Fier, which skirts the Lac d'Annecy before heading for its rendezvous with the Rhône.

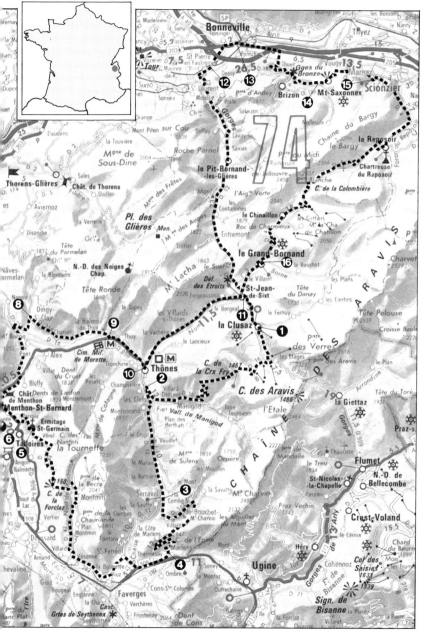

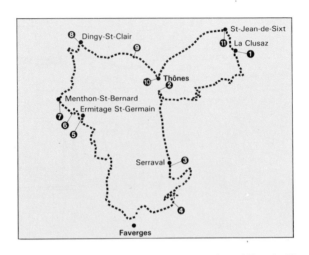

La Clusaz La Clusaz rates as one of the most attractive of French ski resorts. That is not saying much: with its chalet-style buildings it is not offensive (which many other resorts are in summer), but neither is it particularly charming. It has an elaborate swimming pool perched on a south-facing slope, several tennis courts, and a cable-car to give you a flying start on some of the fine local mountain walks (for example to Thônes). There is a fair range of shops (including perfume and soap makers), and a reasonable choice of good-value, pleasant places in which to stay or eat, though nothing out of the ordinary. The only restaurant in the village with any pretensions to serious cooking is the Ecuelle. *Tel 50.02.42.03; price band B.*

Leave the resort ① *on the D909, and if not making the detour to Col des Aravis, bear right in 2.5 km on to the D16 (signposted for the Col); at the next fork, keep left, signposted Col de Merdassier.*

Col des *Go through La Clusaz sticking to the main D909; after 2.5 km keep left,*
Aravis *still on the D909, signposted for the Col.* This pass, at 1,486 metres, is
(detour) the only major break in the Aravis chain. The road up from La Clusaz (unlike the road down the other side) is fairly broad and straightforward, with only a handful of hairpins, the pastures beside it carpeted with crocuses in early summer. What makes this detour worthwhile, especially if you can arrange to do it as the sun is going down, is the view it gives of Mont Blanc. The highest mountain in Europe is not the easiest to appreciate - from many points of view it is simply bulky; but from a little way beyond the Col it is mightily impressive, dwarfing the ski-ing mountains of Megève in the foreground. Off to the left of the main mountain are the spiky *aiguilles* which range along the Chamonix valley. A footpath leading south from the Col gives energetic walkers even broader views of the high Alps.

Col de la   This lower Col is quickly reached through pine forests. It has been
Croix Fry   turned into a big skiers' car-park and has little to detain you in summer.
A little way down beyond the Col is the Chalet Hôtel Croix Fry, where
you might consider stopping for a simple but satisfying meal on the
sunny and beautifully situated terrace (*price band B*) or a night in the
main chalet or one of the smaller self-contained ones (*tel 50.02.05.06*;
pool, tennis). From here a series of long, gentle hairpins leads down
across a broad flank of the pretty, pastoral valley of Manigod.

Manigod -   ② *At the junction with the D12 in the valley bottom, turn sharp left; as*
Faverges   *you do so, signs to Serraval and Faverges become visible; follow them.* The
road climbs gently over the Col du Marais (837 metres).
③ *At Serraval fork left on to the D162 for Le Bouchet and Col de l'Epine.*
The road contours around the hillside giving a series of striking
mountain views in all directions - the southern end of the Tournette
massif (of which this loop is a circumnavigation) is seen to advantage. At
the Col de l'Epine, attention switches to the sharp ridge of the Dent de
Cons, directly south as the road descends the steep hillside (beware the
sharp and unsignposted hairpin).
④ *In the valley bottom, ignore the sign left to Marlens Chef-Lieu; all*
remaining lanes lead to the major road along the valley (N508), at which
turn right; in about 2 km, after crossing a river, turn right for Thônes and
St-Ferreol; follow the main road through the edge of St-Ferreol to Le
Noyeray; follow signs for Faverges, then take a small road to the right,
signposted Viuz; at a fork, go right signposted Vesonne (D282); at the
memorial on the edge of Vesonne, fork right; go straight through the village.

Col de la   Some maps make this road look terrifying. Do not be deterred: the
Forclaz   road is poor but adequate, and the scenery is worth any qualms you
may experience. At first you wind up through woods, then across
sunny meadows beneath the towering cliffs of La Tournette. At 1,150
metres, the Col is relatively low, but is perfectly placed to give a
picture-postcard view of the Lac d'Annecy - an intense milky blue from
this height. There is a small car park just beyond the Col itself. Hôtel
L'Edelweiss, beside the Col, has a pleasant terrace where you can get
simple meals (*price band B*), though the little chalet La Pricaz, up the
opposing hill, enjoys better views. The best views of all are reserved
for picnickers who walk up across the meadows beyond the chalet (and
the sign forbidding picnics) until the distant mountains south of the lake
come into sight. Each establishment has in front of it a wooden ramp
built out over the steep hillside facing the lake, and people come from
far and wide to run down these ramps and hurl themselves down the
mountain - strapped to hang-gliders.

Ermitage-   ⑤ *Past Verel, watch for a sign on the right; take the little road which it*
St-   *marks, go past the church and park a little way down the hill.* As you
Germain   walk back up the shady lane, a footpath on the right takes you along a

ledge to a cave where St-Germain, the first prior of Talloires, retreated. The accommodation looks a bit cramped, but the outlook is exceptional. *Carry on down the hill and turn left (yes, left).*

⑥ *The road descends to lake level some way to the north of Talloires, where the promontory of the Roc de Chère forces the main D909a away from the shore; turn right.* This family resort-village spreads along the road some way from the lake, with pleasant residential lanes running off to the shore, where there are boat jetties and a bathing 'beach'. For walks through woods on the Roc de Chère, follow narrow lanes signposted first for the lake and then for the Roc, and park when you start worrying about the car's suspension. The looming château, dating from the 13thC and 15thC, is worth exploring (*open Sun in summer*).
Follow signs from middle of village away from lake to château.

Annecy
(detour)

Annecy is a busy, confusing town which the dedicated backroadsperson may be inclined to miss. But it has a charming medieval area (cut through by streams flowing out of the lake) at the foot of its imposing château, and boat trips (and boat hire) on the lake. There are car-parks on the way in along the lake shore which are not inconvenient, but for immediate access to the old town (and car-free glossy shopping streets nearby) it is best to aim for the waterfront town-hall car-park.
If you go on up the lake to Annecy, you can regain the tour route by taking the D5 out of town signposted Thorens, and then going off right on the D16 for Thônes.

Menthon -
Thônes

⑦ *From the bridge leading to the château continue up the little valley; cross the main road down a rough lane; in 2.5 km go over a crossroads, and then take a left turn just after a right-hand bend; at the D16 go left.* At the stone bridge over the Fier where the valley narrows, turn right for Dingy-St-Clair, and immediately right again. Downstream of the bridge you may see canoeists competing at weekends. Ahead of you as you go upstream are the exceedingly molar-like Dents de Lanfon and the flat-topped cliffs of the Dent de Cruet.
⑧ *In Dingy turn right for Thônes.* The single-track road goes through a series of peaceful hamlets, their wooden chalets surrounded by orchards and meadows; beware goats and chickens wandering about. Look south as you drive along the sunny shelf (useful for picnics) and you can see distant peaks which are beyond the Lac d'Annecy. As you leave La Balme-de-Thuy, streams cascade down the rock face from the Plateau des Glières, 1,000 metres above you.
⑨ *Join the D909; turn left to go directly to Thônes, or make this detour.*

Cimetière
de
Morette
(detour)

Turn right at ⑨ *and soon locate cemetery on left.* The Aravis region was a stronghold of the French Resistance in World War II - especially the high Plateau des Glières, just to the north of here. This immaculate little cemetery and small museum tell the story of a stubborn fight.

Thônes   A solid, amiable little town with a range of shops under its stone arcades and a busy market on Saturday mornings. Park by the tourist office on the right as you enter the town. Picnic provisions bought here should include the extraordinary variety of breads available from the *boulangerie* in Rue de la Saulne and also *Reblochon*: an unusually creamy soft cheese which is made locally, mild-tasting but strong-smelling. Its name comes from the verb *reblocher*, meaning to milk a cow for a second time. The story goes that in medieval times when landlords called to collect their percentage of the milk, the peasants would stop milking before the cow was exhausted, leaving the creamiest part to be extracted later for their own use. You can try before you buy (and see the cheese being made) at the small co-operative factory beside the road in from Annecy.

   Thônes is well-placed for mountain walks (a detailed map is available from the tourist office) and for excursions by car, as three valleys meet here. There are no very wonderful hotels, but the Nouvel Hôtel Commerce is adequate (*tel 50.02.13.66*) and takes its cooking seriously. ⑩ *In mid-town go left for Les Villards and La Clusaz.*

ROUTE TWO: 66 KM

Classic Alpine scenery, Aravis region.

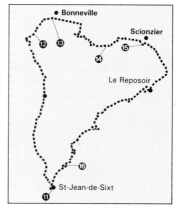

St-Jean-de-Sixt - Bonneville   ⑪ *Take the D4 for Le Grand-Bornand, then in one km turn sharp left on to the D12 for Entremont and Bonneville; in another km, go left again at the T-junction.* Looming ahead as you descend towards the Borne are the steep walls of the Défile des Etroits, separating Mont Lachat to the south-west from the Chaîne du Bargy to the north-east. Beyond it, the valley of the Borne opens out on to pleasant meadows around Entremont (where you can acquire a complete log-cabin kit from the timber yard). Some way past the village is a popular picnic area where you may have to rely on the noise of the rushing Borne to give some sense of privacy. After another defile, a prominently signposted road on the left goes up to the Plateau des Glières. A more rewarding detour starts in Le Petit-Bornand; a road winds east up into the high valley of the Jalandre and on to the optimistically named ski station of Paradis, with close-up views of the Pic de Jalouvre.

The several hamlets making up the community of Le Petit-Bornand-les-Glières are strung along a classically beautiful Alpine valley - vivid green meadows dotted with chalets, and apparently enclosed at both ends by mountain walls. At the northern end you escape via another defile, the Gorges des Eveaux; you wind between rocky cliffs to emerge on the gentle southern slopes of the valley of the Arve.

⑫ *As you enter St-Pierre-en-Faucigny, the D6 goes off left (past a hideous small shopping area) for La Roche-sur-Foron; if not making the next detour, go straight on, cross railway then motorway, and at N203 turn right.*

La Roche- La Roche sits in a slightly elevated position, well to the south of the
sur-Foron Arve, in surroundings which are surprisingly rustic considering the
(detour) proximity of two motorways and the city of Geneva. A round tower is all that remains of its ancient castle (finely set, as you might have guessed, on a rock outcrop, and giving views across the broad valley to the crags of Le Môle). The spacious mid-town area is regularly occupied by markets (and at other times crammed with parked cars), and jolly old streets leading away from it which are being restored. There are tempting food shops for picnic supplies.

Marie If you are in search of a real meal, head 2.5 km east of La Roche-sur-
Jean *(rest.* Foron for this elegant little roadside mansion offering indulgent cuisine
near La and charming service. *Tel 50.03.33.30; closed 28 July-18 Aug, Sun eve and*
Roche) *Mon; price band C.*

Bonneville - ⑬ *From Bonneville, take the N205 south of the river bridge; in 3 km*
Mont- *(after crossing the motorway again) take a small road on the right*
Saxonnex *signposted Thuet; go straight through Thuet; as you leave the village, a sign warns of bends for 4 km.* As you drive towards Thuet, your route back into the mountains is not obvious; but there is a tight, wooded cleft away to the left - the Gorges du Bronze - and the road finds its way into it. There are occasional places to stop for views of the Bronze tumbling over rocks way below the road. On a left-hand hairpin with parking space for a couple of cars, a footpath is signposted off into the woods for La Cascade du Dard. It is a short walk, but a precarious scramble, along the banks of the stream to the point where the Bronze spills over a broad rock shelf; a fine spot for a picnic unless crowded.

Mont- This small, rustic resort-cum-farming-community spreads its chalets and
Saxonnex orchards over a shelf on the mountainside 500 metres above the Arve.
⑭ *At the first settlement - Pincru - follow signs left for Marnaz; in the main village, 500 metres further on, go left down a narrow lane for the church.* From the church there are views in all directions - back up to

*In the Vallée
de Manigod.*

the Pointe Blanche, along the valley of the Arve (with the snowy peaks around Chamonix to the east) and steeply down to the flat valley bottom where the Giffre joins the Arve.

**Mont-
Saxonnex -
Le Reposoir**

The main road through Mont-Saxonnex takes you gently down towards Marnaz. ⑮ *As soon as you enter the village of Blanzy (unsignposted), take a small road leading off to the right; there are signs for Le Reposoir and Col de la Colombière, but they are not visible as you approach the junction; this is the D4.*

**Le
Reposoir**

The village of Le Reposoir may be unremarkable but it enjoys a lovely setting - an elevated meeting of valleys beneath the northernmost peaks of the Chaîne des Aravis and the Chaîne du Bargy. The Charterhouse, in suitably contemplative surroundings a couple of kms south of the village, has been restored to use as a religious retreat, but is now Carmelite rather than Carthusian; visitors welcome.

**Col de la
Colomb-i-
ère**

This is the tamest of Alpine passes, with no serious drops, few hairpins and a gentle gradient. Fine views across the valley as you go up the flank of the Chaîne du Bargy to the Col (1,613 metres), and plenty of picnic spots from which to enjoy them. Once over the Col, the developing ski resort of Le Chinaillon soon comes into view; it is not a pretty sight. But beyond it the road gives views of the Aravis chain.

**Le
Grand-
Bornand**

⑯ *As you enter the village, ignore signs advising you to go right; instead go on down to the small central square; turn right for St-Jean (or park).* More than most mountain resorts, Le Grand-Bornand feels like a real community; and never more so than on Wednesday mornings, when the market comes to town. To complete the loop, *keep left for St-Jean one km out of the village.*

The Vercors massif is one of the most attractive areas of the French Alps for the touring motorist. Slightly detached from the body of the northern Alps, its high plateaux were a natural (though ultimately not invulnerable) sanctuary for Resistance fighters in World War II. It has some of the classical charm of the book's other Alpine tour, in the Aravis area, but its main appeal lies in a few grand set pieces - the spectacular chasms and caverns cut in the limestone of the massif by the water flowing off it.

The nature of the landscape means that there is precious little choice of practical route between the principal sights, which is why the southern loop of this tour consists entirely of classified 'yellow' roads. This does not mean that they are major roads; on the contrary they are narrow, slow and hazardous - and definitely not for the nervous. Motor caravans and other van-like vehicles are effectively prohibited from the most interesting roads by low overhangs and tunnels.

The northern loop from Pont-en-Royans starts with splendid distant views of the dramatic Gorges de la Bourne and ends by bringing you back through the gorges themselves; in between there is some lush countryside. Do not attempt this loop before June: the high road between St-Quentin and Autrans is shaded by cliffs, and can be blocked by snow even when every other road in the Vercors is open.

The southern loop tours the rather harsher countryside of the Vercors proper, and links the two other major spectacles - the precipitous Combe Laval and the cavernous gorges of the Grands Goulets.

▬▬▬▬ ROUTE ONE: 111 KM

Pont-en-Royans
At the western extremity of the massif, the rock of the Vercors makes a final futile attempt to prevent the waters of the Bourne joining those of the Isère. River and road squeeze through a narrow cleft to emerge on to the undulating shelf of Royans. There is not the space to accommodate a village around the river bridge, but Pont-en-Royans has nevertheless grown up here. The tiled roofs of its houses, built into the rock and in terraces up the steep hillside opposite, are reminiscent of Provençal villages.

Bonnard
(rest., Pont-en-Royans)
This pleasant little hotel, in the main street leading away from the bridge, is a reliable choice for meals or accommodation. *Tel 76.36.00.54; closed Nov-Feb and Wed, April-May; price band B.*

Pont-en-Royans - St-Gervais
① *From the river bridge go upstream on the D531; shortly after crossing the river again (about one km from the village) turn left along the D292, signposted Presles.* The narrow road winds steeply up the mountainside, affording increasingly impressive views of the ridges, precipices, gorges and combes to the south and east; the driver, whose eyes should not stray from the single-track road, will have to make the most of the few

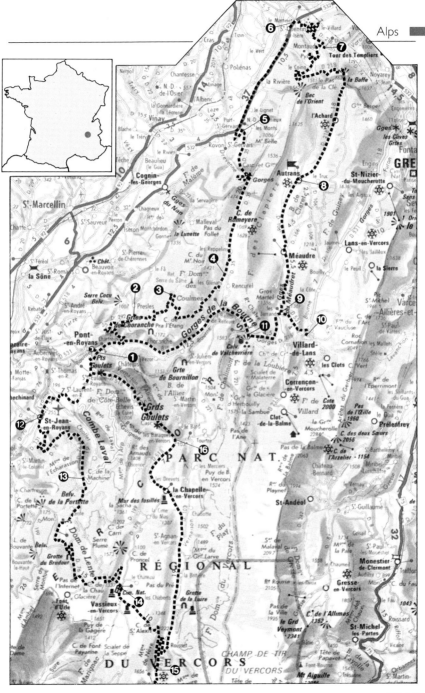

Typical stone house of the Briançon area: the large wooden upper storey is the hay loft.

places where it is possible to stop and look around - the two obvious points are at the Col de Toutes Aures, where the road changes direction but continues upward, and the end of the climb where a tunnel leads to the high plateau surrounding the hamlet of Presles.

(2) *Less than one km across the plateau, take a right turn (poorly signposted) to Rencurel; in about 3 km, at a T-junction, turn left, indistinctly signposted to Rencurel (the signpost pointing in the opposite direction is faintly marked cul de sac).*

(3) *In a further 4 km, where a left fork is signposted to the Col du Mont Noir, carry straight on along the Rencurel road, unless you fancy the slightly more adventurous route on forest roads over the Col (1,421 metres).* During this stretch you pass through pleasantly mixed woods - the Forêt Domainale des Coulmes. There are occasional parking areas and picnic tables, and paths leading off into the forest. The narrow road descends gently along the flank of a broad, prosperous valley around the settlement of Rencurel.

(4) *On joining the 'main' valley road above Rencurel, go straight on up the valley.* From the Col de Romeyère (1,074 metres), a tiny ski-station, there is a relentless straight descent of some 4 km to the entrance to a gorge. The dark tunnel into which you plunge after only a glimpse of the precipitous sides of the gorge is a little unnerving - not only is it unlit, but there is apparently no end to it. When you finally emerge at the far end, park and go back on foot up the old road - cut in the cliff face of the gorge. It makes you appreciate the tunnel after all. For

those with a head for heights, there are stunning views down into the gorge and across to the rolling hills on the far side of the Isère valley. The road you are following can be seen crossing the cascading stream hundreds of metres below. *Continue to St-Gervais.*

St-Gervais -
Autrans

⑤ *At the church, turn right on to the D35C, signposted to St-Quentin and Grenoble; when you reach the main N532, turn right; stay on this road until you reach the traffic lights at St-Quentin.*

⑥ *Turn right at the lights, then bear left immediately following signs for Montaud; at the crossroads in the village, go straight across, following signs for Montaud and Route d'Autrans.* The road zig-zags up the steep side of the Isère valley, then wanders through charming rustic hamlets on the lush little plateau of Montaud. The cliffs above may look impenetrable, but that is where you are heading.

⑦ *At the T-junction, turn right to Montaud.* Beyond Le Coing the road enters a forest of tall pines and starts to climb again under the towering cliffs of the Pas de la Clé. Serious mountain walkers properly equipped can make expeditions from the forest road to the peak of Bec de l'Orient (1,568 metres) for superb views in all directions. Those who stay in the car do not do badly, however. As the road climbs, there are better and better views across the plateau of Montaud (and the steep little valley of the Voroize to the east of it) to the mountains beyond the Isère. The occasional stopping places along this stretch make convenient picnic spots. Eventually, the road turns south at La Buffe, the northernmost crag of the Vercors massif, opening up new views across the Isère to the Chartreuse massif and along the river to Grenoble, before disappearing into a long tunnel into the interior of the massif.

Beyond the tunnel, gentle forested slopes lead into a long, grassy valley; the only indication that you are 1,000 metres above the Isère are the ski runs and lifts scarring the sides of the valley and, straight ahead on the little hill beyond Autrans, the ski-jumps used for the Grenoble Winter Olympics in 1968. Behind, in the distance, the pale swathes through the forest are the ski runs of Méaudre.

Autrans -
Villard-de-
Lans

Autrans and Méaudre are small, plain villages whose houses, with their sloping-step parapets designed to keep water and snow off the porous stone of the gables, are characteristic of the area. Both villages attract Sunday visitors from Grenoble, and each has a handful of simple places in which to stay or eat, and adequate shops for picnic supplies. Autrans is smaller, less affected by ski-ing development, and the more pleasant place in which to pause; the Hôtel de la Buffe just north of the village *(tel 76.95.33.26)* has better amenities than the older, more central Ma Chaumière *(tel 76.95.30.12)*.

⑧ *In Autrans, turn right and then shortly left for Méaudre and Villard-de-Lans; just before Méaudre, turn right on to the D106. In Méaudre, veer slightly left, following the main road.* The Gorges du Méaudret, just south of Méaudre, are by local standards not spectacular, but they are more easily appreciated from the road than their famous neighbours downstream - all you have to do is look up. There are organized picnic areas by the stream in the woody defile.

⑨ On reaching Les Jarrands, turn left at the T-junction for Villard-de-Lans; do not take the first road to the right signposted to the centre of Villard, but stay on the bypass for a further one km before turning right. As you near the middle of Villard there are large car parks on the right; park here to avoid the one-way system.

Villard-de-Lans

A popular winter and summer resort, Villard is at its liveliest at weekends. Outdoor attractions include a cable-car ride (starting 4 km outside the village) up on to La Côte 2,000 - a shoulder of La Grande Moucherolle (2,284 metres). From the top station (1,720 metres) you can walk to the summit of La Côte 2,000, though for the best views to the east and south you need to cross the summit plateau to the Pas de l'Oeille and the Col des Deux Soeurs (not a trivial undertaking). Hearty walkers who shun mechanical assistance can launch off directly from Villard to follow minor lanes through woods and meadows to the Calvaire de Valchevrière - a memorial to the valiant but unsuccessful defence of the hamlet in 1944. From here, there are views of the Gorges de la Bourne.

Le Dauphin
(hotel-rest., Villard-de-Lans)

There is plenty of accommodation in Villard, and all sorts of places in which to eat. Le Dauphin is a charming and good-value restaurant opposite the information office, with a comfortable small hotel attached. *Tel 76.95.11.43; closed mid April-mid May; price band B, with a half-price menu for children.*

Christiana *(hotel, Villard-de-Lans)*

Slightly to the south of the central area, the Christiania is a smart, chalet-style hotel, with a south-facing grassy garden and its own small pool (not far from the big public pool). *Tel 76.95.12.51; open mid March-Sept, Dec-Easter; price bands C/D.*

⑩ Retrace to the D531, then turn left. At Les Jarrands, go straight on, for Pont-en-Royans.

Gorges de la Bourne

Shortly after leaving Les Jarrands, the road enters the gorges and soon becomes narrow and hazardous; built on a ledge cut into the side of the gorge, it occasionally resorts to tunnels. Although the high cliffs closing in above you are impressive enough, to get the full impact you need to park in one of the few stopping places, from where you can peer down at the roaring stream. The height from which the Bourne drops through the gorges is sufficient to have justified the creation of a small hydro-electric installation, which sadly makes the banks of the river dangerous - when they turn the tap on, the water level rises almost instantly.

⑪ One km after crossing to the left bank of the Bourne, take a right turn (signposted La Balme) to regain the right bank. The more open area around La Balme offers one of the few opportunities on this part of the tour to have a picnic without risking vertigo. Shortly afterwards the cliffs close in again and the road is once more forced into the rock face before the valley swells to much grander proportions; as you descend, look out for a stream way off across the valley, spilling down the vertical cliffs.

Grottes de Chor-anche   The caves - reached by a new approach road that forks right along the flank of the valley - are not essential viewing for cave connoisseurs who have sampled the more famous subterranean sights of France, but they do have their own fascination: crystal-clear pools as well as the usual weird and wonderful concretions. And having gained the hillside car park you can always admire the view from the terrace café instead of walking on to the caves, if the picture postcards don't impress you. *Return to the valley road and descend to Pont-en-Royans.*

ROUTE TWO: 87 KM

View from the northern end of the Vercors massif.

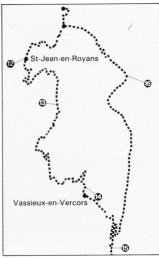

Pont-en-Royans - St-Jean-en-Royans   *Leave Pont-en-Royans on the D54, following the left bank of the river. In Ste-Eulalie and St-Laurent, follow signs for St-Jean.* As the road climbs gently towards Ste-Eulalie, the conclusion of this loop comes into view on the left - the cleft of the Petits Goulets.

St-Jean-en-Royans   An inoffensive small town, the main settlement of the rustic, rolling Royans; if attempts to find a picnic spot along the way have failed, the shady benches in its little squares may come in handy (market: Sat).

Hang-gliding, a year-round sport in the Alps.

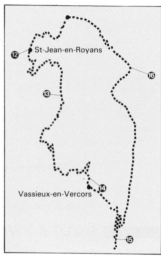

St-Jean-en-Royans

Vassieux-en-Vercors

⑫ *Go straight through the town, eventually bearing left on to the D76 for Col de la Machine and Col de Rousset.*

Combe Laval - Foret de Lente

As you ascend the western side of the Montagne de l'Echarasson there are fine views - but nothing prepares you for the sheer excitement of the eastern side, which is practically a precipice. The road runs along ledges and through tunnels, and it is perhaps just as well that there are few places where you can stop to appreciate the steepness of the drop beyond the flimsy stone wall. At the head of the valley the road burrows through a tunnel which takes you to the Col de la Machine.

⑬ *Beyond the Col de la Machine, take the turning to the right, signposted Lente.* The Forêt de Lente is famous for the length, straightness and resilience of its timber, which made it ideal for use in ships' masts; it was to speed the delivery of this timber to the valley that the extraordinary road along the lip of the Combe Laval was created. These days the area probably makes more money out of its ski-lifts. In early summer, the little plain of Lente grows masses of wild flowers. As you descend the Col de la Chau, at the eastern edge of the forest, the high point of the Vercors - Le Grand Veymont (2,341 metres) - lies straight ahead.

⑭ *At the junction by the cemetery, take the turning to the right, signposted Col de Rousset.*

Vassieux-en-Vercors - Col de Rousset

Rebuilt since the war, the unremarkable-looking village of Vassieux, in its high, dry and rocky valley has become a place of pilgrimage. Vassieux was largely destroyed in 1944, and those who died are interred at the Cimetière National mentioned above.

Continuing along the Col de Rousset road, there is another little col (de St-Alexis) and another change of scenery as you go from the Vassieux valley to the lower, lusher valley of the Vernaison, the long, straight axis of the southern Vercors.

⑮ *Turn right at the hairpin junction halfway down the hill.*

Col de Rousset

Many ski resorts have a curiously Wild West air about them in summer, when they are virtually deserted; the clutch of bars and shops around the entrance to the disused tunnel of the Col de Rousset is an extreme example, and you are unlikely to want to pause here even if the chair-lift is working. Instead, go through the new tunnel on the near side of the 'village'. On the far side of the tunnel there are parking places. They say that the Col represents the meeting of the northern (wet) and southern (dry) Alpine climates, and that the contrast is, under certain conditions, visible.

Col de Rousset - St-Agnan-en-Vercors

The Grotte de la Luire to the right of the road is another focus for memories of the Resistance: it served as a hospital for the wounded until its discovery by the Germans in July 1944. It is also of some interest simply as a cave.

St-Agnan-en-Vercors

This little village retains a more old-established feel than its larger neighbours. The Veymont, in the tiny central square, is a satisfactory simple hotel *(tel 75.48.20.19)*.

La-Chapelle-en-Vercors

Here the cost of the Vercors' resistance movement is made painfully clear by the evident newness of much of this substantial village. There is no particular reason to pause, but there are comfortable rooms and reliable, traditional food at the chalet-style Bellier, in the main street *(tel 75.48.20.03; price band C)*.

Les Grands Goulets

⑯ *Turn right at Les Baraques-en-Vercors in search of a parking space.* Les Baraques is right at the top of the narrowest part of the gorges of the Grands Goulets, and it is well worth parking here and walking a short way down the road to inspect this impressive work of nature - though it means dodging the traffic.

The road from Les Baraques accompanies the torrential River Vernaison through tunnels and clefts which are barely penetrated by the light of day, so high and close are the walls. Soon the the valley widens and deepens, offering grand views that can be admired in comfort from the terrace restaurant of Le Refuge, a useful roadside hotel *(tel 75.48.68.32; price bands A/B/C)*.

On the last lap of this tour the road goes through Les Petits Goulets - another dramatic conflict between rock and river. *Turn right in Ste-Eulalie to return to Pont-en-Royans.*

Auvergne:
AROUND THE PUY DE SANCY

The imposing presence of the Puy de Sancy, the highest peak in the Massif Central, can be felt throughout this tour, whether it is just peeping over a distant horizon or hanging before you, almost unreal, like a piece of rumpled tapestry. At its northern foot lie the source of the River Dordogne and the spa and ski resort of Le Mont-Dore, which is the starting point for both routes. The rival spa of La Bourboule is located a few km downstream.

The landscape of this region, like much of the Massif Central, is of volcanic origin, as can be guessed from its many dome-like mountains. But another sign is the paradoxical presence of lakes at the top of passes or plateaux, as a result of rainwater filling a crater or lava forming a natural dam. There are a couple of these lakes on the tour, as well as the largest artificial lake in the Auvergne, the Lac de Bort, and a delightfully convoluted stretch of water formed by glacial erosion, the Lac de Crégut. All these are ideal for picnics.

As well as thrilling mountain scenery - the driving, incidentally, is always easy and does not require a head for heights - this tour takes in some of the finest architecture the Auvergne has to offer. At the top of the list are two sophisticated Romanesque masterpieces: the churches of Orcival and St-

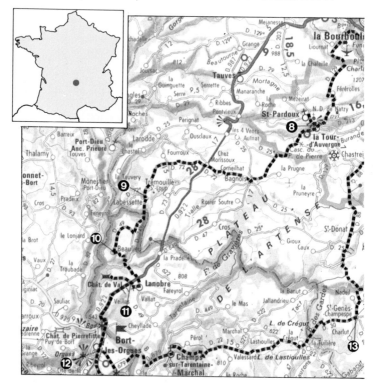

Nectaire. There are also many lesser-known churches, whose engaging craftsmanship deserves attention, and two fine châteaux.

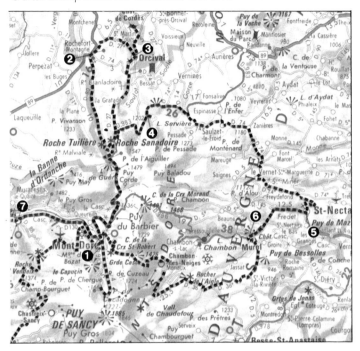

ROUTE ONE: 87 KM

Le Mont-Dore
The hot springs of Le Mont-Dore were exploited by the Gauls, the Romans and Louis XIV, but the spa only really took off in the 19thC. Today the main attraction is still the Etablissement Thermal, a fine example of grand turn-of-the-century spa architecture. Le Mont-Dore is an ideal base and has plenty of accommodation. Market day: Fri.

Skieurs
(rest., Le Mont-Dore)
This welcoming *auberge* (actually called Des Skieurs) serves hearty regional dishes, such as *chou farci* and *tripous* (sheep's tripe). There are a few simple rooms. *Rue Montlosie; tel 73.65.05.59; closed Nov; price band B.*

Puy de Sancy
(detour)
Le Mont-Dore is only 4 km as the crow flies from the top of the Massif Central's highest peak, the Puy de Sancy (1,885 metres). *For this detour,* ① *leave the town by the D983, then take a cable car, which will deposit you within walking distance (20 minutes) of the top. On a clear day the view in every direction is overwhelming. Return to Le Mont-Dore.*

First World War Memorial in the church at Beaulieu, Route Two.

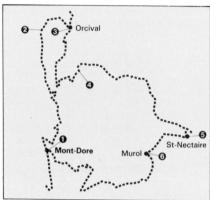

Le Mont-Dore - Rochefort-Montagne	*Take the D983 in the direction of Clermont-Ferrand* and climb the flank of the Puy de la Tache. *Fork left at the junction with the D996, and* continue up through a scree-covered gorge. Suddenly, you emerge at the Col de Guéry with its lake, trapped in a volcanic crater, sitting incongruously at the top of a mountain pass. Just beyond the lake look back at the superb view (the first of many) over the Sancy range, then *turn left along the D80 to Rochefort-Montagne.* This road goes between two spectacular conical outcrops, the Roche Tuilière and the Roche Sanadoire. The valley between them was ground out of the mountain by a glacier during the ice age.
Rochefort-Montagne - Orcival	② *When you reach Rochefort-Montagne,* a busy little town with some interesting old buildings, *veer right in the middle and, just before the junction with the N89, turn right on to the D216. Drive on for about one km, then turn right again on to the D27e to Orcival.* Along the way there is a fine view to the left over the Monts Dômes, a comparatively recent chain of volcanoes (their creation would have been witnessed by earliest man). The tall, thermometer-like object sticking up from the highest of them, the Puy de Dôme, is a broadcasting tower.
Orcival	The village of Orcival is dominated by its impeccably proportioned 12thC Romanesque church, whose interior, thanks to its many windows, is lighter (in both senses of the word) than most comparable buildings in the Auvergne, which tend to be chunky and dimly-lit. The striking 12thC statue of the Virgin and Child attracts many pilgrims.
Château de Cordès *(detour)*	③ The multi-turreted L-shaped Château de Cordès, set among tree-lined avenues and formal gardens designed by Le Nôtre, is definitely worth a detour. *Take the D27 signposted Clermont-Ferrand; 1.5 km beyond Orcival, turn left into the château's drive. Open Easter-Oct 10-12 and 2-6.*

Orcival -
Lac Servière
Leave Orcival in the direction of Le Mont-Dore along the D27. Drive on for about 4 km then turn sharp left at the junction with the D983, which now sweeps majestically along the mountainside with pinewoods to the right and the Monts Dômes to the left. Shortly after a small road comes in from the left, pull in opposite the only house on the road. Here, a badly signposted track leads up through conifers (5 minutes' walk) to another high crater-lake, Lac Servière - a peaceful spot for a picnic.

Lac Servière
- St-
Nectaire
④ *Continue along the D983, then turn right to Saulzet-le-froid along the D74e.* The distant Monts du Forez and du Livradois can be seen straight ahead. *When you join the D74, keep on it via several crossroads and forks, through Saulzet-le-Froid and on to the T-junction with the D5* (where there is fuel). *Turn right towards Murol, then left along the D74, following the signs to St-Nectaire.* After crossing what feels like a table mountain with vistas in every direction, the road wends its way down an attractively miniature mountain valley. Two right turns later *(on to the D150e and D150),* you will see St-Nectaire - or rather its two separate halves - down below you.

St-
Nectaire
This small town is famous for three things: its superb Romanesque church, its hot springs, and its delicious nutty-flavoured cheese. The church, which occupies a promontory in the older part, St-Nectaire-le-Haut, contains some vivid capitals depicting scenes from the Bible and the life of St-Nectaire, and several remarkable treasures. *Out of season the church is open 10.30-11.30 and 2.30-4.30; closed Tues and Thurs.*

Drive down to the D996 and turn left into St-Nectaire-le-Bas, a curiously elongated spa with a turn-of-the-century atmosphere. The Syndicat d'Initiative will give you details of another, less-known aspect of St-Nectaire: its druidic past. The town itself and the surrounding countryside are dotted with dolmens, menhirs and sacred caves.

As for the cheese, try to buy some St-Nectaire *fermier* (as opposed to *laitier,* or dairy-made), either from a cheese shop or direct from a farm: look out for signs on both Route One and Route Two. If buying from a farm, you will be expected to purchase at least half a cheese (750 g). Don't be daunted: its unfatty texture is ideal for picnics.

Marinette
(hotel-rest.,
St-Nectaire)
This simple hostelry in the upper part of St-Nectaire offers copious *cuisine bourgeoise* and, as you would expect, excellent St-Nectaire cheese. *Tel 73.88.50.35; price band A.*

St-Nectaire
- Murol
⑤ *From St-Nectaire, take the D996 to Murol,* a pleasant, large village dominated by the massive rounded walls of its 12th-16thC fortress. To see the castle *(open June-Sept 9-7; Oct-May Sun and national holidays only, 2-7),* turn sharp right just after entering Murol and drive round the back to the car park. *The exit, marked with an arrow, is by another road that leads back down to the D996. Turn right and, at the next junction, left up the D5 signposted Besse.*

Murol - Col de la Croix St-Robert

⑥ *Continue on the D5, and just after entering St-Victor-la-Rivière turn right in the direction of Le Breuil. At the next junction, turn right along the D36.* The driving here is exhilarating, as the unusually straight road seems to be heading directly into the side of the Puy de Sancy. *At the next T-junction turn left towards Le Mont-Dore.* The road, which begins to snake up through a landscape of bare grass and crags, is excellent and not at all precipitous; it seems to climb up and up forever - then suddenly you come out on the Col de la Croix St-Robert. This pass, 1,426 metres high, offers breathtaking views on both sides. La Bourboule can be seen in the distance.

After crossing a steppe-like tract with the Puy de Sancy looming to the left, the road dips down through lichen-covered birch trees to Le Mont-Dore.

ROUTE TWO: 113 KM

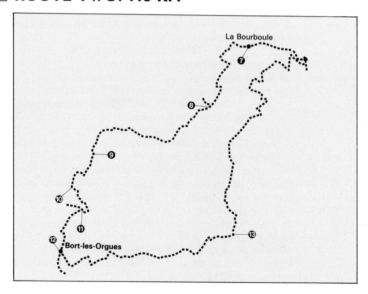

Le Mont-Dore - La Bourboule

Follow the River Dordogne along the D130 to La Bourboule. This spa, which like its neighbour Le Mont-Dore has hot springs, is altogether more congenial in character. It has many tree-lined squares, one with a bandstand, a delightful park, the Parc Fenestre, and a number of attractive Art Nouveau and Art Deco buildings and café interiors.

La Bourboule - La Tour d'Auvergne

⑦ *Drive along the left bank of the Dordogne, past the gingerbread casino, and straight on to the D129 to La Tour d'Auvergne.* The road skirts pleasant woodlands and winds its way to the Plateau de Charlanne. If

you are doing this tour in July or August you will be rewarded by the
sight of fields of great yellow gentian; this plant, which flavours various
Auvergne drinks such as Avèze and Salers, is happy only above an
altitude of 1,000 metres.

Soon you are confronted, suddenly, with a wide vista over the
Plateau de l'Artense ahead. The Puy de Sancy peeps over the horizon
to the left. Note that the typical farmhouse design of this area consists
of a single long, tall building with living quarters at one end and a
cowshed or barn at the other. *On joining the D213, turn right to La Tour
d'Auvergne,* a small town whose well-preserved houses cling to a hillock
on a mountain plateau.

**Notre-
Dame de
Natzy
and St-
Pardoux**

⑧ *For the short detour to Notre-Dame de Natzy and St-Pardoux turn
sharp right in the middle of town (signposted Bagnols and Bort), and at the
junction a few hundred metres later keep straight on along the D203. Just
beyond the sign saying you are leaving La Tour d'Auvergne, stop at the car
park on the right.* Go up the path (follow the Stations of the Cross) past
a dilapidated open-air altar to the huge statue of the Virgin and Child at
the top of the hill (10 minutes' walk): this is Notre-Dame-de-Natzy, a
folly erected by a local notable in 1850 after he was miraculously cured.
There is an extensive view in every direction. *Return to the car park
and continue along the D203, then take the first turning to the left for St-
Pardoux.* Its Gothic church of harmonious proportions contains an
unusual 16thC altarpiece that is a riot of gilt and cabled columns. Note
the sinister bust of the Virgin in the neighbouring school playground.

*La Tour
d'Auvergne
- Labessette*

*Leave La Tour d'Auvergne as indicated for the detour, but turn left at the
first junction on the edge of town (no warning) along the D47 to Bort.*
Soon the road offers a fine view back over the town with the Puy de
Sancy behind. You are now on the Plateau de l'Artense, which is
strewn with boulders and curious rock formations caused by glacial
erosion. *As you come into the sleepy village of Bagnols, turn sharp right
just before the church, then fork left immediately along the D72, through
attractive park-like country. Continue over the N122, taking great care
at a dangerous crossroads about 3 km later (sign obscured). At the
minute village of Labessette, turn right* to its correspondingly minute
Romanesque church, which has a gable belfry and a touchingly
asymmetrical apse.

*Labessette -
Beaulieu*

⑨ *Continue along the D72. About 3 km beyond Labessette in the middle
of a very straight stretch of road, turn right along the D49 (no warning)
towards Beaulieu. Keep straight on (follow sign to La Plage). In Beaulieu
turn right in front of the church and follow signs to Château de Thynières.*
Park the car, then walk through a farmyard and up a promontory to
the ruins of the castle. This site (an ideal picnic spot) is interesting not
so much for the castle itself as for the superb views it offers along the
huge Lac de Bort, which is 18 km long.

Château de Val.

Beaulieu -
Lanobre

⑩ *Leave Beaulieu by the picturesque D49 signposted Lanobre. Cross the N122 into Lanobre,* which has a fine 12thC Romanesque church with some interesting capitals and superb 13thC wrought-iron decorations on its door. *Turn right at Lanobre church and right again to the N122.*

Château
de Val
(detour)

⑪ *For this detour, a 5-km return journey, go straight over the N122.* The dam of Port-les-Orgues was designed so that the waters of its artificial lake would (just) spare this picturesque 15thC castle, which is now romantically situated at the end of a narrow peninsula. Well worth a visit, but crowded in high summer. Leave the car at one of the many car parks on the way down to the castle, as you will not be able to park at the bottom. *Open 9-12 and 2.30-6.30; closed Nov to mid-Dec and Tues Nov-Whitsun.*
Return to the N122 and drive on to Veillac.

Beau
Rivage
(hotel-rest.,
Veillac)

Nice garlicky *terrine*, tasty pheasant (when in season), a well-stocked cheese platter and excellent pastries are some of the things on offer at this friendly hotel-restaurant. There is also a quiet garden where meals are served in summer. *Tel 71.40.31.11; closed Jan and Feb; price band B.*

Bort-les-
Orgues

This straggling town, overlooked by a massive dam and an overrated ridge of basalt columns that are supposed to look like organ pipes (hence 'les Orgues'), need not detain you.

Saut de la
Saule
(detour)

For a short detour to this awe-inspiring series of waterfalls, where the River Rhue has sliced its way through massive gneiss boulders, *leave the middle of Bort on the N122. Fork left up a small road signposted to*

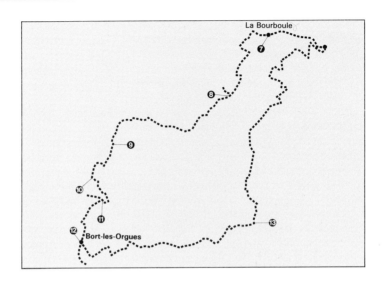

Camping de la Cascade; then fork right before the level crossing. Drive on for 2 km then park by a football field. Take the path marked Saut de la Saule over a small suspension bridge, then turn left (follow blue arrows). *Return to Bort the way you came.*

Bort-les Orgues - St-Genès-Champespe

⑫ *Drive from Bort to Champs-sur-Tarentaine on the D979, then turn left along the D22 signposted Marchal.* You are now back on the characteristic terrain of the Plateau de l'Artense. The Puy de Sancy soon reappears to the left, while the distant Puy Mary range can be seen to the right. The lake formed by the dam at La Crégut has a charming Scandinavian quality - and not too many tourists. *Follow signs to St-Genès-Champespe.*

St-Genès-Champespe - Chastreix

⑬ *Turn left in the village and take the D88 to St-Donat. Veer left round its Romanesque church and continue on the D89.* The countryside becomes more rugged as you approach the Puy de Sancy. *Turn left at the junction with the D203, then turn right along the D88 to Chastreix.*

Chastreix

This small village is notable for its outsize Gothic church, which has an interesting porch and wall paintings. Sadly its jewel - a superb 11thC statue of the Virgin and Child - was stolen (but postcard available).

Chastreix - Le Mont-Dore

Continue on the D88 to the left of the church. At the first main T-junction, branch left to Le Mont-Dore (sign hard to see). Extraordinary views open up to the west. *Ignore the turning to the right to a 'télé-ski'. At the junction with the D213 turn right, and later fork right for Le Mont-Dore.* As you drive, there is a view over La Bourboule.

Southern Auvergne:

GORGES DE LA TRUYERE AND THE CHATAIGNERAIE

The two loops of this tour, which is centred on the attractive little town of Entraygues-sur-Truyère (normally known just as Entraygues), take in two quite different types of countryside. Route One explores the untamed scenery of the Gorges de la Truyère, whose lack of human habitation, narrowness, and resistant granite sides made them the ideal site for a series of major hydroelectric dams.

Route Two meanders through a little-known area called the Châtaigneraie (as its name suggests, it is full of sweet chestnut trees), whose friendly landscape of gently rounded hills, woods, pastures and tree-lined hedges is bisected by trout streams. Here you will see a profusion of dormer-windowed houses whose steep roofs are covered with the distinctive local form of slate, mica schist; distinctive gable-belfries, often perched on roofs; and pigs roaming loose in the woods, rooting for chestnuts and acorns, hence the excellence of the local *charcuterie* (restaurants, incidentally, offer real value in the Châtaigneraie); but you will see few tourists, even at the height of summer - except possibly at Conques, whose picturesque houses, extraordinary church, and even more extraordinary treasure are the highlight of this tour.

▬▬▬ **ROUTE ONE: 95 KM**

Typical Auvergnois building: stone construction, simple austere style and, at higher levels, steep-pitched roofs.

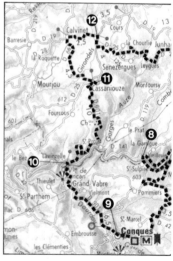

Entraygues   The small town of Entraygues (its name means 'between the waters') is situated at the confluence of the Truyère and the Lot. It has an elegant Gothic bridge, an imposing castle - originally built in the 13thC, then razed and rebuilt in the 17thC - and a fascinating old quarter.

**Entraygues
- Pons**

① *Follow the signs out of Entraygues for Mur-de-Barrez, crossing the
bridge over the River Truyère, then turning sharp right along the D904.* The
road runs straight along the Truyère, which has already taken on its
typically fjord-like appearance; you will probably have noticed that the
bridge you crossed was in fact a dam. *As you approach Couesque,* which
is overlooked by terraces where vines used to be grown, *take the first
turning to the left signposted Montsalvy, then bear right in Les Carrières
(not on map) for Pons,* which soon comes into view, tucked away cosily
at the end of the valley. *Bear right across the bridge, then left into the
middle of Pons.*

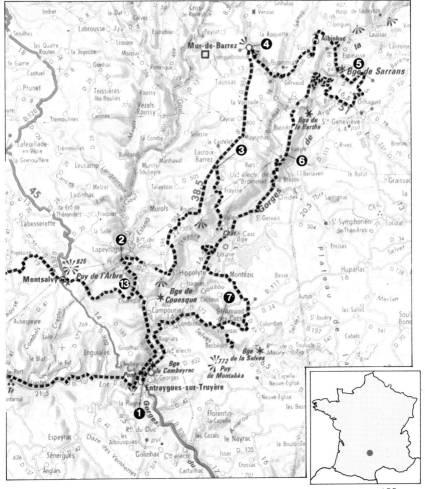

Pons

This charming little village, notable for its idiosyncratic church and well-preserved old houses, marks the eastern edge of the Châtaigneraie.

Pons -
Rouens

② *Leave Pons on the steep St-Hippolyte road (not marked on map),* which offers views first to the left over the conical Puy Haut and Puy de la Pause, then to the right over the Château de Vallon, the Gorges de la Truyère and the vast and windswept Aubrac plateau beyond. *Ignore the sign to Mur-de-Barrez and continue into St-Hippolyte, bearing right past the church* (which like most in these parts, has a gable-belfry). *Shortly after leaving the village,* which affords a fine view back over the Couesque dam, *turn left on to the D904 to Rouens.* As the road comes over the top of the hill, the entire Puy Mary massif appears ahead.

Rouens -
Lacroix-
Barrez

Turn right into this hamlet, which has many fine mica-schist roofs covering barns as well as houses, and follow the signs to the neatly laid out *belvédère.* This is a pleasant place for a picnic if there is not too much wind; views all round. *Return to the D904, which now becomes an exhilarating ridge road, and continue to Lacroix-Barrez.*

Château
de Vallon
(detour)

③ *For this detour, which entails a 9-km round trip, turn right in Lacroix-Barrez on to the D97.* The road runs down an attractive steep valley to Vallon, a totally unspoilt hamlet (no cars), perched on a rocky spur overlooking the Gorges de la Truyère and dominated by a ruined castle (inhabited by wall-creepers, birdwatchers please note). *Return to Lacroix-Barrez and continue on the D904.*

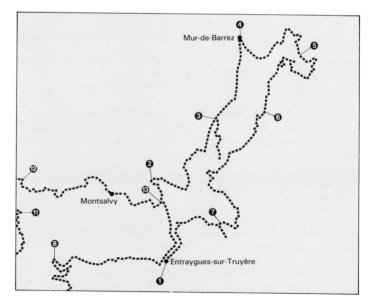

Mur-de-Barrez

An atmospheric little town, taken by the English in 1418 and turned into a Protestant stronghold; later it was given by Louis XIII to the Prince of Monaco. It has a large number of interesting 17thC buildings and a 12th-13thC church (note the unusual keystone representing a recumbent Christ above the organ loft). Sensibly, the oldest part of the town has been made into a pedestrian precinct.

Auberge du Barrez
(hotel-restaurant, Mur-de-Barrez)

Follow the signs to the *gendarmerie* for this easy-to-miss hostelry, a bland new building which its owners, the town council, have obviously been at pains to make as unobtrusive as possible (look for the Logis de France sign). The cuisine, which is excellent value, delicately combines the traditional and the *nouvelle*. The rooms are quiet (except when the *gendarmes* are called out - which is not often in this part of the world). *Tel 65.66.00.76; closed Mon and Jan; price bands A/B/C.*

Mur-de-Barrez - Barrage de Sarrans

④ *Take the D900 to Brommat, whose church has an extraordinary asymmetrical clock tower. Cross the bridge and bear left towards the middle of the village, then turn sharp right on to the D98.* This high road, with sweeping views both left and right, goes through the attractive hamlet of Albinhac, which has yet another church with a gable-belfry and a charming little turreted manor.

As the road (now the D98) approaches the Barrage de Sarrans, a portion of the 35-km long lake created by the dam comes into view below. Drive over the dam and up to the car park and *belvédère*. The only sign of human habitation is a group of incongruous (for this area) ochre-coloured chalets, built before the Second World War for the dam engineers.

Barrage de Sarrans - Rueyre

⑤ *Continue on the D98, then turn right on to the D537 to Orlhaguet* (note the quirky church which has a castle turret up one side). *At the T-junction with the D900, turn right towards Brommat.* The road twists and turns through wild and craggy ravines with the Truyère, for once looking like a river rather than a fjord, flowing below: this section gives some idea of what the Gorges must have looked like before man decided to harness the Truyère's waters. *Continue on the D621 across a surprising (in this context) stretch of plain.* Soon the horizon is filled with a forest of pylons and electrical installations - the Rueyre interconnection station. Set in the middle of nowhere, with its cables swooping to their destinations in every direction, this silent non-polluting complex has a powerful science-fiction beauty.

Rueyre - Volonzac

⑥ *Do not drive into Rueyre itself, but fork right towards Le Brezou.* Soon the road reveals a fantastic plunging view ahead over the Truyère and undertakes a series of hairpin bends down past the mysterious underground power station of Brommat - a colossal construction hollowed out of the granite mountainside.

After crossing the Truyère (which by this time has become an elongated lake again, because of the Barrage de Couesque downstream), there is a relaxing drive along a recently built section of the D621 (not marked on map) gouged out of the sides of the gorge. The Château de Vallon (see detour in Route One) can be seen on the right from a new angle - i.e. from below. *At the first crossroads keep straight on along the D97 towards Montézic. In Montézic veer right for St-Amand-des-Cots*, through less spectacular countryside. *Go straight through St-Amand-des-Cots on the Entraygues road, the D34, to Volonzac.*

Besbéden
(detour)

⑦ *For this short detour, bear left in Volonzac along a narrow and at times rather precipitous road up the gorges of the River Selves.* The microscopic hamlet of Besbéden soon appears below, perched on a narrow rocky ridge in the middle of the valley. Drive past its tiny 12thC church (gable-belfry, of course) and down to a 14thC bridge - a delightful spot for a picnic. *Return to Volonzac.*

**Volonzac -
Entraygues**

Continue on the D34 as it joins and follows the Selves, then crosses the river in the direction of Bagnars (where the church belfry is protected by an eccentric umbrella-like construction) and Entraygues. As you come into Entraygues, keep straight ahead for the town.

Medieval Auvergnois architecture. Conques.

▰▰▰ ROUTE TWO: 87 KM

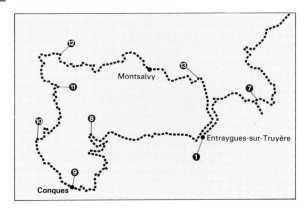

Entraygues *Follow the signs to Aurillac over the dam-bridge. When you reach the*
- Vieillevie *crossroads by the Gothic bridge, keep straight ahead on the D107,*
signposted Conques. This road snakes attractively along the steep side of
the Lot valley. Don't swim in the river - it is treacherous.

Vieillevie Once a lively little river port when boats carried oak planks to
Bordeaux for barrel-making.

Hôtel- A family-run restaurant, which provides simple fare at ludicrously low
restau- prices. Regular dishes include a tasty boar stew and *chou farci*, but if
rant de la you happen to be in the area between November and Easter, make a
Vallée point of sampling *stofinado*, a unique local speciality found only in the
(Vieillevie) triangle formed by Villefranche-de-Rouergue, Maurs and Entraygues. It is
a delicious, subtly flavoured mixture of potatoes, hard-boiled eggs,
cream, parsley, garlic and stockfish (unsalted wind-dried cod, which has
to be soaked in water for a week before it is soft enough to eat).
Tel 71.49.94.57.

Vieillevie - ⑧ *Return to the bridge you passed as you entered the village, cross it and*
Conques *veer left for Conques along the C7,* which takes you past the diminutive
church of Notre-Dame d'Aynès and its equally diminutive cemetery,
then forks right up the hillside, revealing ever more spectacular views.
At various junctions and forks, follow the signs to Conques. At Peyssonet
(not on map) bear left (no sign). Later, at a dangerous and unmarked
T-junction, turn right along the D42. Use car park on edge of Conques.

Conques The village - a cluster of perfectly preserved half-timbered houses
clinging to the hillside and dominated by the large church of Ste-Foy - is
all the more remarkable because of its unexpected location in the wild
gorges of the River Duche. Allow time to explore.

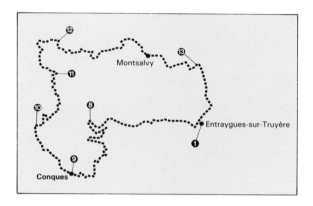

Eglise Ste-Foy, Conques

This mainly 12thC Romanesque masterpiece is one of the great buildings of France. An informative leaflet is available which recalls its history as a stopping-place for pilgrims on their way to Santiago de Compostela and describes in detail the various things to be admired: its 12thC tympanum, teeming with lively, almost Bosch-like sculpted figures; its 212 capitals, many of them depicting scenes from the Bible; and above all its priceless treasure, the centrepiece of which is the gold-encased reliquary statue of Ste-Foy herself, who was martyred in 303. Over the centuries pilgrims brought the Saint gems, cameos and intaglios, many of them Greek and Roman, which were added to the statue and the throne; to see these properly you need a pocket flashlight. *Treasure open Feb-Dec 9-12 and 2-6.*

Conques - Lavinzelle

⑨ *Drive straight through Conques and down towards Grand-Vabre, first on the D550, then on the D901.* The craggy, narrow gorges of the River Dourdou open out as you approach Grand-Vabre and the Pont de Coursavy over the Lot. Those who feel like a strenuous walk should make a detour to the hamlet of Lavinzelle.
⑩ *Turn left after the bridge on to the D42 and park about 100 metres later.* You will see varnished wooden signs pointing up a steep path to Lavinzelle (round trip: 1½ hr). One section of the path, once used by pilgrims, consists of a boxwood tunnel. Ignore the turning off to the right, half-way up.

Lavinzelle is a totally unspoilt little village perched precipitously on the side of a steep, south-facing hillside. Because it is completely protected from the north wind, it has an exceptionally warm microclimate that is a boon to market gardeners. There is yet another unusual bell tower, this time separate from its church (except for the bell-ringer's cable), on a rock at the topmost point of the village. From this eyrie (a good picnic spot) you can enjoy a superb view over the Lot valley, and may be lucky enough to spot a peregrine. The village can also be reached by car: *continue along the D42, turning off at signpost to Lavinzelle.*

Lavinzelle - *Return to the D42. Turn right after the Pont de Coursavy (not on map),*
Cassaniouze *then bear left up the D601.* ⑪ *Shortly after the D25 joins the D601*
from the left on the edge of Cassaniouze, turn left along the D66 to
Calvinet, which takes you past the 18thC Château de Lamothe.

Calvinet Renowned in the past for its cattle market (you can still see the
weighbridge in the central square), the village of Calvinet is known
today for its formidably steep main street - a regular feature of the
Tour de France cycle race.

Hôtel Louis-Bernard Puech recently took over the family business (hotel,
Beau- restaurant and *charcuterie* rolled into one) after working with some of
séjour the best chefs in France. Both influences show: there are
(hotel- straightforward local specialities such as *pied de porc farci* and *tripous*
restaurant, (sheep's tripe), but you can also sample more sophisticated, skilfully
Calvinet) executed dishes such as his imaginative salad of sautéed chicken livers,
curly endive, French beans, and raw cèpe mushroom, *cassolette*
d'escargots aux noix, mousseline de brochet aux écrevisses, and a deep
and richly flavoured *salmis de canard* based on his mother's recipe. The
desserts are particularly good. Rooms are simple (with shower). *Tel*
71.49.91.68; closed 15 Oct-Easter; price bands A/B/C.

Calvinet- *Leave Calvinet by the D19 signposted Montsalvy.* ⑫ *At the first T-junction,*
Montsalvy *turn right in the direction of Rodez, then, a little later, left on to the D25*
towards Junhac. This road goes through a particularly attractive stretch
of country, sensuously rounded hills and dips and, on the right, the
compactly turreted Château de Senezergues, which can be seen from
several angles silhouetted against the valley below. As you come into
Junhac, turn right on to the D19; straight on through the village.

Mont- Once a fortified village (the English besieged it unsuccessfully in 1357),
salvy Montsalvy no longer has its surrounding walls, though several of the
original gates are still standing.

Hôtel du This cosy establishment offers a menu which includes many Auvergnat
Nord specialities often neglected by other local chefs - for example, *aligot*
(hotel- (mashed potatoes with garlic and unmatured Cantal cheese), *pounti* (a
restaurant, kind of savoury pudding), *tripous* and trout with bacon. *Tel 71.49.20.03;*
Montsalvy) *closed Jan-Mar; price bands A/B/C.*

Montsalvy - *Take the Pons road down the valley of the Palefer through tall, cool pine*
Entraygues *forests. At first rather narrow, it quickly widens and becomes a much*
easier drive. ⑬ *At Les Carrières (not on map), turn right to Couesque,*
then right again along the D904 to Entraygues.

Dordogne:

PERIGORD BLANC

Set in the northern part of the Dordogne *département*, this tour more or less covers the area known as the Périgord Blanc because of the local prevalence of limestone. It is based on the city of Périgueux, which has a long and turbulent history going back to Roman times.

The route ranges eastwards along the Auvézère river, whose landscape changes from a majestic broad valley to narrow and densely wooded gorges. (The latter can be sampled by taking the detour at point 4.) Then you turn westwards through more typically Dordogne countryside - gently rolling, but with quite frequent outcrops of whitish limestone that can give a certain grandeur to the scenery.

After the market towns of Excideuil and Thiviers, the route goes through the picturesque village of St-Jean-de-Côle and the magical, water-lapped

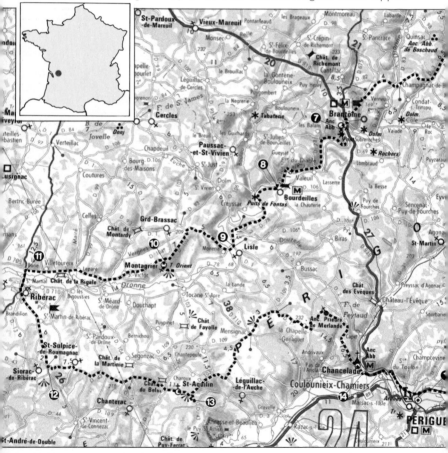

town of Brantôme. This is a relatively long loop to complete in a single day and the most enjoyable way to do it is with a night at Brantôme, where there is a choice of hotels and fine restaurants - as indeed there is elsewhere on the tour, including a Michelin two-star restaurant, the Moulin du Roc, at Champagnac-de-Belair *(tel 53.54.80.36; price bands C/D)*.

From Brantôme you follow a charming course along the valley of the Dronne via Bourdeilles to Ribérac, and then via some untroubled countryside to Périgueux. This makes a restful second day's drive.

Included in the route are three of the finest châteaux in south-west France - Hautefort, Puyguilhem and Les Bories. But just as important in building up a picture of this, the least spoiled part of the Dordogne, are the less obvious charms of many an ordinary Périgord village, manor and farmhouse.

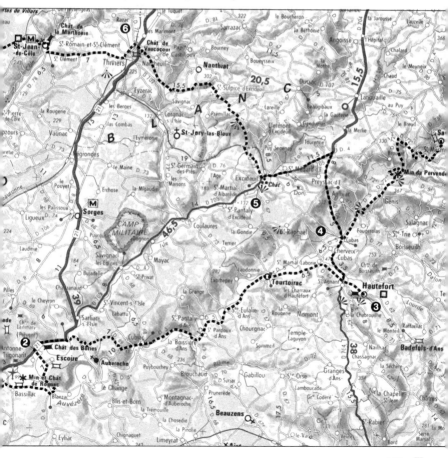

ROUTE: 165 KM

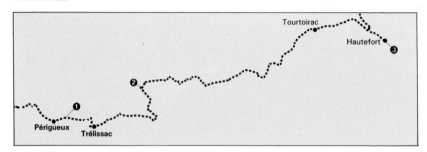

Périgueux Périgueux is blighted by traffic jams (it is an important road junction), graceless modern buildings (following indiscriminate demolition), and sprawling suburbs. But its considerable charms are immediately revealed once you step into the self-contained and mostly pedestrianized old town, which contains a large number of yellowish (and now attractively worn) stone buildings. If possible, take a stroll here after dark, when the buildings' many decorative details - on doorways, windows and staircases - are theatrically set off by street lighting of exemplary intelligence. There are two pleasant cafés in the tiny Place St-Louis (where the celebrated truffle market is held on *Wed and Sat, Nov-Feb*).

The Cathédrale St-Front, a cavernous Byzantine construction restored almost beyond recognition in the 19thC, has a certain eccentric charm (eg its huge *trompe l'oeil* organ case). But the delicately proportioned Romanesque Eglise St-Etienne-de-la-Cité, although partly demolished in the 16th and 17thC, is a far more interesting building.

Musée du Périgord, Périgueux A little museum containing many different kinds of exhibits, most interesting of which are the prehistoric and Gallo-Roman collections, mostly from local sites. *Open 10-12, 2-7; closed Tues.*

L'Oison, (restaurant, Périgueux) Try this plush restaurant if you feel like treating yourself to some superb cuisine that does not confine itself to such Périgord favourites as *confits, foie gras* and *pommes sarladaises*. Régis Chiorozas is particularly skilful with fish, often cleverly serving three or four different kinds together in a single sauce; but his meat courses (sweetbreads with an onion purée, *noisettes d'agneau à la glace d'estragon*) and desserts are also imaginative - and generously served. *31, Rue St-Front; tel 53.09.84.02; closed Sun evening, Mon, and 15 Feb-15 March; price bands C/D.*

① *Leave Périgueux on the Limoges road; at the main junction on the edge of town turn right as though for Bergerac, and a little later left on to the D5 signposted Bassillac. When you get there, fork right into the village.*

Bassillac This little village, not yet engulfed by Périgueux' ribbon development, has a charming domed Romanesque church.

Rejoin the D5 and continue to the junction with the D6. Turn left and follow the signs to Antonne. After bearing left in Escoire, be sure to stop and look back at the elegant and original late 18thC château.

At the T-junction ② *with the N21 in Antonne, turn right.* Just after leaving the village, and on a right-hand bend, there is a drive leading to the Château des Bories.

Château des Bories, Antonne

This stout-turreted 16thC castle has two remarkable features: a staircase which encloses, instead of a stair well, a dark and tiny vaulted room on each floor; and an ornate kitchen. *Open 10-12, 2-7, July-Sept.*

Continue briefly on the N21, taking the first right turn on to the D69 signposted Cubjac. After driving up through woodland, bear left on to the D5 and down to the Auvézère river, bypassing Cubjac and continuing through Ste-Eulalie-d'Ans to Tourtoirac.

Ancienne Abbaye de Tour-toirac

Sadly dilapidated, but to be restored, this early 11thC abbey is worth visiting for its chapter house and its prioral chapel, whose vaulting is most unusual in that it contains small cavities designed to dampen the echo. *Open 9-12, 2-5, Mon-Sat; ask for key at nearby* mairie.

Hôtel des Voyag-eurs
(hotel-restaurant, Tourtoirac)

You will get straightforward local fare, including *omelette de Négrondes* (with pork scratchings), good value, and a friendly welcome from Georgette and Louis Couty at this hotel-restaurant, whose garden backs on to the Auvézère. *Tel 53.51.12.29; closed Jan; price bands A/B.*

Continue on the D5. When it turns left towards Cubas, keep straight on in the direction of Hautefort on the D62 and, after crossing the D704, the D62E1. Soon Hautefort will appear high above you on the right.

Château de Hautefort

This imposing 17thC château is one of the largest in south-west France. Although much of it was burnt down in 1968, it has been lovingly restored by its owner. One turret which escaped destruction contains, beneath its domed roof, a superb example of chestnut timberwork. There is a large shady park, ideal for picnics. *Open 9-12, 2-7, 2-6 Nov-Easter; closed 15 Dec-15 Jan.*

③ *Return to the D704 and turn right for Cubas.*

Auvézère Gorges
(detour)

This is a long but attractive detour (round trip, 15 km) through the wooded gorges of the Auvézère to Savignac, where there is an interesting piece of industrial archaeology.

④ *Emerging from Cubas, turn right on to the D5 and make for Génis. Bear right in the middle of that village, then turn immediately left along the D72E4 signposted Payzac.* This true backroad winds its way down through dense woodland into the wild and sparsely inhabited gorges - a landscape untypical of the Dordogne as a whole. *Soon after climbing out of the woods on to a plateau of pasture, take the hidden turning right on to the D72E5 to St-Mesmin,* which takes you back into the gorges. *Turn*

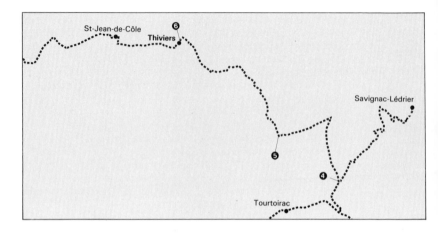

right just after St-Mesmin's naive little Romanesque church (worth a quick glance inside), then left for Savignac-Lédrier. Turn left in Savignac, then left again on to the Lanouaille road. At the bottom of the hill after Savignac, turn left for La Forge, an exceptional example of a 16thC ironworks complete with original charcoal-fired blast furnace, which stopped production only in 1930. Although the interior is not visitable for much of the year, a stroll round the outside is interesting enough. *Open 2-6, July and Aug. Either retrace via Gorges, or rejoin main route by continuing towards Lanouaille as far as crossroads with the D4. Turn left and follow the signs to Excideuil, crossing D704 and soon joining the D705.*

Excideuil As you approach, extensive views open up to the west. It is a lively little market town (market: Thurs) containing a number of 17thC houses and a curious château that is half medieval keep, half Renaissance manor. It has had a particularly eventful history: it was besieged by Richard Coeur du Lion (unsuccessfully), and changed hands several times during the Hundred Years War and the Wars of Religion. It cannot be visited, but a stroll round the walls reveals a good deal.
⑤ *Turn right at the Monument aux Morts in Excideuil, then immediately left on to the D77 to St-Sulpice-d'Excideuil. There bear left by the church, and on reaching the T-junction with the D707 turn left for Thiviers.*

Thiviers Bustling Thiviers holds weekly markets (Sat) which enjoy a considerable local reputation, especially from Nov to March, when there is a staggering array of geese, ducks, *foie gras* and truffles.
⑥ *Turn right at the church in the middle of Thiviers; continue on D707.*

St-Jean-de-Côle An attractively compact village; the Château de la Marthonie (15th-17thC) overlooks a small square and an old covered market, which nestles against an eccentrically asymmetrical and partly 11thC church. A broad cobbled street leads down to the Côle river, which is spanned by a narrow Gothic bridge with pier-heads.

Cross the river, then turn left on to the D98. Follow the signs for Château de Puyguilhem.

Château de Puy-guilhem, Villars
On reaching Villars, turn left, then right, for the château, which is just outside the village. The elegant architecture and decoration of this early 16thC building, with its turrets of different shapes, are reminiscent of the best of the Loire valley châteaux. Inside, the main staircase and several fireplaces are notable for their sculpting. *Open 10-11, 2-5 Feb-March; 9.30-12, 2-6 April-June and 8 Sept-15 Oct; 9-12, 2-7 July-7 Sept; 10-12, 2-7 16 Oct-15 Dec; closed 16 Dec-Jan 31 and Tues 8 Sept-June.*

Leave Villars on the D3 and follow the signs to Brantôme via Champagnac-de-Belair.

Brantôme
Brantôme's charm has, of course, a great deal to do with its setting. The former abbey, now occupied by the town hall, school and a museum, tucked away against a cliff and topped by an extraordinary late-11thC bell-tower erected on a rock above the church, is separated from the town itself by an arm of the Dronne. An L-shaped 16thC bridge leads from the abbey to the former monks' gardens, which are dotted with ornamental trees (including giant sequoias) and Renaissance stone *reposoirs* (shelters).

Ancienne Abbaye, Brantôme
The abbey church, massively over-restored in 1846, contains two powerful bas-reliefs. The monastery is chiefly interesting for the caves behind it, where scenes were carved out of the rock by the monks.

Musée Des-moulin, Brantôme
Don't miss this fascinating little museum in the former abbey, which has a collection of prehistoric art as well as the disturbing works of Fernand Desmoulin, a 19thC local painter who executed 'automatic' portraits of the dead (even in pitch darkness) after being put in a trance by a medium. Both abbey and museum *open 10-12, 2-6 16 June-15 Sept and Easter; closed Tues.*

Moulin de l'Abbaye
(hotel-restaurant, Brantôme)
You can peer from the L-shaped bridge across to the dining room windows of this idyllically positioned restaurant. It is expensive, but, besides the setting, you get imaginative dishes from a wide-ranging menu; the wine list carries some of the best from Cahors and Bergerac. There are ten sumptuous bedrooms. *Tel 53.05.80.22; closed Nov-May, Mon; price bands C/D.*

Hôtel Chabrol
(hotel-restaurant, Brantôme)
Also known as the Frères Charbonnel, this place is less glamorous than the Moulin de l'Abbaye, but nonetheless pleasant, with a charm of its own, and some rooms overlooking the river. The welcome is friendly, rooms are comfortable (if, in some cases, small) and the food in the large, sober dining room is excellent without being flashy. *59, Rue*

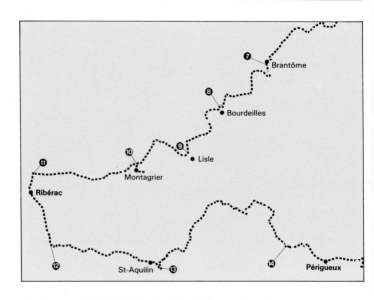

Gambetta; tel 53.05.70.15; closed mid Nov-mid Dec, Feb, Sun evening and Mon Oct-June; price bands C/D.

Brantôme -
Bourdeilles
⑦ *Take the D78 (Bourdeilles) road out of Brantôme, later continuing on the D106 and enjoy a marvellous drive along the north side of the Dronne (frequent access to picnic places on riverside meadows, shaded by poplars). At points you will be dwarfed by dramatic cliffs.*
⑧ *Turn left across the river into Bourdeilles.*

Bour-
deilles
Just across the bridge, keep left up the main street, which leads past the great bulk of the château; park at the top. The guided tour is worthwhile, revealing a medieval fortress and a beautifully furnished Renaissance palace. The gold room is a highlight, but perhaps just as rewarding is the view from the terrace. *Open 9-11, 2-6; closed 15 Dec-1 Feb, first week in Oct and Tues 15 Sept-15 June.*

Griffons
(hotel-restaurant, Bourdeilles)
With a prime position on the south side of the Dronne this is a reputable place with ten rooms. *Tel 53.05.75.61; closed Oct-March; price bands B/C/D.*
   Leave Bourdeilles on the D78 in the direction of Lisle and ⑨ *turn right on to the D1, re-crossing the Dronne. Just across the bridge is a pleasant spot with ample parking where you can picnic under weeping willows by a weir, or, if fine, bathe in the river, or watch children leaping into the water from the bridge. Immediately after the bridge, turn right, keeping on the D1. At the next crossroads* ⑩ *turn left if you wish to visit Montagrier, otherwise go straight on.*

Mon-tagrier
A pretty village with two simple *auberges*, and fuel. Drive through, down the hill, looking for an unsignposted tarmac turning on the left; take it and in 20 metres turn right along an avenue of chestnuts to Montagrier's clumsily restored 12thC church. It stands, however, in a fine isolated position, commanding marvellous views of the Dronne valley. *Retrace through village and turn left on to the D104e; continue, ignoring side turnings, via St-Victor. At La Borie* (11) *turn left on to the D708, re-crossing the Dronne for the last time.* Riverside picnicking is virtually impossible between St-Victor and La Borie.

Ribérac
A market and tourist town, with a dignified, mainly 18thC main street, and plenty of bars and cafés. For a proper meal, there is the Hôtel de France (*tel 53.90.00.61; price bands A/B*).
Continuing straight ahead on Ribérac's main street, leave the town on the D709 and in about 6 km (fast driving through a lush valley) *turn left* (12) *at the staggered crossroads on to the D43 signposted St-Aquilin.* Just outside the village (notice the turrets of nearby Château de Belet) you pass the Etang de Garennes, a pleasant, man-made lake where you can bathe and hire pedal boats, or have a drink, or a simple meal.

St-Aquilin - La Chapelle-Gonaguet
St-Aquilin is dominated by its cream-coloured, fortified Gothic church; fuel here. *Continue out of the village on the D43* (views to the right) *and in one km from the middle of the village, where the D43 turns right, turn sharp left* (13) *then immediately bear right, on the D103. Continue ignoring one minor turning left and two to the right and in 2.5 km, at the crossroads, take the third right in the direction of Mensignac. Follow the D109 through Mensignac, and in 0.5 km go left. In 2.5 km take the second right on to the D1 for La Chapelle-Gonaguet. Go straight through the village, taking the first left just outside it, followed by the first right. In another 1.5 km, you come to the* Ancien Prieuré on the left.

Ancien Prieuré de Merlande
In a meadow in the forest, only the restored chapel and the prior's house remain of this priory built by the monks of Chancelade. Inside the gaunt chapel with its rough stone floor a surpise is in store: fearsome, and finely carved monsters and lions embellish the capitals of the chancel's blind arcades - a rather aggressive touch for so peaceful a place. *Continue on the partly single track road* (blind corners) *leading to the D2, where turn right.*

Chan-celade
The Augustinian abbey founded here in the 12thC was a powerful force and had a chequered history up to the Revolution. Remaining today are the abbey church, with a fine arcaded belfry, and the endearing little Romanesque chapel of St-Jean. Grouped around a courtyard and some pretty gardens are further monastery buildings, including a small museum of religious art. Nearby are the ruins of a fortified abbey mill.
Leaving Chancelade fork left (14) *on to the D710 and soon right on to the D939 to the outskirts of Périgueux.*

Dordogne:

VINEYARDS, RIVERS AND *BASTIDES*

The valley of the Dordogne and its vicinity are among the most popular tourist destinations in France, particularly for those renting *gîtes* or farmhouses. Famed for the gentle beauty of its landscape, it also boasts some spectacular sights, especially along the great river itself - clifftop castles, *villages perchés*, prehistoric caves; and it is the land of *foie gras, confits* and the truffle.

This, the most southerly of the book's two Dordogne tours steers away from the area's most famous - and crowded - attractions and has been devised to include and contrast three distinct features of the region: the river itself, the historic *bastides* and the vineyards of Bergerac.

The first route is a gentle meander through pretty wine country south of Bergerac. There are fine views, some enchanting châteaux, both private and open to the public, and opportunities to taste and to buy the local wines. For those wishing to continue on the second route, there is a pleasant linking stretch of some 15 km between Issigeac and Beaumont.

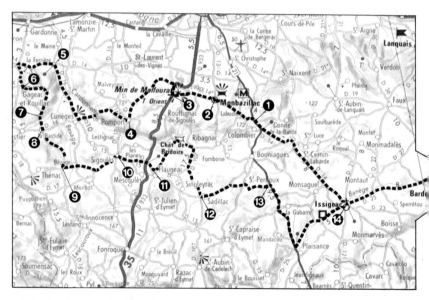

The *bastides* of the Dordogne are walled towns each built to a similar plan with grid pattern streets surrounding an arcaded central square. They were constructed by both the French and English during the 13thC wars. The second route takes in the *bastides* of Beaumont and Monpazier and then turns towards the Dordogne and Vézère rivers and the peaceful hill country between. The route recrosses the Dordogne at one of its most attractive points and returns to Beaumont past the lovely abbey of Cadouin.

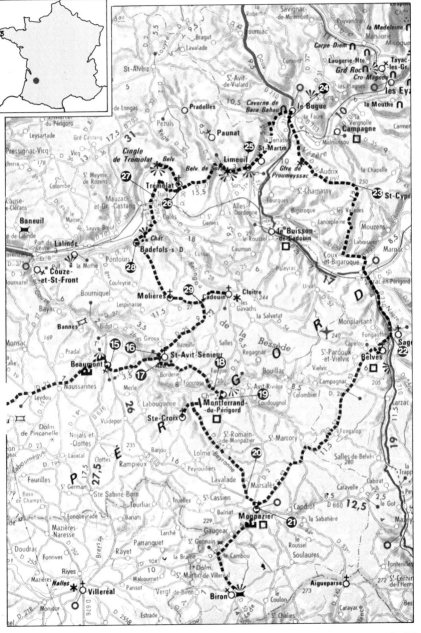

■■■■ **ROUTE ONE: 70 KM**

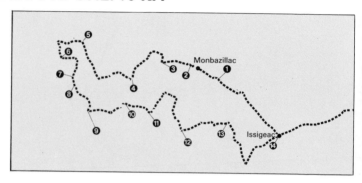

Issigeac

This is a pretty country town on the River Banège. The bishops of Sarlat found it an agreeable place: one built the lovely Gothic church in the early 16thC, and another the huge bishops' palace, now the town hall, in the late 17thC. *Leave Issigeac by the D14 (Bergerac) road and, in 9 km, after joining the RN21* ① *take the next turning left, poorly signposted to Labardie. At T-junction turn right into Labardie (signpost broken). Follow signs to Château de Monbazillac. At junction before Monbazillac turn right into village.*

Château de Monbazillac

Like a child's cardboard cut-out, all brown and grey with pointed roofs and four fat towers, this endearing château stands guard over the vast surrounding Monbazillac vineyard. Now owned by the regional wine co-operative, it houses a small museum of Protestantism - Bergerac was the centre of that faith in Périgord - and a collection of wine-making implements. If you don't have time for the guided tour (about 3/4 hour), content yourself with a stroll round the château and the view from the north terrace. You will, though, forfeit the chance to taste Monbazillac, the star of Bergerac's wines, and once considered the equal of Sauternes. Its fame has rather unjustly diminished in recent years: sweet, golden and fragrant, it is perfect with *foie gras* or as an aperitif. *Open daily Mar-Nov 9-12, 2-6; Nov-Mar 9.30-12, 2-5; restaurant.* ② *After visiting the château, return to the village and carry straight on signposted Moulin de Malfourat.*

Moulin de Malfourat

From this sail-less mill (viewing table on roof terrace of the bar/créperie) there is another panoramic view of the Monbazillac vineyards, Bergerac sprawled out in the Dordogne valley and the hills beyond. From the other side of the road there is a fine and different view to the south.

Moulin de Malfourat - Saussignac

③ *At the D933 turn right. Take the first left signposted Pomport. The* route plunges into the vineyards of Monbazillac, which, typically of the Bergerac region, are mostly small family-owned plots. It is possible to buy wine direct from many of these châteaux, but remember that it is not easy to taste without being obliged to buy. It is generally best to choose your wines from a large selection at a *cave coopérative* or even at a good shop with helpful staff. And resist the temptation to buy gallons of *vin ordinaire* and crow because they only cost a few francs: the real bargains here are among the better local wines which you would have less opportunity of sampling at home.

④ *In Pomport turn right by the war memorial signposted Cunèges. At the T-junction turn left on to the D16. At crossroads just before Cunèges, turn right.* This is an attractive road with wide views to the right.

⑤ *At La Ferrière, turn left on to the D14.* Before turning, notice the hilltop château on the left.

Saus-signac

The nobly proportioned château of Saussignac which stands in the centre of the village has a delightfully tamed and domesticated air. The graceful three-sided facade is a pretty row of terraced houses, with the post office housed in one corner. Washing lines, chicken runs and vegetable plots encircle the never-finished 16th and 17thC building, once inhabited by the beautiful Louise de la Béraudière, who entertained Rabelais and captivated Montaigne here.

Like Monbazillac, Saussignac is another of the wine *appellations* within Bergerac, and the surrounding vineyards produce a pleasant white country wine.

Bergerac, sweet and dry.

Relais de Saus-signac
(restaurant)

A sound modernised village inn (and a *Logis de France*). The food in the spacious restaurant is not unadventurous and the place is a fair choice for a family lunch. There are 20 inexpensive, peaceful bedrooms. *Tel 53.27.92.08; closed Mon; price band B.*

⑥ *At the Co-op shop turn left signposted Gageac-Rouillac. This road is not marked on the map. Go through Les Cavailles, and at the unmarked junction with minor road, follow your road round to the left.*

173

Gageac-
Rouillac
-Sigoulès

You will emerge at a small T-junction directly opposite the portcullis gateway of the enchanting dry-moated château of Gageac-Rouillac. Built as a fortress in the 14thC, it was the seat of Geoffroi de Vivans, Huguenot leader in the Wars of Religion.

Facing the château at the T-junction, turn right. At the electricity pylon turn right again signposted Monestier and after 1.5 km.

⑦ *Turn left at bottom of hill signposted Tourmentine and La Bastide.*

⑧ *At La Bastide turn left opposite the church and then turn right signposted Thénac. Follow the next signpost to Thénac.* Fine views of the gentle countryside open to the left. Notice, further on, the imposing turreted Château Panisseau, also on the left. This produces perhaps the best Bergerac *sec*, crisp and dry. You have now left the Saussignac vineyards and entered the large Bergerac region, which produces excellent everyday red wines; amongst the whites choose the driest (such as Panisseau), or the sweetest.

⑨ *At the crossroads (poorly signposted), turn left. After Bézage, follow the signs for Sigoulès.*

Sigoulès

If you are feeling hot and want a dip, or the children are becoming restless, *turn left in Sigoulès signposted Base de Loisirs Sigoulès-Pomport. Follow signs to Base de Loisirs on the D17.* This is one of several man-made lakes which dot the region, with sandy beach, picnic tables, bar, fishing and tennis (there is another excellent one with an outdoor restaurant not far away at St-Sernin near Duras).

⑩ *To continue the tour, turn right in Sigoulès signposted Flaugeac.* On the right is the local *cave coopérative* where you can taste and buy.

⑪ *Having crossed the D933 (main road) turn left at the blue Renault repair garage signposted Ribagnac. At the T-junction turn left.* Beware - this road is pot-holed. The towers of Bridoire and Malfourat Mill are visible ahead. *Turn left at T-junction.*

Château
de
Bridoire

It was much restored in the 19thC but today this formidable yet romantic 15thC château is deserted and to date its future is uncertain. After driving round the château, *return to the junction and carry straight on. At the next crossroads turn right for Sadillac.*

Sadillac

In Sadillac turn left uphill into the village proper. Carry on over small crossroads to the village square. Typical of this pocket due south of Bergerac, Sadillac seems almost fast asleep. The fine 12thC church in the square looks neglected, though the adjoining 16thC château has been saved by the de Conti family, local wine producers.

⑫ *Return to the small crossroads in the village and turn right.*

⑬ *At the unmarked crossroads in St-Perdoux, go straight over and follow the single track road through the hamlet, round a left- and then a right hand- bend to emerge on the main RN21. Turn right. In about 5 km turn left signposted Issigeac.*

ROUTE TWO: 100 KM

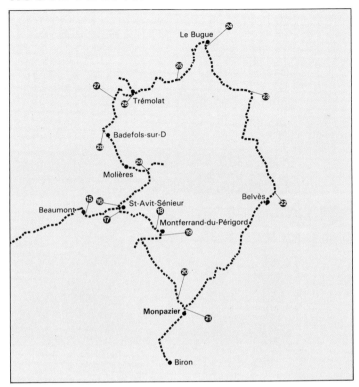

⑭ *To continue on Route Two, leave Issigeac by the D25, signposted Autres Directions and then Beaumont.*

Beau-mont

The market town of Beaumont is a fortified English *bastide* built in 1272. One of its original gateways, the Porte de Luzier, still survives; from there (signposted from the square) you have a clear idea of a walled town and of how, even today, the open countryside begins immediately beyond. The fortified church is splendid.

Hôtel des Voya-geurs Chez Popaul
(restaurant, Beaumont)

Usually crowded with local families, this popular restaurant prides itself on its vast selection of hors d'oeuvres (except Sun). Choose one of the cheaper set menus, dabble with the soup (plonked on the table in a big saucepan) and the uninteresting *plat du jour* and concentrate on piling your plate with crayfish, prawns, mussels and endless *salades variées* from the groaning buffet table. There is a special menu for children. *Tel 53.22.30.11; closed Mon and Jan, Feb, Oct, Nov; price bands B/C.*

⑮ *Leaving Beaumont turn left at the filling station signposted Cadouin.*

⑯ *Turn right signposted St-Avit-Sénieur, a tiny hilltop village sporting a sleepy café, a couple of fuel pumps and a mammoth fortified church. Next to it are the ruins of an 11thC abbey.*

⑰ *Keeping the church on the left follow the road into a pretty wooded valley past a stonemason's yard. At the staggered crossroads go straight on following the sign to Montferrand-du-Périgord.*

⑱ *In 2.5 km, at the T-junction with a grassy island in the middle, turn*

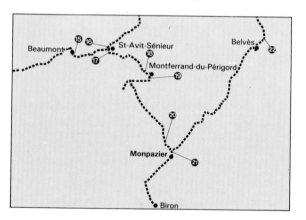

left, then bear right immediately, signposted Montferrand.

Montfer-rand-du-Périgord
Montferrand begins with a lovely covered market supported by fine squat pillars and continues with a succession of mellow old houses straggling uphill towards the ruins of a medieval château.

⑲ *At the top of the hill turn right down a lane signposted Eglise. This road is marked on the map only by a single line. It passes a tiny romanesque chapel with an interior covered in peeling frescoes. All around are fields and woods, perfect for picnics. At the crossroads go straight over to see Ste-Croix; turn left to continue the route.*

Ste-Croix
(detour)
Here, in an isolated setting, is a 12thC church notable for the purity of its lines; there are also the ruins of an *ancien prieuré* with ornate mullioned windows and a large classically-styled 17thC château.

Mont-ferrand - Monpazier
A long gentle road which follows the Beyronne stream through tranquil countryside. Just past the turning to Marsalès is the peaceful little man-made Lac de Veronne, with sandy beach, picnic tables and bar.

(20) *At the junction with the D660 turn left (signposted Château de Biron).*

Mon-pazier

Leave the car outside the town walls and walk into the perfect arcaded central square. You are among tourists again, but Monpazier is a delight, the best preserved of all the Dordogne *bastides*. The rectangular plan of the streets is still intact, and in the square the usual covered market hall has grain measures still to be seen. Monpazier was founded in 1284 by the English, but suffered at the hands of both English and French during the Wars of Religion. Today it is a useful place to stock up for a picnic, filled as it is with shops selling local *spécialitiés*; there are also plenty of cafés and pizza houses.

The market square, Monpazier.

Château de Biron *(detour)*

Leaving Monpazier follow signs to Château de Biron (8 km). It suddenly appears, towering above the landscape and seeming almost to crush the little village that clusters at its feet. The château was owned by the same eminent family, Biron-Gontaut, from the 12th to the 20thC. Until the 18thC each generation busily added bits on, resulting in an amusing jumble of styles and a visual surprise at every turn. Though essentially a fortress, there are some charmingly light touches of Renaissance architecture, notably the double chapel and inner loggia. *Open 9-11.30, 2.30-6.30 Feb-Oct; 10-12, 2-4.30 Oct-Feb; closed Tue in Dec and Jan.*

(21) *To continue route take the D53 from Monpazier signposted Belvès.*

Belvès

An attractive walled town whose old houses and terraced gardens overlook the Nauze valley. In the covered market notice the pillory chain, still attached to one of the pillars. Walnuts are a major local product.

(22) *From Belvès, follow the ring road (signposted Autres Directions) and at the T-junction turn left signposted Périgeux.*

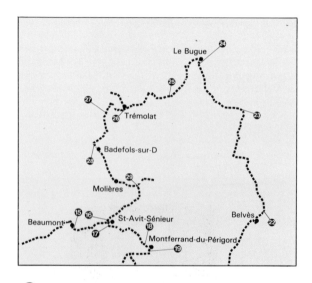

㉓ *Five km beyond Coux-et-Bigaroque turn left off the D703 signposted Audrix and Gouffres de Proumeyssac.*

Audrix A pretty wooded lane with views on both sides leads to this little visited hilltop village, a delightfully tranquil spot, particularly for those joining the route from nearby Les Eyzies, heaving with tourists. Stand behind the attractive Romanesque church for a view over the Vézère valley and in front of the *mairie* for a view over the Dordogne valley. Pause for a drink or a simple meal at the Auberge Médiéval with its pretty vine-covered terrace, or picnic in the surrounding fields.

Gouffres de Prou- meyssac A chance to visit one of the many extraordinary caverns for which the Dordogne is so famous. This is a huge watery domed chasm covered in stalagmites (up) and stalactites (down) and many other strange shapes. Cups, jugs and other objects placed on the cavern floor help to demonstrate the rapidity of calcification. *Open 8.30-11.30, 2-6 daily Easter-Sept; Sun only Oct. Tour leaves every half-hour and lasts three-quarters of an hour.*

㉔ *At the T-junction with the D31 turn right into Le Bugue. After crossing the river take the first turning left signposted St-Alvère on the D703. In 2 km turn left signposted Trémolat.*

Limeuil Notice on the road to Limeuil the domed 12thC church of St-Martin, ringed by cypress trees. Limeuil stands at the confluence of the Dordogne and Vézère rivers and it makes a picturesque spot at which to stretch your legs, picnic or bathe.

㉕ *Leave Limeuil on the D31, signposted Trémolat.* The road passes a viewpoint (layby) of the river below, known as the Belvédère de Sors.

Trémolat The route now rejoins the Dordogne at the point where it describes its famous and spectacular loop, known as the Cingle de Trémolat. The attractive old village is worth a look; less charming is its church, a great windowless barrack of a place, though in contrast you will find in the cemetary a charming Romanesque chapel, recently restored.

Vieux Logis *(restaurant, Trémolat)* This is a heavenly place: an old creeper clad building full of antiques with a dining-room converted from a barn and the most beautiful flower-filled garden with a stream where you can sample excellent *Périgordine* cuisine. Despite being part of the prestigious *Relais et Châteaux Hôtels* group, the atmosphere is relaxed and prices are reasonable; lovely bedrooms. *Tel 53.22.80.06; closed Jan, Tues; price bands B/C.*

Belvédère de Racamadou *(detour)* *Following the 'Route du Cingle de Trémolat' signpost drive from the village to the belvedere 2 km north.* A platform on top of a water tower gives a wonderful view of the curling river set in a patchwork landscape. **㉖** *Return to Trémolat and the junction with the D31 where turn right.* At the bridge, tracks to left and right lead to riverside picnic spots.

㉗ *At the Y-junction in Traly bear right signposted Calès. At the junction with the D29 turn right and follow the scenic riverside road to Badefols-sur-Dordogne.*

㉘ *As you enter Badefols turn left at the sign for Lou Cantou hotel* (a genteel small hotel which merits a Red R in Michelin for its food) *and then turn right signposted Molières.*

Molières A peaceful village which began its existence as an English *bastide* but was never finished. It possesses a plain but eye-catching Gothic church and a grassy square bordered by attractive old houses, with views from the far corner over the *Périgord Noir*.

Cadouin As in other villages in the area, the yellow stone of the houses gives Cadouin a pleasant mellow quality. In the central square is a pretty covered market and the abbey, once a revered place of pilgrimage owing to its possession of a (bogus) piece of the Holy Shroud. Dispense with the long guided tour, but take time to stroll in the lovely flamboyant gothic cloisters, admiring the four fine corner doors, the highly realistic sculptures, the faded frescoes and the serene atmosphere. Entrance at side of church in the square; *closed Dec and Jan, and Tues Oct-Mar.*
　　Retrace on the D25 out of Cadouin and **㉙** *at junction with the D27 keep left on the D25 for St-Avis-Sénieur and Beaumont.*

Avoiding the undeniably spectacular but much visited Gorges de l'Ardèche in the south of the *département*, this tour features the less known, more varied and equally beautiful northern Ardèche.

The tour revolves around Mont Gerbier de Jonc (where the River Loire has its source) and the majestic Mézenc massif, extending to the spa of Vals-les-Bains in the south and the mountain plateau of the Velay in the north (with a brief sally into the Haute-Loire *département*).

To get the best out of this tour, you have to be prepared to do a certain amount of easy hill-walking - though no proposed walk will take you away from the car for more than 50 minutes. However, those unwilling or unable to engage in such energetic activities will still be able to enjoy wonderful views from the roadside. The tour's hub lies on the watershed between the Atlantic and the Mediterranean. This dividing line can be seen almost physically in the marked difference in the landscape that occurs as you cross it. To the north-west there are vast moors and windswept plains at an average altitude of about 1,200 metres, over which tower the numerous *sucs* (cones of extinct volcanoes) of the Mézenc massif; to the south-east, the deeply eroded valleys take on an almost Provençal look with their vineyards and orchards.

Those with a penchant for geology, botany and ornithology will probably enjoy this tour most, although the scenery alone is worth the trip, especially in late October, when autumn colours are at their most vivid. At this time of year, check in advance that hotels and restaurants are open; the food, incidentally, tends to consist of straightforward home cooking (excellent and copious) rather than *haute cuisine*.

▬▬▬ ◢ ROUTE ONE 72 KM

Gerbier de Jonc

The Gerbier de Jonc, which is 1,551 metres above sea-level, is a massive hunk of rock that rises abruptly out of the bleak moors of the Mézenc massif like a huge marshmallow. It is made of fine-grained rock called phonolite, also known as clinkstone, which as its name suggests emits a sound when struck. The view from the top, particularly towards the south-east, is well worth the effort (40 minutes there and back by the steep path that leaves from the large car park at its foot).

Nearby, several streams emerging from different points in the hillside together form the source of the River Loire, which perversely flows south at the start of its 1,020-km journey north and west to the Atlantic.

Gerbier de Jonc - Les Estables

① *Leave the Gerbier de Jonc westwards (i.e. to the left when facing the mountain) on the D378.* This excellent road becomes the D36 when it crosses from the Ardèche *département* into the Haute-Loire, shortly before swooping down to Les Estables. It offers a majestic view over the broad valley of the Gazeille.

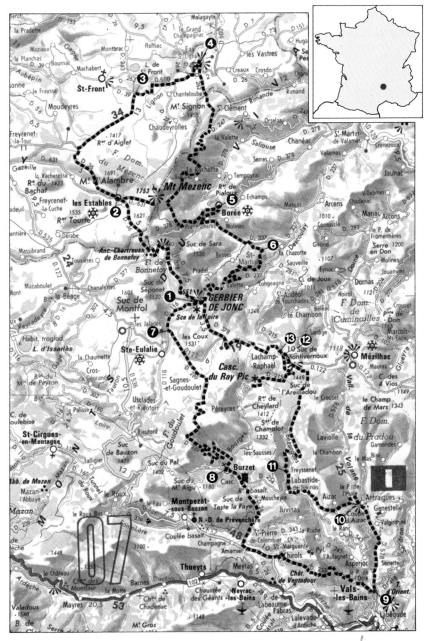

Gorges de l'Ardèche à Aubenas

Les Estables

This sprawling, fast-expanding, cross-country skiing resort is a good starting point from which to tackle Mont Mézenc.

Les 3 Monts
(rest., Les Estables)

Although housed in rather a graceless building, this large restaurant offers genuine local fare at reasonable prices. Specialities include *civet de porcellet*, home-made duck terrine with chestnuts and bilberry tart. *Tel 71.08.35.06; closed Tues and 1 Nov–15 Dec; price band A.*

Mont Mézenc
(detour)

② *For this detour, take the D631 out of Les Estables for almost 3 km to the Croix de Boutières.* From there, a 25-minute energetic walk will take you to the top of the mountain (signposted), 1,753 metres above sea-level. The panoramic view from the top is truly flabbergasting: laid out before you is the whole of the Auvergne, with its lakes, valleys, mountain plateaux and extinct volcanoes. On a clear day, the Alps can be seen hovering like a mirage on the horizon. Those who have seen the sun coming up over the Alps from the top of Mont Mézenc say it is an unforgettable experience; but to do this you have to rise early and put on plenty of layers. The mountain is a favourite haunt of botanists. In addition to the expanses of bilberries and wild raspberries, several rare species of Alpine plants are to be found. Bilberries (French, *myrtilles*) are an important local industry: several hundred tons are picked each year in the region, much for export.

Les Estables - Chaud- ayrac

Return to Les Estables and continue on the D36 (fork right as you leave the village) towards Fay-sur-Lignon. After turning right on to the D500, you will drive through a vast tract of almost treeless pastureland with Mont Meygal in the distance: this landscape is typical of the Velay. Note the interesting architecture of many of the farmhouses: the front door is in a kind of porch-cum-penthouse which sticks out from the front wall. The point of this design was to prevent snow from getting into the house and, in the old days, to enable the farmer to use the projecting room as a cowshed in winter, thus avoiding the necessity of going outside at all in cold spells.

Chaudayrac - Fay

③ *At a dangerous crossroads at Chaudayrac (not on map), the D500 makes a 90° right turn to Fay-sur-Lignon (no warning is given).*

Fay-sur- Lignon

Hardy mountain cattle of the kind that you will have seen grazing on the moors are on sale at the big livestock market regularly held in this delightfully unspoilt little town. An ordinary market (ideal for picnic fare) is also held here every Wednesday. Away from the two marketplaces, houses huddle together to resist the fiercely cold winds that come up from the Lignon valley in winter - the town's altitude is almost 1,200 metres. Explore the narrow streets, and don't miss the view over the Lignon valley from the cemetery next to the church. The Hôtel-Restaurant des Négociants (see below) has only one or two rooms, but the Hôtel du Lignon is cheap and pleasant. *Tel 71.59.51.44.*

The Ardèche in late summer, leaves about to turn to autumn's vivid colours.

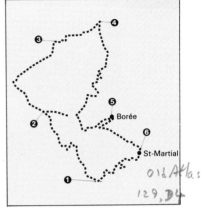

old Atlas
129, B4

Des Négo-ciants
(rest., Fay)

Mme Ladreyt is expert at such hearty dishes as leek soup and beef *daube*, and everything is served in mountainous quantities. The restaurant's cosy first-floor dining-room overlooks the cattle market. *Tel 71.59.50.61; price band A.*

Fay-sur-Lignon - Borée

④ *Leave Fay-sur-Lignon on the D262, and bear right along the D410 (not on map) at the junction with the D247 to St-Clément.* This marvellous new - though not always perfectly surfaced - stretch of road is flanked by Mont Mézenc on the right and offers plunging vistas to the left. It meanders past clumps of yellow-flowered gentian (the bitter roots of which flavour the local apéritifs, Avèze and Salers), herds of white cattle and long, low farmhouses with distinctive rust-coloured lichen on their walls and stone roofs. The road, although an easy and pleasant drive, zigzags so relentlessly that one is soon disorientated; valleys and peaks heave in and out of view in magically quick succession. *Ignore the turning off to the right to Les Estables, and a little later turn left along the D378 to Borée.*

Borée - St-Martial

⑤ *Turn sharp right along the D215 to St-Martial.* On the right, the uncannily rounded Suc de Touron towers above the road. Shortly after crossing a small river, beware of an invisible crossroads (unmarked at the time of writing).

St-Martial - Gerbier de Jonc

An unassuming little village overlooking a small lake that is an ideal picnic spot.
⑥ *Fork right in the middle of the village along the D237.* The road twists and turns through fragrant conifers as it climbs up towards the Gerbier de Jonc. To the right, there is a splendid view of the Suc de Sara with the massive Mont Mézenc looming behind. *On reaching the junction with the D378, turn right to the Gerbier de Jonc.*

183

ROUTE TWO 87 KM

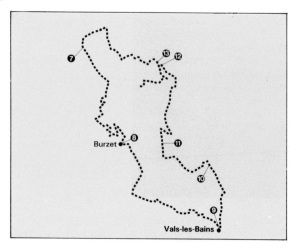

Gerbier de Jonc - Burzet

⑦ *Leave the Gerbier de Jonc by the D116, which follows the infant River Loire through moorland as far as Ste-Eulalie and beyond, but turn left on to the D122 before reaching Ste-Eulalie* (unless you are interested in medicinal plants and it happens to be the first Sunday after 12 July, when a special herb market, the Foire aux Violettes, is held there). *A little farther on, fork right along the D289 in the direction of Sagnes-et-Goudoulet and Burzet.*

About 3 km beyond Sagnes-et-Goudoulet, stop and look back over the hauntingly beautiful, bleak moors and mountain peaks in the distance. Then drive on for about 1.5 km, to reach one of the points where the watershed between the Atlantic and the Mediterranean is most striking. Suddenly, a whole new landscape will open out before you, a landscape that foreshadows the Midi farther south (vines, walnut trees, poplars). Nestling in the valley bottom 700 metres below, but only 3 km as the crow flies, is the village of Burzet. The road down the mountainside is strictly for those with a head for heights, but it is expertly engineered - as well it might be, for it forms part of the circuit of a motor rally which Burzet holds every year in mid-winter, called the Monte Carlo (sic).

Burzet

If you are in this area around Easter, make a point of visiting Burzet on Good Friday, when a ceremony takes place which dates back to the Middle Ages: the inhabitants, many of them dressed in biblical costume, walk in procession to a calvary perched high above the village. The visit to the Ray Pic waterfall mentioned in a later detour, (see ⑫) can be made from Burzet if it suits you better, but the drive is longer - 22 km there and back: *turn left out of the village along the D215.*

Burzet - Vals-les-Bains

⑧ *Turn right across the bridge in Burzet along the D26 in the direction of Vals-les-Bains.* After the excitement of the D289, this is an easy, relaxing drive along the verdant valley of the Bourges. *On reaching the T-junction, turn left along the D536. A minute or two later, almost immediately after entering the hamlet of Pont-de-Veyrières (not on map), turn left again on to the D253 to Vals-les-Bains (the signpost is virtually invisible).* This narrow road at times twists completely back on itself and offers superb views over the wild Tanargue Massif on the far side of the River Ardèche.

Vals-les-Bains

Slotted into the narrow valley of the River Volane, the sausage-shaped spa of Vals-les-Bains - 'town of 100 springs' - need not detain you unless you want to take its celebrated waters (especially good for diabetics) or have a fling at the casino.

If you wish to stay overnight in Vals-les-Bains, try the Hôtel Europe *(tel 75.37.43.94; closed Oct-Mar)*, which offers old-fashioned food at middling prices. However, for a more pastoral setting it is worth leaving Vals-les-Bains and driving 13 km along the N102, in the direction of Thueyts, to the Hotel Levant in leafy Neyrac-les-Bains *(turn left immediately after the garage in Neyrac; the hotel is signposted).* As well as serving good simple food, the hotel is quiet, unpretentious, and inexpensive *(tel 75.36.41.07; restaurant open all year, but hotel closed Oct-Easter).* Out of season, you should be able to find a room in one of the many hotels in Aubenas, 6 km south of Vals-les-Bains on the N102.

Local farmhouse, front door in the projecting porch: see entry for Les Estables - Chaudayrac.

Chez Mireille
(restaurant, Vals-les-Bains)

This is the one restaurant in Vals-les-Bains - and, indeed, in the whole of the area explored on this tour - where you can find gourmet food at reasonable prices. The friendly Mireille Augustin officiates in the restaurant's smallish dining-room, and her inventive husband Jean-Paul does the cooking. His wide range of specialities includes *gelée de daube et pieds de veau*, *rascasse* in a crayfish sauce, and a sumptuous *ronde des desserts* (five or six mini-servings) that is a must for anyone with a sweet tooth. Local wines are on offer at ludicrously low prices. *3 Rue Jean-Jaurès; tel 75.37.48.98; closed Mon, Tues, and lunchtime Wed Oct-March; price bands B/C.*

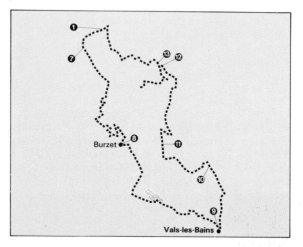

Vals-les-Bains - Antraigues

⑨ *Take the D578 out of Vals-les-Bains up the valley of the River Volane*, a narrow gorge lined with vineyards. The road skirts the base of the village of Antraigues. If you have time to visit it, *turn sharp right up the hill (signposted).*

Perched on an outcrop of volcanic rock, this little village has been described as the Saint-Tropez of the Ardèche, with all that that entails: trendy bistros, antique shops, high prices, and so on. The central square with its plane trees has undoubted charm on a balmy summer evening. Antraigues is the adopted home of the well-known singer and iconoclast Jean Ferrat.

Antraigues - Freyssenet

⑩ *Just before the sharp right turn up into Antraigues, the Route de la Bézorgues branches off the D578 to the left in the direction of Labastide de Juvinas.* This delightful little road winds up from the Volane valley through an Italianate landscape of chestnut groves, Lombardy poplars and houses with flat red-tiled roofs, and eventually leads over a ridge and down into the adjacent valley of the River Bézorgues. *On reaching Labastide turn right along the D254 to Freyssenet.*

Freyssenet -
Lachamp-
Raphaêl

⑪ *Follow the road round to the left, then turn sharp right up the D354 in the direction of Lachamp-Raphaêl.* This section of road running up the Bézorgues valley is like an action replay, in slow motion and in reverse, of the sudden switch from moor to vineyards just before Burzet: as the road loops gently uphill - passing, incidentally, one of the few surviving farmhouses with a traditional thatched roof - trees gradually thin out and the landscape becomes more inhospitable. Then, after a stretch of pine forest, you suddenly emerge on to something resembling Arctic tundra: you are back on the plateau of the Mézenc massif. *When the D354 joins the D122, keep straight ahead into Lachamp-Raphaêl.*

Les Cimes
(restaurant,
Lachamp)

The keynote here is simplicity, quality produce and value for money. There are also a few rather spartan rooms (showers and WC on landing). *Tel 75.38.78.58; closed Nov; price band A.*

Ray Pic
(detour to
waterfall)

⑫ *For a detour to the Ray Pic waterfall, take the D215, a sharp left turn as you drive into Lachamp-Raphaêl from Freyssenet.* Although it involves a 15-km return journey along a small and sometimes rather uneven road, this detour is strongly recommended. Park in the large car park and walk to the waterfall along the signposted path (40 minutes there and back). The austerity of the site is reinforced by the booming 'caw' of the ravens that live there. The waters of the River Bourges emerge through two gaps in the rocks and crash down into a surprisingly placid pool below. But more striking than the waterfall itself is the rock formation flanking it - a monstrous overhanging outgrowth of dark-grey columnar basalt pointing down to the pool as though it, too, were still flowing as it did when it was molten. The Ray Pic waterfall is an ideal place for a cool picnic on a hot day, always supposing there are not too many people with the same idea.

Lachamp-
Raphaêl -
Gerbier

After you have returned to Lachamp-Raphaêl, there is an easy ridge drive along wide roads to the Gerbier de Jonc. *First take the D122 through the village, and a few km later* ⑬ *veer on to the D378 for the final section of the loop.*

Gorges du Tarn:
AND THE CAUSSE MÉJEAN

The verdant Gorges du Tarn.

The great attraction of this tour lies in the contrast between the Gorges du Tarn themselves - an immensely deep, verdant valley (strictly speaking a canyon) gouged out by the River Tarn - and the high arid *causses* (limestone plateaux) on either side. The Causse Méjean, which forms the central part of the tour, is a geological oddity. Its limestone crust is so porous that it retains no rainfall, hence the sparseness of trees and vegetation which, in some parts, results in an awesomely empty, moon-like landscape. Streams and rivers are found not on the surface but below ground, flowing through a complex network of subterranean galleries.

There are, however, some pockets of arable land known as *dolines*. These small depressions are caused by the erosion of the limestone crust by rainfall. When erosion goes one stage further, an *aven* (pothole) leading down to a subterranean river is formed.

The plateau is extremely inhospitable in winter. On a hot summer's day however, it is fragrant with wild thyme, savory and an abundance of rare plants. The Causse Méjean has few human inhabitants, but many sheep.

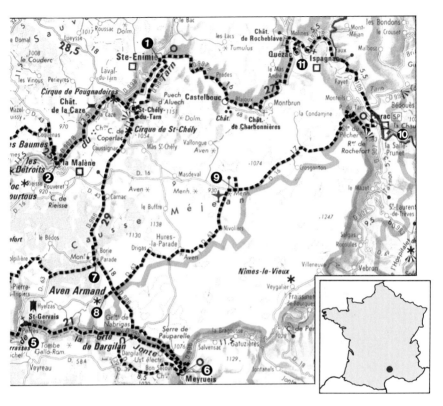

The Gorges du Tarn have a more obvious beauty than the bleak *causses*, so it is hardly surprising that they have become a major tourist attraction. In high summer be prepared for plenty of traffic, at least in the gorges themselves. A visit to the area in October is particularly recommended, when the usual palette of autumn colours that lines the canyon is enhanced by the bright crimson leaves of the local Montpelier maple.

ROUTE ONE: 109 KM

Ste-Enimie
Named after a 7thC Merovingian princess who founded a convent here after being miraculously cured of leprosy by the waters of a spring, Ste-Enimie is a small town whose spotless cobbled streets rise in rows up the hillside beneath the cliffs of the Causse de Sauveterre. Be sure to see the Halle au Blé (former cornmarket) and the ancient Place au Beurre nearby. The Vieux Logis, a folk museum *(open July-Aug 10-12.30 and 2-8; Apr, June and Sept 10-12.30 and 2.30-6)*, is also worthwhile.

189

Auberge du Moulin (restaurant, Ste-Enimie) The Auberge is housed in a handsome building just by the D907. Specialities include the *terrine maison*, delicious jugged hare, and the tasty local blue cheese, *Bleu des Causses. Tel 66.48.53.08; closed Nov-Mar and evenings in Apr and Oct; price band B.*

Grandeur of the Gorges du Tarn.

Ste-Enimie - La Malène ① *Leave Ste-Enimie by the D907B, past the bridge over the Tarn, in the direction of La Malène. The road either bends gracefully round the bulging sides of the canyon or goes straight through them via a series of short tunnels. When the beautifully turreted Château de la Caze comes into view to the left, drive on past it, then admire it in safety from the lay-by. This romantic 15thC château is now a luxury hotel.*

La Malène La Malène was laid waste during the Revolution, and marks made by the smoke from one of its burning houses can still be seen on the cliff overhanging the old part of this small village. Downstream from La Malène, the Tarn flows between absolutely vertical cliffs 100 metres high; the total depth of the canyon at this point is about 500 metres. The best way to see this part of the river is to take a punt to the Cirque des Baumes. It is not cheap (you hire a boatman, and a taxi to bring you back), but the experience is unforgettable. *Details from the boatmen's co-operative at La Malène, tel 66.47.51.10.*

La Malène - Point Sublime ② *Turn right in the centre of La Malène up the D43, which climbs a rocky gorge. When nearly at the top, turn sharp left along a small road marked Point Sublime. The drive along the plateau goes through typical causse countryside of the less rugged kind (stone-walled fields enclosing* flocks of sheep, scattered trees, a few isolated farmhouses). *At the junction with the D46, turn left towards St-Georges-de-Lévéjac, and just as you reach the village turn left again along a little road signposted to Point Sublime, 1.5 km away.* Ample parking space and, in season, a café.

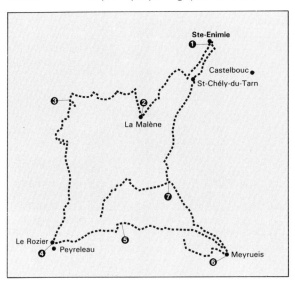

Point Sublime

As its name suggests, this rocky promontory offers a stunning view over the Gorges du Tarn, back along the section you have just driven through, and, to the right, towards the massive jumble of rocks called the Pas de Souci.

Point Sublime - Peyreleau

③ *Drive back to the D46, then turn left in the direction of Les Vignes. At the junction with the D995, bear left again towards Les Vignes.* The road ahead - a succession of hairpin bends leading down to the bottom of the canyon - is not for those who suffer from vertigo, but is perfectly engineered and safe. *In the village of Les Vignes, turn right towards Le Rozier along the D907B.* As you cruise along this easy stretch of road you can admire successively, on the far side of the Tarn, the ruined Château de Blanquefort, the idyllic hamlet of La Bourgarie with its neat kitchen gardens, and the colossal Rocher de Cinglegros, which has broken off the *causse* like an iceberg from a polar icecap. *At the junction with the D996 turn left into Le Rozier, then immediately right across the bridge to Peyreleau.* Drive straight ahead to a large car park.

Peyreleau

You are now (briefly) in the Aveyron *département*. Climb the steps opposite the car park up into Peyreleau's pleasant, if slightly over-restored, labyrinth of streets.

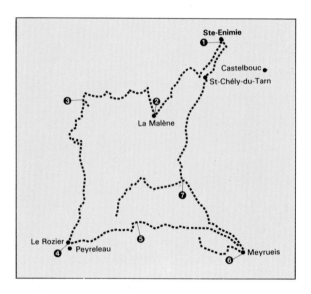

Peyreleau -   ④ *Drive back into Le Rozier and turn right along the D996 in the*
Les Douzes   *direction of Meyrueis.*

Hôtel-   Nestling against the cliff, the Hôtel-Restaurant de la Jonte has succeeded
Restau-   in retaining its character (and local clientele) despite the seasonal influx
rant de la   of tourists. Pierre and Jacqueline Vergély, who have run the place for
Jonte *(Les*   26 years and radiate friendliness, offer a wide range of excellent local
Douzes)   fare (*confit de canard*, lamb from the *causses*, delicious home-made
pâté). In summer you can eat outside under trees. This is also an
inexpensive place to stay. *Tel 65.62.60.52; price bands A/B.*

Les Douzes   ⑤ *Continue up the D996, having asked the Vergélys to explain how to*
- Meyrueis   find the mysterious resurgence of the Jonte - the spot where the river
emerges after flowing underground for several kilometres. The
character of the Gorges changes: they become more classically canyon-
like, with a sheer cliff at the top, followed by a scree-covered slope and
then a second cliff plunging down to the river.

Meyrueis   Meyrueis, like Ste-Enimie, is an important tourist attraction but it has
kept more of its individuality because it is a bigger and busier town.
There is a market on Wed and Fri, part of it in what must be one of
the smallest covered marketplaces in France (on main street).

La   This is a real gem of a hostelry: not only are the Burguet family
Renais-   extremely hospitable, but their 16thC hotel (once their family home) is
sance   furnished from top to bottom with perfect taste and lots of personality.

(hôtel-restaurant, Meyrueis) Here one is surrounded by engravings, paintings, antique furniture and harmonious wallpaper. There are even bookshelves in the bedrooms. The restaurant specializes in a wide range of local dishes, such as *poularde au coulis d'écrevisses* and *godiveau de truites*) and offers a choice of around 400 wines (several are served by the glass). *Rue de la Ville: tel 66.45.60.19; price bands B/C; booking essential in summer.*

Grotte de Dargilan ⑥ *For a detour to the Grotte de Dargilan, 8.5 km from Meyrueis, take the D986 in the direction of Lanuéjols, and on the edge of Meyrueis turn sharp right up the D39. Turn right 7 km later along the D139 to the cave.* The Grotte de Dargilan is in fact a series of caves full of very varied, pinkish stalagmites and stalactites. Their arresting beauty is undeniable, but if you have time for only one cave the Aven Armand is even more spectacular. It features on Route Two, but could just as easily be included on Route One. Grotte de Dargilan *open Easter-Sept 9-7; first two weeks Oct 1-5.*

Meyrueis - La Parade *Leave Meyrueis in the direction of Ste-Enimie, forking left up the D986 shortly after crossing the Jonte.* This excellent road climbs in leisurely fashion up on to the Causse Méjean. Stop at one of the lay-bys for a bird's eye view of the narrow Gorges de la Jonte. Soon you are on the plateau, whose stark landscape is awe-inspiring. At La Parade there is a strategically placed filling station.

Les Arcs de St-Pierre ⑦ *The detour to Les Arcs de St-Pierre is well worth the 20 km round trip across flat terrain. Turn left at La Parade along the D63, and after a kilometre or two turn sharp right along a narrow but perfectly surfaced road signposted to Le Courby. After going through the hamlet of La Volpilière, which contains some superb examples of the domestic architecture of the causse, ignore the turning to Le Courby and continue through St-Pierre-des-Tripiers until you reach a crossroads with La Viale to the left and a car park to the right.* Park here and follow the signpost to Les Arcs. The walk (allow about 25 minutes each way) takes you through a sheltered, almost Arcadian landscape of rocky outcrops, dells and stone pines; it is easy to see why the site attracted prehistoric settlers. The various things to see should (*pace* vandals) be signposted. The Arcs themselves - three massive natural arches formed by rock erosion - stand round a small tree-dotted hollow: a magical spot.

La Parade - Ste-Enimie *Return to La Parade, then bear left along the D986 to Ste-Enimie.* When the road leaves the *causse* and begins its easy descent into the canyon, stop at the lay-by on the first sharp right-hand bend: there is an almost vertical view down over the Cirque de St-Chély.

Ste-Enimie - Aven Armand *Leave Ste-Enimie by the D986, over the bridge, in the direction of Meyrueis.* If you have not already done Route One, stop when you get to the top of the *causse* to look back down into the canyon. *A couple of km after*

ROUTE TWO: 76 KM

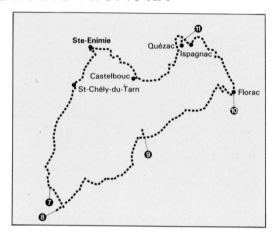

La Parade, there is a well-signposted right turn to the Aven Armand.

Aven Armand

Rightly considered one of France's greatest natural sights, the Aven Armand, a single but immense cavern which could almost accommodate Notre-Dame Cathedral, contains an extraordinary forest of stalagmites. *Open June, July and Aug 9-7; May and Sept 9-12 and 1.30-6.*

Aven Armand - Nivoliers

⑧ *Return to the D986, cross it and go straight ahead along the D63 in the direction of Nivoliers.* The road goes through the small, crouching villages of Drigas and Hures-la-Parade. To the right, there is a hauntingly bare, lunar landscape. A word of warning about driving on the more barren parts of the Causse Méjean: the road can seem deceptively level and straightforward, but the lack of visual reference points (such as trees or hedges can make it easy to misjudge a slope or bend.

Auberge Le Chanet *(restaurant, Nivoliers)*

If you have not planned a picnic, this is a useful stand-by on the otherwise restaurant-bereft *causse*. It offers hearty local specialities served in pleasant surroundings. *Tel 66.45.65.12; closed Mon-Fri Nov-Apr; price band A.*

Nivoliers - Florac

Beyond Nivoliers, the road opens out on to the strikingly fertile (in this context) plain of Chanet. As you pass the tiny Florac-Chanet Aerodrome (used mainly for gliders) you will see a solitary menhir standing quizzically at the end of the runway on your left. If, by the way, you should see a bird bigger than a golden eagle soaring high in the skies above the *causse*, it is probably a griffon vulture (a species that has just been reintroduced into the area). *At the junction with the D16, turn right for Florac.*

The *causse* is peppered with scores of small *avens* (potholes). If you want to see what one of them looks like, take this short detour.
(9) *Not far along the D16, turn left towards Poujols. Drive for just over one km, then park about 250 metres beyond the point where the conifer plantation on the right gives way to a flat rocky field.* The *aven* is about 75 metres from the road, to the right. It is not fenced, so don't venture too near the edge. *Return to the D16 and turn left for Florac.* When the road reaches the edge of the *causse*, there is a totally unexpected, plunging view over the grey roofs of Florac 500 metres below - the *causse* here seems to have been sliced off with a knife.

Florac A rather severe little town with a turbulent, bloodstained history of Catholic fighting Protestant, Florac forms a rectangular complex of narrow streets. A market is held every Saturday in the shade of the plane trees on the pleasant central esplanade. If you just want to look round, bear right on entering the town up a small street leading to the church, where there is usually plenty of parking space. If, on the other hand, you decide to stay or eat at the Grand Hôtel du Parc, continue downhill and left to the high street, then turn left again to the hotel.

Gd. Hôtel This hotel, set back from the road amidst pleasant gardens, does
du Parc indeed look very grand. It is in fact a reasonably priced, old-fashioned,
(hotel- well-run hotel-restaurant. *Tel 66.45.03.05; closed Dec-mid-Mar and Sun*
rest.Florac) *evening and Mon out of season; price bands B/C.*

Florac - (10) *Leave Florac in the direction of Mende along a short stretch of the*
Ispagnac *N106, with the Causse Méjean towering above you to the left, then fork left on to the D907B in the direction of Ispagnac and Ste-Enimie.*

Ispagnac Ispagnac, cradled in a bend of the Tarn, enjoys a warm microclimate, hence its market gardens, vines, orchards and Lombardy poplars.

Ispagnac - Shortly after leaving Ispagnac, you will see an elegant five-arched bridge
Quézac to the left; once it is in sight look out for the turning off to Quézac (the
(detour) signpost missing). Quézac is a tiny village worth a detour for its houses with their overhanging eaves, and its church, which has an unusual 16thC porch. *Turn left and cross the Tarn by the bridge,* which was built by Pope Urban V in the 14thC, destroyed during the Wars of Religion, and rebuilt to its original design in the early 17thC. If you continue on the little road that goes through Quézac, you will find plenty of bucolic picnic spots along the banks of the river.

Quézac - (11) *Return to the D907B and continue in the direction of Ste-Enimie.*
Ste-Enimie Don't bother to turn off to Castelbouc: this well-known and much visited little village, built against the cliff with a ruined castle perched on a rock above, is best appreciated from a distance, i.e. the car park on the D907B about one km beyond the signpost.

The Bastides of Gascony

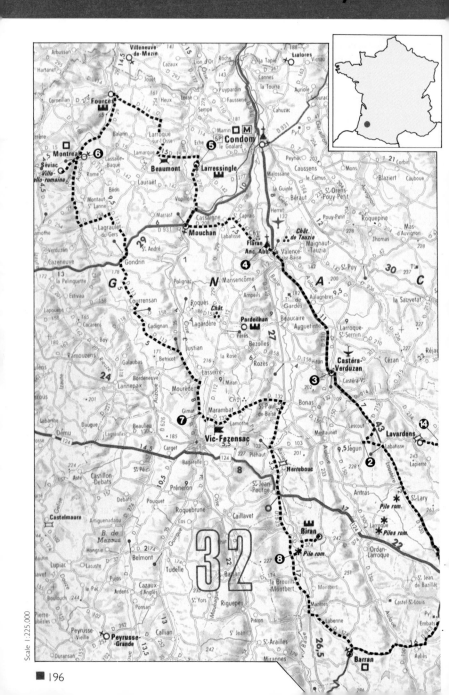

This tour covers the part of Gascony (the old name for the region) that lies in the Gers *département*, a curious, unspoilt and individual area. It is dotted with scores of *bastides* - villages and small towns, often fortified, which were built in the 13th and 14thC according to a strictly geometrical plan, usually with a central arcaded square around a covered market. It boasts no less than 146 castles, and hosts of beautifully proportioned stone manors and farmhouses (some empty and crying out to be restored).

It has been impossible to mention all the architectural treasures to be found on this tour, so do explore for yourself when you see a turret or

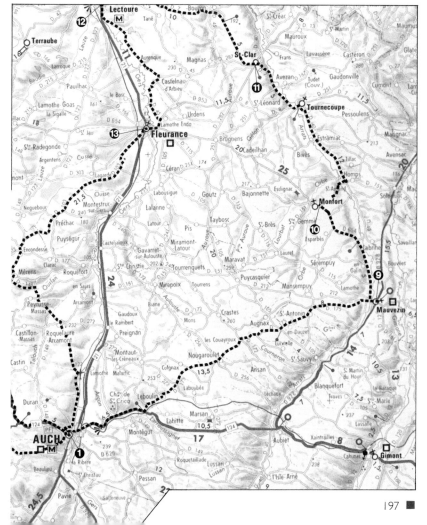

clock tower peeping romantically through the trees. This part of Gascony, incidentally, was the home of the 'real' d'Artagnan, Charles de Batz, on whose memoirs Alexandre Dumas based *The Three Musketeers*.

Just as the *bastides* are a variation on a theme, so the countryside is strikingly uniform - an attractively rolling mixture of fields, hedges, vineyards, copses and little valleys, through which rivers with strangely assonant names flow (e.g. Aulouste, Auloue, Auroue, Auzoue, Lauze, Douze, Ousse, Osse). There are virtually no winding roads and little traffic, so distances are covered easily and pleasantly.

Foie gras and *confits* are the great gastronomic specialities of the area, but fortunately in recent years most local chefs have realized that their customers cannot take such rich food all the time, and have consequently extended their culinary range. There are usually three or four menus to choose from and wine lists give priority to the *appellations* of the south-west. The local brandy, Armagnac, and the Armagnac-based aperitif, *floc*, are worth sampling.

ROUTE ONE: 137 KM

The Romanesque church at Mouchan.

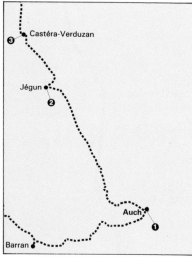

Auch   A compact and pleasant little town, Auch is the capital of Gascony and therefore makes an ideal centre for this tour. Its cathedral (15th-17thC) is chiefly remarkable for what it contains within: some vivid stained-glass windows by Arnaut de Moles, a 17thC organ, and more than 1,500 vigorously carved, and occasionally immodest, saints and mythical figures on its oak choir stalls (a coin in the slot will illuminate them a little, but enthusiasts should take a pocket flashlight with them). As befits the capital of a gastronomic province, Auch takes its markets (Thurs and Sat) seriously.

Hôtel de France
(hotel-restaurant, Auch)

This well-appointed hotel, which has been in the Daguin family for almost a century, sets a standard it would be hard to beat anywhere at any price. The soul of the place is its kitchen, where André Daguin devises an astonishing number of variations on a single theme, the culinary traditions of Gascony. Foie gras, *magret* (duck breast served pink like an underdone steak), *confits* (preserved duck or goose), truffles, and the local vegetable *par excellence,* the broad bean, are served in a multitude of often surprising guises. Even if your holiday budget cannot accommodate the prices at Daguin's main restaurant (which are justifiably high), do try the hotel's less expensive bar-restaurant, Le Neuvième, whose *plats du jour* are cooked in the same kitchens. *Place de la Libération; tel 62.05.00.44; closed Jan, Sun evening, and Mon in winter; price bands: main restaurant, D; Le Neuvième, C/D.*

Auch - Jégun

① *Follow the signs for Condom, first on the N124, then on the D930. At Labatisse, turn left to Jégun.* This *bastide* is unusual in that it does not have a central square (though there is a tiny covered market tucked away in the middle). Instead, there is a delightful balustraded esplanade at one end of the village, with pollarded trees and a bandstand. This is where players of *boules* and the mysterious local game of *palettes* congregate.

Le Bastion
(restaurant, Jégun)

Mireille Fauqué has few strings to her culinary bow - but what strings. Vegetable soup containing tasty morsels of duck, gently sautéed oyster mushrooms, juicy charcoal-grilled *magret* and wonderful pastries. *Tel 62. 64.54.57; closed Mon and first three weeks Jan; price bands A/B/C.*
② *Leave Jégun on the road you came in on, turning left on the edge of the village on to the D215, then back on to the D930 to Castéra-Verduzan.*

Castéra-Verduzan

A strung-out little village which has, believe it or not, been a spa since Roman times and has recently come back into vogue (its waters are reputed to be good for gum disorders). Even if your gums are fine, don't be in a hurry to leave Castéra-Verduzan, for it boasts a restaurant and a hotel that offer philanthropically good value.

Le Florida
(restaurant, Castéra-Veduzan)

Bernard Ramounéda, certainly the best *restaurateur* on this tour apart from Daguin, offers set menus and local wines that are absurdly cheap in view of their quality. His pâtés are breathtaking, his *feuilletés* featherlight, his *confits* crisp and succulent, and his desserts tasty and unusual (e.g. *poire aux épices*). In summer there is a congenial terrace, and in chillier weather the comfort of a log fire. *Tel 62.68.13.22; closed Feb, and Sun evening and Mon Oct-Apr; price bands A/B/C/D.*

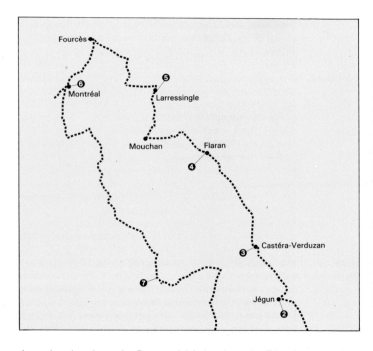

Hôtel Ténarèze (Castera-Verduzan)

A modern hotel, run by Ramounéda's brother, the Ténarèze offers pleasant, bright rooms with bath and WC. The prices, which include a proper breakfast with home-made jam and real orange juice, should make some other hoteliers in the district blush with shame. *Tel 62.68.10.22; closed Feb.*

Castéra-Verduzan - Abbaye de Flaran

③ *Continue on the D930 through Valence-sur-Baïse, a bastide whose arcades have been disfigured by garish shop signs. Branch left after a bridge on to the D142 to the Abbaye de Flaran.* Now a cultural centre, this Cistercian abbey is well worth a visit not just for its 12thC church and 14thC cloisters (now disused), but for its quite exemplary permanent exhibition devoted to local architecture. *Open 9.30-12 and 2-7 (2-6 Sat, Sept-May); closed Tues Oct-May.*

Abbaye de Flaran - Larressingle

④ *Continue on the D142, bearing left at Cassaigne on to the D208 to Mouchan,* whose Romanesque church is unusual in having been built around an earlier defensive tower (now its clock tower). *Turn right on to the D931, soon veering left on to the D142. Now follow the signs to Larressingle, and park the car outside its walls.*

Larressingle

This charming and well-preserved fortified village, which was the refuge of the bishops of Condom in the Middle Ages, is the size of a pocket-

Fourcès - an unusual central 'square'.

handkerchief. The Gascons, with typical tongue-in-cheek exaggeration, call it 'the Carcassonne of the Gers'.

⑤ *Follow the sign to the D15, turn left, cross the River Osse and just after reaching the top of the hill turn right along the D254. Shortly after going through Larroque-sur-l'Osse, turn left along the D114 to Fourcès.*

Fourcès   Founded by the English in the 13thC, this engagingly small and self-contained *bastide* is unusual in that its central 'square' is in fact round. It has been well restored.

Drive along the D29, lined with Lombardy poplars, to Montréal.

Montréal   Here the local rugby football team is treated with respect: the *bastide*'s central arcaded square has been called Place-des-Champions-de-France ever since they came top in their division.

Chez   Simone Daubin has a considerable local reputation as a cook, and
Simone   rightly so. She makes a sublime foie gras *mi-cuit* (pink in the middle),
(restaurant,   salmis de palombe* (wood pigeon), and crisp *confit de canard* that is not
Montréal)   oversalted (as it can be in some Gers restaurants). Her puff pastry dessert, the local *croustade*, is also delicious. *Tel 62.28.44.40; closed Sat; price bands B/C/D.*

Cross the bridge over the Auzoue and turn left along the D29.

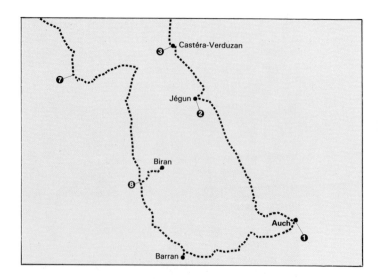

Séviac
(detour)

⑥ *Turn right almost immediately for short detour to Séviac. After one km turn right up a track* to the interesting ruins of a 4thC Gallo-Roman villa (mosaics, etc.). Open 9.30-12, 2-7, daily July and Aug, and Sun, April-Nov. *Return to the D29.*

La Gare
(restaurant, near Montréal)

Turn right just before an overhead bridge 3 km beyond Montréal to reach this amusing restaurant housed in the ticket office of a former railway station. There is much to keep children entertained: old railway lamps, posters, tickets, ticket machines, railway noises (on request) and, in the garden, swings and a see-saw. As you would expect in this area, the food is excellent too. *Tel 62.28.43.37; closed Jan, and Thurs evening and Fri Sept-June; price bands B/C/D.*

Shortly after the overhead bridge, fork left on to the D230. At the first main crossroads turn left on to the D254, signposted Lauraêt, bearing left at forks until you reach the D113. Turn right to Gondrin, a pretty enough bastide except for the fact that in a moment of collective lunacy the local council decided to erect a water tower right in the middle of the village. On leaving Gondrin, fork left along the D113 to Courrensan.

**Cour-
rensan**

Turn right into the village, a wonderfully unspoilt haven with a carefully restored castle and overhanging half-timbered houses. *Continue on the D113, veering right when it joins the D35.*

**Maram-
bat**

⑦ *After about 5 km, where a majestic avenue of conifers leads off to the right, turn left to Marambat (no sign),* yet another little bastide worth exploring. *Turn right on to the D112 on the edge of the village, then almost immediately turn left on to the D132, signposted Bonas.* This pretty road runs through countryside which, by Gers standards, could almost be described as mountainous. *At the crossroads with the D939, turn right.* About 4.5 km after St-Jean-Poutge, you will see to your left a Gallo-Roman *pile*, or stack, of which there are several in the area (their purpose is unknown).

Biran
(detour)

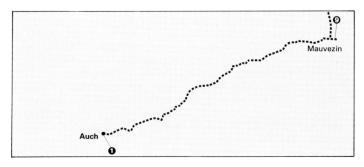 *Turn left here on to the D374 for a short detour to Biran.* a tiny fortified village. Strikingly positioned on a rock, it contains some fine medieval buildings, many in need of repair. *Return to the D939. Continue up the valley of the Baîse, later turning left to Barran along the D174.* The imposing Château de Mazères can be seen to the left.

Barran

A picturesque *bastide* with moat, covered market, arcades, overhanging houses and an interesting outsized church. The latter contains a Renaissance lectern and some fine 15thC choir stalls, but its most curious feature, as you will see from a distance, is its helicoidal slate-covered spire.

D943 as far as Embats, then turn right opposite the church for Auch.

ROUTE TWO: 110 KM

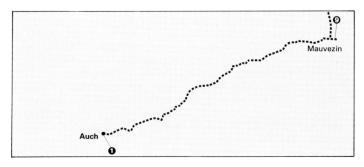

Auch -
Mauvezin

Leave Auch on the Toulouse road, the N124, turning left after 6 km on to the D175 in the direction of Mauvezin.

Mauvezin

Once an important Protestant centre, Mauvezin earned itself the nickname of 'Little Geneva'.

La
Rapière
(restaurant,
Mauvezin)

Book ahead at Michel and Marie-Thérèse Fourreau's constantly packed, attractive restaurant, even out of season: it provides some of the best value in Gascony. The B-price-band menu, including wine, might consist of the following (all excellent): pumpkin soup, salmon *terrine* with *sauce verte*, *huîtres chaudes au sabayon*, two duck drumsticks in a Madiran-based sauce, cheese and dessert. *Rue des Justices; tel 62.06.80.08; closed Sat lunch and Wed; price bands A/B/C/D.*

Mauvezin - Monfort

⑨ *Follow the signs for Fleurance out of Mauvezin on to the D654,* which coasts along the valley of the Arrats to Monfort. Yet another nice *bastide,* though sleepier than most, Monfort has an interesting early 14thC church, whose single nave leads to a polygonal choir with little chapels built between the buttresses.

Monfort - Château d'Avezan

⑩ *Leave Monfort on the Homps road, the D151. At Homps turn left on to the D40, and left again on the edge of Tournecoupe along the D7 signposted to St-Clar. About 3 km beyond Tournecoupe, follow the sign to 13thC Château d'Avezan on the right,* one of Gascony's few privately-owned castles which can be visited. *Open April-Nov, 10-12, 2-6.*

St-Clar

Founded by the English in 1274, St-Clar has two arcaded squares and a fine covered market, where a garlic fair is held on the second Thursday in Aug (St-Clar is the biggest producer of garlic in the Gers).

A hive of activity in this otherwise pleasantly somnolent village is Art Village, a shop-cum-publisher run by the sprightly Maurice Vidal, who not only writes a witty little annual guide to the restaurants of Gascony (*Le Guide Gascon*) but also sells a wide range of excellent Armagnacs, *flocs* and local wines at growers' prices, *confits,* foie gras, etc. *Open Mon-Sat 10-12.30 and 2.30-7 (6 in winter).*

St-Clar - Lectoure

⑪ *Leave St-Clar by the D953 in the direction of Lectoure. Drive into the centre of the town and park near the Hôtel de Ville.* There are lots of things to see in this hilltop capital of Lomagne (the north-eastern part of Gascony) and erstwhile fortress of the Comtes d'Armagnac: its Cathédrale St-Gervais; its Promenade du Bastion, which offers a superb view over the Gers and, on a clear day, the Pyrénées; its many old buildings; and its museum in the Hôtel de Ville.

Musée de Lectoure

The museum contains many relics of Lectoure's pre-Christian history: prehistoric tools, Gallic pottery, Gallo-Roman mosaics, and no less than 20 rare taurobolic altars from the 2nd and 3rdC (well explained by the guide). *Guided tours 10-12 and 2-5.*

Lectoure- Fleurance

⑫ *Leave Lectoure in the direction of Fleurance; and just after the Agen road comes in from the left, turn left along a small road signposted Lac des Trois Vallées.* Ignore the lake, which is overcrowded and ringed with bungalows, and continue along a picturesque, if at times bumpy road that skulks along the flank of the Gers valley to Aurenque, which has a charming little chapel. If you are looking for a pleasant riverside picnic spot, park near the tiny 15thC bridge a few hundred metres to the right. *Otherwise keep straight on until the junction with the D45; turn right and follow signs to Fleurance.*

Fleurance

From the time of its foundation in the 13thC (it was named after Florence) to the beginning of the 17thC, this large, bustling and

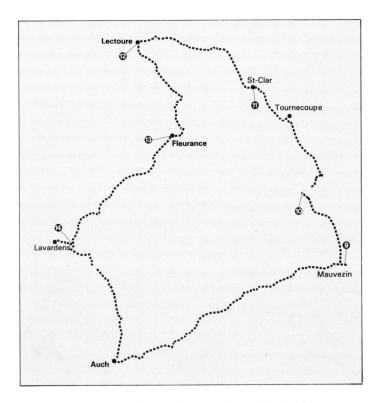

strategically located *bastide* was the scene of many battles, first between English and French, then between Protestants and Catholics.

Fleurance - Lavardens

⑬ *Leave Fleurance on the D103 in the direction of Préchac and Mérens. Shortly after bearing left on to the D148, you will see a turning to the right signposted Lavardens; ignore this, and continue along the pretty ridge road to Mérens*, where you can enjoy a good view over Lavardens.

Lavardens
(detour)

⑭ *For this short detour to Lavardens, turn right at Mérens on to the D518. The Château de Lavardens, whose asymmetrical architecture cunningly hugs the limestone outcrop it is built on, is one of the most imposing castles in the Gers, a massive top-heavy construction erected in the early 17thC. Open mid-June to mid-Sept, 10-12 and 3-8.*

Lavardens - Auch

Return to Mérens and continue on the D148, with the Gers valley spread out to your left, then bear left on to the D272 to Roquelaure-Arcamont. After passing some ruined ramparts, turn sharp right at the crossroads and through the village of Roquelaure-Arcamont towards Auch.

Lower Rhône:
MONT VENTOUX

The area covered by this tour roughly corresponds to the Comtat Venaissin, the part of France that was under papal rule from 1274 to 1791 (and is now contained mainly within the Vaucluse *département*).

Route One, which skirts the crags of the Dentelles de Montmirail and strikes out across the low-lying plains of the Rhône valley, takes in two historic towns, Vaison-la-Romaine and Carpentras, and offers a detour to a third - Avignon, residence of the popes from 1309 to 1377.

Each of these three towns holds a top-quality summer festival. Perhaps as a result, the Vaucluse has a high concentration of country cottages owned (and often restored) by Parisian intellectuals. The climate could have something to do with it too: hot without being torrid as in lower Provence, it provides ideal conditions for holidaymaking.

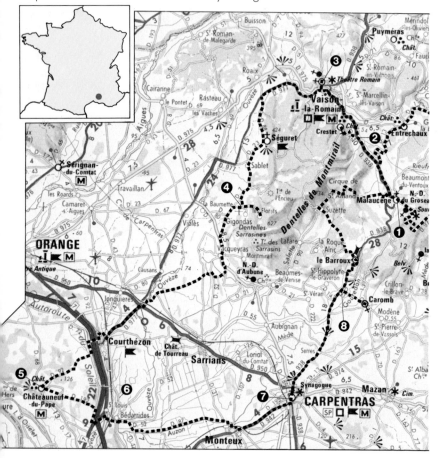

The Vaucluse also includes some of the best of the Rhône wine-growing appellations, such as Châteauneuf-du-Pape, Gigondas and Vacqueyras, as well as the less well-known, less heady Côtes-du-Ventoux. If you buy wine at a cooperative or a vineyard in this area, you will rarely be disappointed.

Route Two, which takes you up to the top of the Mont Ventoux with its staggering views, can only be undertaken in full from June to mid-Nov; the rest of the year the snowbound section of the D974 between Mont Serein and Chalet Reynard is closed.

On both routes many of the villages - in particular Sablet, Gigondas, Vacqueyras, Le Barroux, Aurel, Brantes and Entrechaux - have retained much of their old-world charm and deserve exploration if time permits.

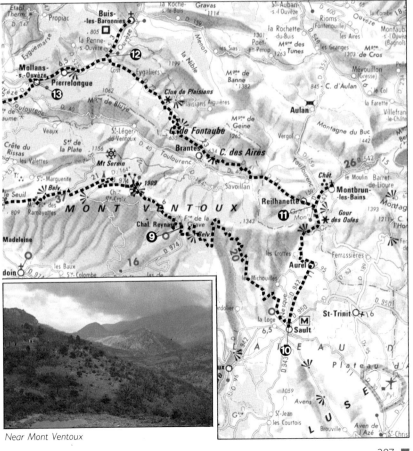

Near Mont Ventoux

ROUTE ONE: 93 KM

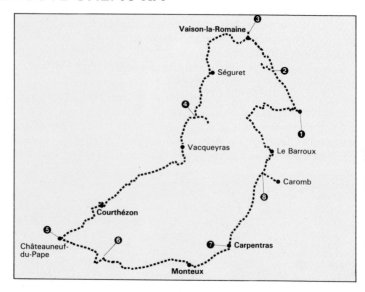

Malaucène

The tour is based on this little town famed for its cherries. Malaucène has avenues of age-old plane trees, cool fountains and above all an interesting 14thC Romanesque church, which used to form part of the town fortifications (hence its iron-plated door and fortress-like appearance) and contains a well-known 18thC organ.

① *Take the D938, signposted to Vaison*, which coasts along the lush valley of the Groseau river.

Crestet
(detour)

② *After about 5 km, you can turn left on to the D76 for a short detour to Crestet. Drive up through olive groves to the T-junction at the top, turn right and park by the 12thC castle* (currently being restored). There are no roads to speak of in this tiny village, just a maze of alleyways and steps that children love to explore. Everywhere the emphasis is on tasteful restoration. *Retrace to the D938 and continue to Vaison.*

Vaison-la-Romaine

Once one of the most important Roman towns in Gaul, its Roman bridge still carries traffic (first right turn as you drive in). As well as two large and fascinating excavated sites, complete with streets, columns and vestigial walls, there is a Roman theatre scooped out of the hillside (where many of the events in Vaison's annual drama, ballet and music festivals are held), and an excellent museum containing the main finds from the site; also worth visiting are the Cathédrale Notre-Dame and adjoining cloisters. *The same opening times apply to all these places: 9-7 July-Sept, 9-6 March-June and 9-5 Nov-Feb.*

The quaint and recently restored old town, clinging to a rocky outcrop on the south side of the Ouvèze river, is where the inhabitants of Vaison lived during the troubled Middle Ages. One of the largest and most varied markets in Provence is held every Tues.

③ *Leave Vaison on the D977, the Avignon road, and after 5.5 km turn left on to the D88, signposted Séguret.*

Séguret

By describing itself, on a bill-board, as 'France's most beautiful village', Séguret goes a little overboard, but its old gate, fountain, bell-tower, church, castle and steep streets are undoubtedly picturesque.

Le Mesclun
(restaurant, Séguret)

Friendly Jean Vassort, ably assisted by his equally friendly wife Joëlle, provide expertly cooked and generously served cuisine (e.g. *charlotte d'asperges à la crème de ciboulette, rognons d'agneau au cerfeuil*, and excellent fruity desserts). Depending on the weather, there is a choice between an impeccably decorated interior and an airy terrace. Booking is essential. *Tel 90.46.93.43; closed mid-Feb to mid-Mar and Mon, and lunch Tues-Sat mid-Sept to mid-June; price bands B/C.*

Séguret - Gigondas

Leave Séguret on the D23 and drive through Sablet to Gigondas, a fortified village as small as its celebrated wine is big.

Les Dentelles de Montmir-ail *(detour)*

④ *For a detour that offers the opportunity to have a picnic with a view, or visit a popular hotel-restaurant, follow the signs to Les Florets restaurant and the Col du Cayron. Drive past the restaurant and up to a car-park overlooking the Dentelles.* Rock-climbers come from afar to tackle these extraordinarily jagged mini-mountains. There are plenty of picnic spots on the tracks that lead off from the car-park.

Les Florets
(hotel-restaurant, Gigondas)

This large, bustling but friendly restaurant offers classical cuisine with a rustic touch (eg *civet de porcellet*, which goes well with one of the many Gigondas vintages on the wine list); the sumptuous-looking dessert trolley lives up to expectations. If you stay the night, peace is guaranteed. *Tel 90.65.85.01; closed Jan-Feb, and Wed; price bands B/C.*

Gigondas - Château-neuf-du-Pape

Follow the signs to Vacqueyras. Just beyond this fortified village turn right on to the D52, signposted Sarrians. A little later, bear right (on a left-hand bend, no signpost) and keep going until you come to a road signposted Château de Roques. Go along this road for several kms, over a vast plain.

After crossing a railway bridge, turn right over a river, then turn left immediately on to the D977 to Courthézon. This road takes you through a pretty landscape of tidy vineyards, neat rows of cypresses and trim wine-growers' houses. *At the T-junction, turn into Courthézon, bearing left at roundabout and following Châteauneuf-du-Pape signs across motorway.*

The road now meanders through a tiny enclave of vine-covered hills in the middle of the flat Rhône valley; soon you can see the imposing ruins of the castle of Châteauneuf-du-Pape silhouetted against the sky.

Château-neuf-du-Pape

A strangely dead little town that has grown fat on the fame of its wine; it has more *caveaux de dégustation* than cafés. But don't miss the unusual view of Avignon and the Rhône valley from the castle.
(5) *Leave Châteauneuf on the Avignon road, then at the crossroads on the edge of town take the D192 for Bédarrides. After converging with the motorway, turn left underneath it towards Orange.*

Avignon
(detour)

This is, of course, one of the most rewarding cities to visit in France, worth at least a day to itself. From (6) *it is a 31-km round trip: turn right on to the N7 immediately after going under the motorway.*

Bédar-rides

Cross the N7 into this unassuming village, which has two oddities: a triumphal arch and a church with a 17thC Baroque front stuck on a Romanesque nave.

Bédarrides - Carpentras

Go over the old bridge in the direction of Entraigues, and about 1.5 km later turn left on to the D87 to Monteux. The road runs alongside the little Auzon river, which is enclosed within high dykes and hidden by trees. There are plenty of shady places to picnic by the river. *On reaching the D31 bear right into Monteux and follow signs to Carpentras.*

Carpen-tras

A busy, unspoilt town which has a number of interesting old buildings - a Roman arch, France's oldest synagogue (*open 10-12, 3-5 Mon-Fri*) a 17thC Palais de Justice, and the Cathédrale St-Siffrein, known for its fine stained-glass, 17thC organ, and striking portal in the flamboyant style (called the Porte Juive: it was used by converted Jews). Market: Fri.
(7) *Leave Carpentras on the D938, the Vaison road.*

Caromb
(detour)

(8) *At a crossroads 9 km beyond Carpentras, turn right on to the D21 for a short detour to Caromb,* a charming village whose large 14thC church contains yet another historic organ. There is a 16thC bell-tower topped by a delicate 18thC wrought-iron 'cage' for the bell.

Le Beffroi,
(hotel-rest., Caromb)

The fare on offer at this establishment is straightforward and classical, the welcome most amiable, and the rooms, many of which have beamed ceilings, cosy. *Tel 90.62.45.63; closed Tues evening and Wed Sept-May; price bands B/C/D.*

Caromb - Malaucène

Return to the D938. In a short while turn left to Le Barroux on the D78, then continue to Suzette on the D90A and the V3, a rather poor road. There is a superb view up towards the Dentelles as you climb steeply to Suzette. *On the edge of Suzette bear right on to the D90.*
 There follows a particularly exhilarating stretch, first under the sheer cliffs of the Cirque de St-Amand, then past fields of rosemary up to a pass with views to the north over the Ouvèze valley and east towards the Mont Ventoux - scenery whose depth of perspective is reminiscent of Italian Renaissance landscape paintings. *Continue down to Malaucène.*

▬▬▬ ROUTE TWO: 100 KM

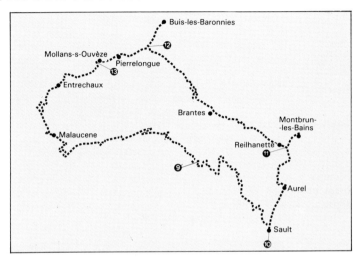

Malaucène - Notre-Dame du Groseau

Leave Malaucène along the excellent D974, signposted to the Mont Ventoux. You soon reach the appealingly tiny, 11thC Romanesque chapel of Notre-Dame du Groseau, which has a sculpted frieze outside and well-preserved capitals within (*open 6-7 Sat in May and Aug*).

A few hundred metres further on, opposite a café, the Source du Groseau issues from the mountainside, forming a little pond beside which are picnic tables. The spring water is drinkable - and delicious.

Continue along the D974, which now begins its relentless climb to the summit of the Mont Ventoux.

Mont Ventoux

Almost immediately the view begins to look pretty good, but by the time you are at the ski resort of Mont Serein, two-thirds of the way up, the panorama has become breathtaking.

After emerging from the forest and entering a lunar landscape of blindingly white rocks, you reach the viewing table at the summit (1,909 metres). By this time, the surrounding countryside has retreated so far into the distance as to appear almost map-like. On an exceptionally clear day it is just possible to make out the Mont Canigou in the Pyrenees some 300 km away.

Winds at the top of the Mont Ventoux can reach 250 km per hour, so the drive should not be attempted in a lightweight car on a gusty day. Some say that the mountain's name comes from '*venteux*', meaning 'windy' - but it is just as likely to derive from the Celtic '*ven top*', meaning 'white mountain'.

The Mont Ventoux forms a nature reserve of great interest to botanists and ornithologists. The former come out in early July in search

of rare species of poppy, saxifrage and iris, while birdwatchers hope to see crossbill, rock thrush, Tengmalm's owl or subalpine warbler.
Continue on the D974 to Chalet Reynard, where there is a café.

Chalet Reynard - Sault

⑨ *From Chalet Reynard, take the D164, signposted Sault.* This road takes its time meandering downhill, with yet more wonderful views, in particular over the Montagne de Lure to the east. Pine forest gives way to gnarled and stunted oak, then to acres of wild thyme. The neat rows of mauve lavender bushes can be made out in the valley below.

Sault

If your ears are popping after coming down the mountain, relax for a moment in the medieval streets of Sault.
⑩ *Leave Sault on the D942 signposted Montbrun-les-Bains.*

Montbrun-les-Bains
(detour)

⑪ *Instead of turning off along the D72, continue along the D542 for a short detour to the tiny spa of Montbrun-les-Bains,* whose once celebrated baths (containing hydrogen sulphide) are due to reopen in 1987. Access to the village is through a fortified 14thC clock-tower.

Brantes, with Mont Ventoux in the background.

Montbrun-les-Bains - Buis-les-Baronnies

Return to the junction with the D72 and turn right. The road goes along a flat stretch of the Toulourenc valley up to the Col des Aires, where there is a fine view of the awesome, almost sheer north face of the Mont Ventoux. Continue past the hamlet of Brantes (arts and crafts) on the left, and the Clue de Plaisians on the right (a *clue* is a deep cleft in a mountain ridge).

Buis-les-Baronnies
(detour)

⑫ *For this detour, which involves a 4-km round trip, turn right at the junction with the D5.* As you drive towards Buis-les-Baronnies, the knife-edge ridge of the Rocher St-Julien can be seen to the right. The town enjoys an exceptionally sheltered micro-climate that is ideal for growing olives, almonds and apricots. It also holds Europe's biggest lime-blossom

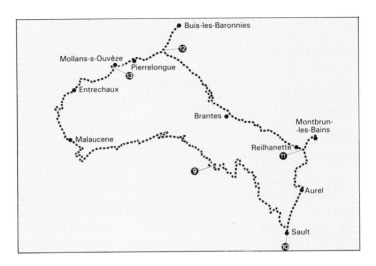

market on the first Wed in July. Its streets are fragrant for two weeks beforehand while the blossom is being dried in lofts and warehouses.

Make a point of dropping into the Moulin à l'Huile du Puits Communal, a marvellous shop-cum-museum in the old quarter near the Place du Marché. At one end there is a display of fossils, rocks and semi-precious stones found in the area, as well as an olive press and other utensils used in the manufacture of olive oil; at the other end a tempting selection of local products are on sale (lime-blossom *eau de toilette*, various soaps, lavender essence, finest olive oil, and Provençal preserves such as *tapnade* and *saussoun*). *Rue de Puits-Communal; closed Sun.*

Les Oliviers
(hotel-restaurant, Buis-les-Baronnies)

This secluded modern hotel with well-appointed rooms is on the northern edge of Buis (follow signposts). In the restaurant, the *escargots à l'anis* (in a pastis-flavoured sauce, a Provençal speciality), the *pintade aux grisets* (guinea-fowl with a type of tasty local mushroom), and the sorbets, are especially good. *Tel 75.28.08.77; closed Wed and Jan to mid-Feb; price bands B/C.*

Buis-les-Baronnies - Mollans-sur-Ouvèze

Returning from Buis to the junction with the D72, continue along the D5 to Pierrelongue, whose church is preposterously perched on a high rock in the middle of the hamlet, and then on to Mollans. Pause here to take a look at the fine fountain, arcaded public wash-house, heterogeneous clock-tower and restored 13thC castle.

Mollans - Malaucène

⑬ Continue on the D5, D13 (through the old village of Entrechaux) and D938, across a smiling landscape of orchards, vines and market gardens, to Malaucène.

213

Provence:

AIX AND MONTAGNE STE-VICTOIRE

If your idea of paradise involves sipping a *pastis* in the shade of a giant plane tree, watching old men in berets play *boules*, and allowing yourself to be lulled by the grating of cicadas and the hot perfumes of lavender and thyme, then this is the tour for you.

Route One concentrates on the Montagne Ste-Victoire - whose colour varies from bleached white to dull grey or luminous violet depending on the weather - and the elegant town of Aix-en-Provence, with its renowned music festival, large and lively student population, and many old buildings. It also provides glimpses of the extraordinary Canal de Provence network of watercourses, begun in the 16thC and constantly extended ever since; by channelling the unpredictable Durance and Verdon rivers, it provides much of the Rhône basin with irrigation, electricity and drinking water.

Route Two explores a lesser-known, less spectacular part of Provence, where there is a lower concentration of tourists - and some rather second-rate roads. Villages and little towns such as La Verdière, Barjols and Cotignac have a truly authentic Provençal feel and have not yet been invaded by chic boutiques. Similarly, the surrounding countryside, planted largely with vines and olive trees, has on the whole escaped the clutches of property developers, mainly due to water supply problems. Much of Provence is parched in summer - and much of it goes up in smoke every year, so be sure to heed the numerous fire warnings.

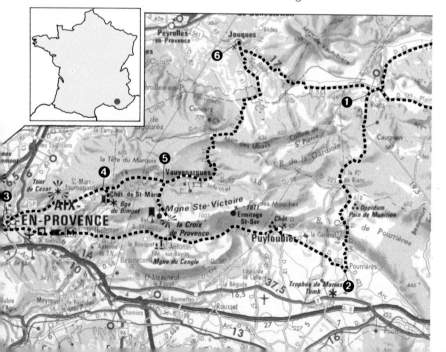

ROUTE ONE: 82 KM

Rians

The tour is based on the sleepy little town of Rians, which has been chosen for its geographical convenience rather than for any specific interests of its own. For good plain fare and accommodation at reasonable prices, L'Esplanade hostelry is a useful standby. *Tel 94.80.31.12; price bands A/B.*

Rians - Pourrières

① *Leave Rians on the St-Maximin-la-Ste-Baume road, turning right shortly on to the D23 signposted Pourrières.* This road takes you through an evocative, uninhabited landscape dotted with that most beautiful of Provençal trees, the parasol-shaped stone pine. Then comes some strenuous driving as you twist and turn down an attractive rocky gorge to Pourrières.

Pourrières - Aix-en-Provence

② *Go through Pourrières, then turn right to Puyloubier,* for your first good view of the Montagne Ste-Victoire. *In Puyloubier, fork right on to the D17.* The road runs through sparse woodland and the occasional meadow, edging closer and closer to the mountain, a curious ghostly presence covered with crinkles and folds, which fascinated Aix-born painter Paul Cézanne to the point of obsession. Beyond St-Antonin-sur-Bayon a series of tight hairpin bends leads through pine forest to Le Tholonet, a plush suburb of Aix. *Drive on into the town.*

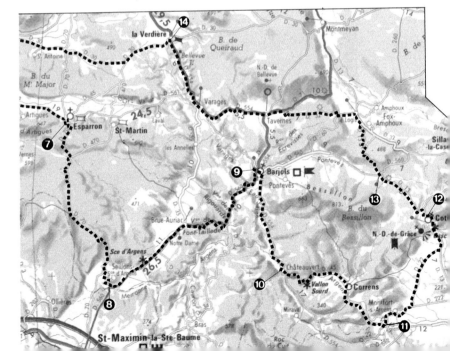

Aix-en-Provence

Parking in Aix can be a nightmare even when the festival is not in progress; the best advice is to drive into town until you get on to its one-way circular boulevard system, then make for the huge open-air car park near the bus station (well signposted). From there it is only a short walk to the old town, which is extremely compact and can easily be explored on foot.

Many of Aix's delights are to be sampled in the open air: its impressive fountains, its plethora of imposing 17thC *hôtels particuliers* (town houses), its Hôtel de Ville, and of course its celebrated Cours Mirabeau, a broad leafy boulevard lined on one side by austere private houses and banks, and on the other by one of the most congenially extrovert series of café terraces in France. This is where all those who matter (or think they matter) in Aix - students, intellectuals, festival-goers, beautiful people - get together.

Indoor attractions are numerous too, but priority should be given to the following:

Cathédrale St-Saveur

This remarkable church, built between the 5th and 17th centuries, contains a fascinating multitude of styles; be sure to walk round its marvellously elegant cloisters.

Musée Granet

Works by Hals, Rembrandt and Cézanne (eight paintings) are on show here; the interesting Aix-born artist, François Granet, is also well represented. *Open 10-12, 2-6; closed Tues.*

Market, Barjols: see Route Two.

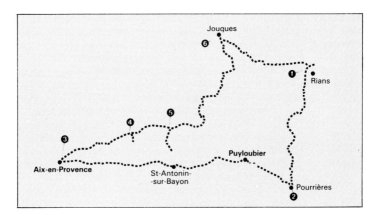

Atelier de Cézanne
The studio of Aix's best-known painter contains moving mementoes of the man and several objects (e.g. apples, changed every day) that feature in his still lifes. *Open 10-12 and 2.30-6 (2-5 Oct-May); closed Tues.*

Eugénie's
(restaurant, Aix)
Serge Drevon and Patrick Tournel's attractively decorated beamed restaurant offers original and well-prepared cuisine (for example, rabbit terrine with *confiture d'oignons*, lamb in a *crème d'ail* sauce, and a dreamy chocolate and mint dessert): above-average value. *I Rue Brueys; tel 42.27.48.05; closed Feb, and Tues Sept to mid-June; price band C.*

Le Prieuré
(hotel, Aix)
This quiet, reasonably priced and welcoming hotel can be a lifesaver when Aix is buzzing. Most of the rooms are fairly small (as you would expect in a former priory), but some overlook a garden designed by Le Nôtre. *Route des Alpes (about 2.5 km from Aix's circular boulevard on the Manosque road); tel 42.21.05.23.*

Aix - Barrage de Bimont
③ *Leave Aix on the D10, the St-Marc-Jaumegarde and Vauvenargues road, which climbs easily and quickly into the hills.*
④ *About 8 km from Aix, turn right for the following detour:*

Barrage de Bimont
(detour)
A 5-km return journey: the dam offers a spectacular view of the Montagne Ste-Victoire across the lake's usually turquoise waters (like the mountain, they tend to vary in hue), and pleasant picnic spots in the woodlands on the far side of the dam.

The energetic may wish to continue on foot for 30 minutes down a pretty defile to the Barrage Zola, designed by Emile Zola's father and claimed to be the world's first arched dam.

There is ample parking by the Barrage de Bimont, but no café, so bring plenty of liquid refreshment - despite the proximity of the cool waters of the lake, this is a notoriously hot spot.

Return from the dam and continue along the recently improved D10.

La Croix-de-Provence
(detour)

⑤ Only attempt this detour, which involves a strenuous three-hour return journey on foot up the Montagne Ste-Victoire, at times of the year or day when temperatures are below scorching. Those who reach the Croix-de-Provence, one of the mountain's highest points, will be well rewarded: the 360° view over the surrounding countryside and mountain ranges is staggering. Park at Les Cabassols, about 4 km beyond the turning to Bimont on the D10, and strike off up the signposted footpath to the right (Grande Randonnée 9).

Vauvenargues - Jouques

The D10 soon sweeps past the fast-expanding little village of Vauvenargues. Pablo Picasso is buried in the grounds of its 14thC château (not open to the public).

Shortly after Vauvenargues, turn left on to the D11, which elbows its way up through a narrow rocky gorge. On the way down to Jouques, on the other side, there are views of the Lubéron mountains in the distance. The road crosses one of the arms of the Canal de Provence. *At the junction with the D561, turn left into Jouques.*

Jouques

This relaxed village, once the residence of the archbishops of Aix, has a ruined castle and an interesting 12thC chapel.

Jouques - Rians

⑥ *Leave Jouques as you came in, continuing this time on the D561 to Rians.* After passing *underneath* the Canal de Provence (which is held aloft in a huge silvery tube by a suspension bridge), the road goes through a pretty landscape of green pastures and brick-red soil.

ROUTE TWO: 112 KM

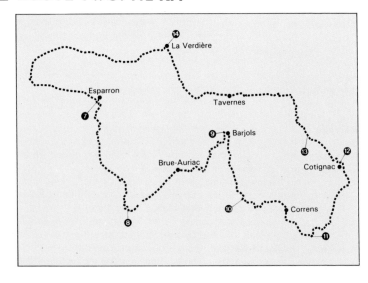

Rians -
Esparron

Leave Rians in the direction of Manosque. Just outside the town bear right on to the D561, signposted Esparron.

A word of warning about the road-sign policy in force in the area around Rians: the local traffic authorities have not yet adopted the almost universal system of making one set of traffic give way to the other at major intersections, so great caution is required at all crossroads within a 15-km radius of the town.

The D561 runs along the broad flat valley of the aptly named River Plaine. The Bois du Mont Major and the Montagne d'Artigues rise to the left and right respectively.

Esparron -
Seillons-
Source
d'Argens

⑦ *On reaching Esparron*, a gently decaying village built on the side of the hill and overlooked by a large château, *turn right on to the St-Maximin-la-Ste-Baume road*, which leads up to a deserted plateau. Here you can observe several different types of Provençal landscape: *garrigue* (desolate heath), rock-strewn woodland (densely populated by spindly truffle oaks), and, at times, thick carpets of thyme bushes.

On reaching the D270, turn left for Seillons, then keep straight ahead as far as the T-junction with the D560. This downhill drive affords views of Mont Aurélien to the south-west, and Montagne Ste-Victoire to the west - i.e. on your right.

Seillons -
Barjols

⑧ *Turn left in the direction of Barjols.* After going through the quiet, wine-growing village of Brue-Auriac, the road winds its way down the narrower and more verdant Vallon de Font-Taillade, then up towards Barjols.

Barjols

If the weather is very hot - as it often is in this part of the world - there is no greater pleasure than to drive into the little town of Barjols, turn off the engine and listen to the cool, splashing waters of one of its 25 fountains. Despite the many *boules* players, parking is usually easy on the tree-lined Place de la Rouguière, which boasts one of the finest fountains, a large moss-covered, mushroom-shaped structure.

Nestling in an amphitheatre of limestone cliffs, Barjols is delightfully unspoiled. Allow time to explore its maze of tiny streets and alleys, as well as its church, the Collégiale, whose fine organ case and choir-stall carvings date from the 16thC. If you happen to be around in mid-Jan, you can enjoy the unusual Fête de St-Marcel (a costumed procession and, every four years, a spectacular spit-roasted steer). Lively markets are held in Barjols every Tues, Thurs and Sat. There are a few hotels and restaurants in the town.

⑨ *Leave Barjols on the D554, the Brignoles road, and follow the valley of the quirkily named Eau Salée river as far as Châteauvert.*

Auberge
de Chât-
eauvert

Delicious trout and crayfish from the open-air fish tank (other dishes are good, but not quite on a par) served in an idyllic riverside setting. *Tel 94.77.06.60; closed Tues in July and Aug; price band B.*

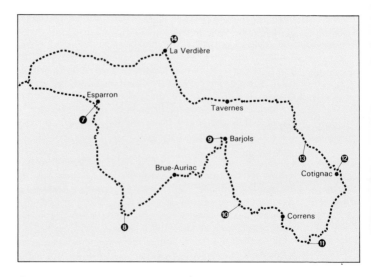

Châteauvert - Cotignac

(⑩) *Fork left by the restaurant up the D45 to Correns.* This little road meanders along the enchanting Vallon Sourd, a small-scale gorge with miniature jagged cliffs whose many caves were used as hiding places during the Wars of Religion. There are plenty of shaded picnic spots by the River Argens.

Beyond Correns, the gorges open out into an attractive verdant valley that contrasts with the parched *garrigue* which can be seen rising to the left.

(⑪) *At the junction with the D22, turn left to Montfort-sur-Argens and Cotignac.*

Cotignac

Like Barjols, Cotignac is a typical Provençal village tucked away in a rocky cleft, but it has more facilities for visitors (as well as a regular programme of open-air ballets and concerts in July and Aug). Through-traffic no longer disturbs the peace of its central esplanade (Cours Gambetta), which is shaded by massive plane trees. Do not miss the charming Place de la Mairie, with its old bell-tower and fountain.

The village wine co-operative, Les Vignerons de Cotignac (*closed Sun*), sells various excellent local wines, from *vin de pays* - suitable for picnics - to the more expensive Côtes-de-Provence.

Lou Calen
(hotel-restaurant, Cotignac)

Book well ahead in season if you want one of the tastefully decorated rooms in this gem of a hostelry. But in any case make a point of sampling the cuisine, which combines classical French dishes with such tasty Provençal specialities as *daube, pieds et paquets* (sheep's tripe and trotters), and *soupe au pistou*. The service, like *patronne* Huguette Caren's welcome, is spontaneously friendly, and prices, in view of the facilities provided (a private swimming pool and a magical secluded garden with exotic trees), are remarkably reasonable. *Tel 94.04.60.40; closed Wed and Nov-Easter; price bands B/C.*

Rest. des Sports
(Cotignac)

Also on the Cours Gambetta, this is a useful little restaurant (with a terrace) to fall back on if Lou Calen is closed or full. The fish soup is especially good. *Tel 94.04.60.17; closed Mon and Nov; price band A.*

Cotignac - La Verdière

(12) *Leave Cotignac on the D13.* As the road climbs out of the village in the direction of Riez and Barjols, there is an excellent view of the strikingly pock-marked tufa cliff which overhangs the town, and which is itself topped by two 13thC watchtowers. Soon the D13 crosses a plateau of olive groves, vineyards and woodland.
(13) *At the junction with the D560, turn right then left almost immediately and continue towards Fox-Amphoux. At the next T-junction, turn left towards Riez. At the following crossroads turn left on to the D32, signposted Avignon. On reaching the main D71, turn left*, and drive down to the completely vine-encircled Tavernes, with a view of the Montagne Ste-Victoire in the distance. *Keep straight on to Varages. Turn right in Varages for La Verdière.*

La Verdière

Park on the main road, which skirts this *village perché*, and walk up through its narrow streets to the promenade and château at the top. This vast, mainly 18thC building (believed to have 365 windows and a hectare of roofing) is currently being restored by its new owner and will shortly, one hopes, be reopened to the public.

A la Ferme
(restaurant, La Verdière)

When Wolf Raukamp - a biblical figure with a flowing white beard - and his wife Rolande decided to call their restaurant A la Ferme they meant the words literally: much of the produce that finds its way on to your plate (chicken, goose, kid, goat cheese) comes from their own adjacent farm. The restaurant's décor, and indeed the welcome, have a personal touch more commonly found in a private home. On top of that, the cuisine is very good (with rarities such as scrambled eggs with *grisets*, the local mushroom) and the prices are astoundingly low in view of the mountainous portions. It is better not to try to make friends with Donald, a gander whose self-appointed task is to guard the Raukamps' car. *The restaurant is 2.5 km north of La Verdière on the Manosque road. Tel 94.04.10.50; price bands A/B/C.*
(14) *Take the D30 back to Rians.*

Côte d'Azur:
AND THE HINTERLAND

The overcrowded stretch of Mediterranean coast between Monte Carlo and Marseille known as the Côte d'Azur is still one of Europe's most beautiful: a succession of rocky headlands and wooded coves, strung with palms and cypress trees, cacti and flowers. Despite the overexposure, it has an undeniable draw: sweeping seafront boulevards, little harbours crowded with yachts, magnificent beaches, hotels and restaurants. Nothing in all Provence is more striking than the contrast between this hectic, brilliant coast and its mountainous hinterland, serene and mostly unspoilt.

These two loops are designed primarily to discover those lovely inland hills and mountains, but to highlight the contrast, the route dips down to the

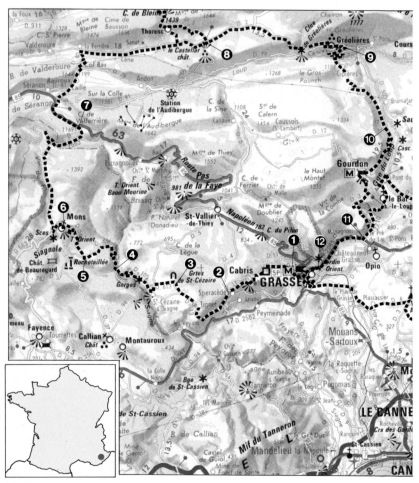

coast at one of its most beautiful parts, Cap d'Antibes, and takes in some of Provence's rich art collections. Picasso, Matisse, Léger and Renoir, whose museums the route passes, are only some of the artists who have been inspired by the clear light and beautiful landscapes of the south of France.

Both loops start at Grasse, an inland town perched above countryside whose greenery and abundance of blossoms partly compensate for the recent mushrooming of villas. From there the route reaches far into the upper hinterland with its breathtaking scenery.

Just as the scenery on this spectacular tour is diverse, so are the restaurants, from the world-famous Colombe d'Or to little-known inns offering real value. Gift shopping in also catered for, with stops at the craft villages of Tourette, Biot and Vallauris.

There is so much to see and do in this area that it is obviously not possible to take in all the suggested sights in a one-day trip. The tour presents a real case for an overnight stop, perhaps at Thorenc, Vence or Grasse (outside Grasse there is a lovely hotel at Pégomas: Le Bosquet, tel 93.42.22.87).

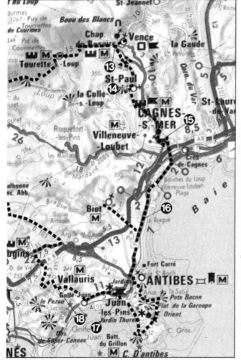

Sunset, Antibes.

ROUTE ONE: 104 KM

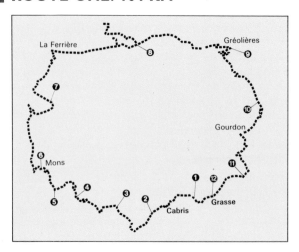

Grasse

Grasse, once a well-known winter resort, is not a good place to stay or eat in; but it is worth taking in the old town, the Cathédrale Notre-Dame (three paintings by Rubens and one by Fragonard, who was born in Grasse), and the Place aux Aires (market: Tues and Sat). Grasse is also capital of the French perfume industry, and the Parfumerie Fragonard (*20 Bd. Fragonard*) offers daily conducted tours (dreadful smells) and has a small museum and a shop (delightful smells).

Grasse - Grottes de St-Cézaire

① *Leave Grasse on the D4 signposted Cabris.* The D4 winds its way along the hillside, which although increasingly built up still sports more flowers and foliage than brickwork.

Cabris

From its position on the spur of a steep hill, the views from this tastefully restored village are superb: to the south the Iles des Lérins, and to the west Lac St-Cassien. *Continue on D11 to Spéracèdes.*

La Soleil-lade,
(restaurant, Spéracèdes)

In a charming village, which most tourists overlook, this jolly restaurant relies on straightforward menus and fresh local produce. Service, under the directions of English-speaking, ex-circus artiste M. Forest, is brisk and helpful. *Rue des Orangers; tel 93.66.11.15; closed Wed (except in July, Aug and Oct; price bands A/B.*
② *Follow signs to St-Cézaire, bearing right on to the D613 to the Grottes.*

Grottes de St-Céz-aire

Children particularly will love the guided tour round these fascinating caves, discovered by chance at the end of the last century by the father of the present owner: thousands of stalagmites and stalactites. *Open 10-12, 2-6, June-Sept; 2-5 March, April, May and Oct.*

Grottes de St-Cézaire - Mons ③ *After leaving the caves continue on the D613, then turn left at the crossroads on to the D5 and then right on to the D105,* a narrow road which twists and turns its way down the side of the sheer Siagne gorge. ④ *After crossing the bridge over the Siagne, continue on the even narrower D656 (there are passing points) up past striking rock formations to a wooded plateau.* ⑤ *On reaching the T-junction with the D56, turn right for Mons.*

Mons A typical Provençal hill village, with its maze of tiny streets, steps, courtyards and jumbled rooftops, all refreshingly unrestored. Park on the Panorama, a large esplanade favoured by *boules* players, with breathtaking views to the south-east (there is a viewing table and a telescope). Mons has no fuel.

Mons - Col Valferrière ⑥ *From Mons take the D563 signposted Castellane.* Shortly after leaving Mons the valley of the River Fil broadens into tiny meadows, and for a 2-km stretch there are plenty of easily accessible waterside picnic spots.

Col Valferrière - Thorenc ⑦ *At the Valferrière pass (altitude 1,169 metres), turn left along the N85, then fork right 3 km later on to the D79 signposted Caille. Bear left as you come into Caille and follow signs to Thorenc, skirting an extraordinarily flat-bottomed valley. Just before reaching the village of La Ferrière, turn right along the D2, which sweeps easily up the Lane valley.* This is a far cry from the hemmed-in feel that is characteristic of the busy roads down on the coast. *Ignore the tiny road with a red-bordered sign indicating Thorenc and turn left into the village a little later up the D502.*

Thorenc Thorenc (altitude 1,250 metres) has retained much of the charm that used to attract the English. It has a lake and tennis courts.

Hôtel des Voyageurs *(hotel-restaurant, Thorenc)* Claudette and Albert Rouquier offer genuine and carefully cooked local dishes on their two *prixe fixe* menus (no *à la carte*). The light and airy dining room is decorated with stuffed animals and birds. There is also a charming terrace overlooking an orchard. *Tel 93.60.00.18; closed 15 Oct-1 Feb; price band B; accommodation available if you take full board (or half-board out of season).*
Return to D2; in 3 km turn left to the Quatre Chemins crossroads.

Col de Bleine *(detour)* ⑧ *For this detour, a 9-km round trip, turn left on to the D5.* As you climb to the pass you get a view of Thorenc's gingerbread villas below. The Col de Bleine reveals staggering vistas over the surrounding mountains, with the snow-capped Alps in the distance. There is an even better vantage point - and a fine place to picnic on a windless day - up the road branching off to the right at the pass; it has no passing points and is better tackled on foot (15 minutes).
Returning to the Quatre Chemins crossroads, turn sharp left on to the D2 for Gréolières, a quiet old village.

Gréolières - *Gourdon*	⑨ *Two hairpin bends after Gréolières, turn sharp right on to the Cipières road. On the edge of Cipières bear left along the D603 to Gourdon. This* enchanting road leads through the dramatic valley of the Loup; at ⑩ *it joins the D3 beneath beetling cliffs at the beginning of the Gorges du Loup proper.*
Gorges **du Loup**	The D3 winds along the Gorges, which plunge away to the left. At one point there is a well-marked parking bay and viewing platform perched almost vertically above the Courmes waterfall. There are many accessible picnic spots away from the road.

Gourdon	The grey stone houses here are barely distinguishable from the sheer rocks to which they cling. Gourdon is one of the most dramatic of all the *villages perchés* in this area; views are as spectacular as one might expect. The 13thC château (*open June-Sept 11-1, 2-7; rest of year 2-6 and closed Tuesdays*) contains an interesting collection of naïve paintings.
	    At Gourdon the coast seems suddenly near again: every cranny of the village, which is not much larger than its ample car park, is filled with gift shops selling anything from kitsch to genuine works of art.
	    Take the D3 to the junction with the D2085, then ⑪ *turn right for Grasse.*

ROUTE TWO: 88 KM

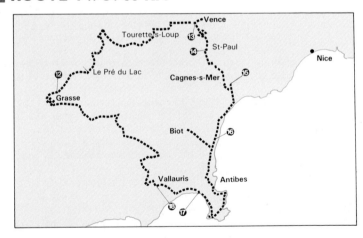

Grasse - *Vence*	⑫ *Leave Grasse by the D2085 and at the roundabout in Châteauneuf follow signs left and half-right for Le Bar-sur-Loup and Vence on D2210.*
Le Bar- **sur-Loup**	The Gothic church in this weathered village holds an arresting curiosity: an anonymous 15thC painting called the *Danse Macabre*, depicting the fate that befalls sinners when they die.

Tourette-sur-Loup A fortified hill village whose lonely setting, yet in close proximity to the coast, has attracted many artists and craftsmen.

Vence A sizeable resort which, although thronged by tourists much of the year, has a lived-in feel because of its many permanent residents (both French and foreign). Its long history stretches back to pre-Roman times. The attractive *vieille ville* is filled with shops selling antiques and local pottery. See the Place du Peyra and the Romanesque cathedral.

La Farigoule,
(restaurant, Vence)
Success has not gone to Georgette Gastaud's head: on her two set menus she still proposes the same genuine, generously served Provençal specialities - rabbit *à la farigoule* (with thyme), sardines *à l'éscabèche*, and *mesclun* salad (with rocket). In fine weather you can eat on the congenial patio. *15 Av. H. Isnard; tel 93.58.01.27; closed Friday and 15 Oct-15 Nov; price band B.*

Chapelle du Rosaire
(Vence)
This is a little chapel decorated with characteristic flair and simplicity by Matisse in 1950, when he was 80. It was a present from the artist to the adjacent convent of Dominican nuns, who had nursed him through a long illness. *Route St-Jeannet; open Tues, Thurs 10-11.30, 2.30-5.30; or by special arrangement - tel 93.58.03.26.*
⑬ *Take the D2 on the edge of the old town, signposted St-Paul.*

St-Paul-de-Vence
Park in one of the car parks on the road signposted Nice outside the village ramparts; expect parking difficulties in high season. Stroll through mosaic-paved alleys and pretty piazzas to the church on the hilltop, and then to the ramparts. Despite its being choc-a-bloc with tourists and gift shops of every description, St-Paul still gives an inkling of the charm that attracted Bonnard and Modigliani here in the 1920s.

Fonda-tion Maeght
(museum, St-Paul-de-Vence)
This famed modern art museum (on the Pass-Prest road opposite the turn-off into St-Paul) is remarkable not only for its contents but for its setting and the building itself. Designed by the Spaniard J.L.Sert, the boldly modern building is crowned by two inverted domes. Most of the major artists and sculptors of the 20thC are represented. *Open 10-12.30, 3-7 May-Sept; 10-12.30, 2.30-6 Oct-Apr.*

La Colombe d'Or
(hotel-rest., St-Paul-de-Vence)
If you are touring in a Rolls Royce, then this renowned hotel with its own important art collection is the natural choice for a lunchtime stop; if you are not, consider giving yourself a special treat anyway. Sip *kir* by the lovely pool amid Braque and Calder sculptures, and eat on the terrace with its marvellous Léger mural. The food itself, despite the prices, must be said to be enjoyable rather than superb. *1 Pl. Géneral de Gaulle; tel 93.32.80.02; closed Nov-mid Dec; price band D.*
⑭ *Fork left at the end of the series of car parks on the Nice road on to the D2 signposted Villeneuve-Loubet. After 3 km turn left along the dual carriageway signposted Cagnes-sur-Mer.*

Cagnes-sur-Mer

This is an unremarkable resort except for the old part, Haut-de-Cagnes, which perches on a hill; but see also the former home of Renoir in Cagnes-Ville, Les Collettes, now open to the public. It is an unpretentious villa standing in a large garden. Renoir spent his last years here, from 1907 to 1919. He suffered from rheumatoid arthritis, and so that he could continue to paint his brushes were tied to his stiffened fingers. The artist's peaceful studio has been faithfully reconstructed and it recreates, with a touching, even disturbing feel of reality, the nature of the man who worked in it. *Les Collettes, Av. des Collettes, Cagnes-Ville; open 2-6 June-Oct, 2-5 Nov-May; closed Tues, mid-Oct to mid-Nov.*

Cagnes-sur-Mer - Antibes

⑮ *Keep driving towards the sea, through Cagnes' ugly suburbs. Get into the right hand lane to avoid the motorway, and just before the flyover turn right on to the N7 signposted Cannes.*
⑯ *Keep on the N7 to La Brague, turning right on to the D4 if you want to make a detour to Biot (8-km round trip).*

Biot
(detour)

This is a lively village with an arcaded square and 16thC gates and ramparts. Pottery and glass-blowing flourish here, and there are many shops where you can browse and buy. Novaro has a particularly fine selection. *The turning to the Léger Museum, on the D4, is opposite.*

Musée Fernand Léger

Léger's artistic development is traced in over 300 pieces on show in this museum made especially for his work. Built by his widow Nadia after his death in 1955, this was the first major museum in France for one artist. *Open 10-12, 2.30-6.30 (2-5 in winter); closed Tues.*

Café des Arcades
(restaurant, Biot)

André Brothier's interestingly decorated inn has an easygoing atmosphere. A good place to try the Provençal speciality of *aioli. Pl. des Arcades; tel 93.65.34.91; closed Sun eve, Mon and Nov; price bands C/D. Return from Biot and continue along the N7 into Antibes.*

Antibes

The town began life as a Greek trading post and is still busy and commercial, but also has an undeniably charming old quarter.

Musée Picasso

In 1945 Picasso was given temporary use of Château Grimaldi as a studio, and in gratitude he left the whole huge output of that period on permanent loan here. The paintings are mainly exuberant fantasies inspired by the sea and Greek mythology, such as *La Joie de Vivre* and *Ulysse et Les Sirènes. Château Grimaldi, Vieille Ville; open 10-12, 3-6 or 7 in summer; closed Tues, Nov.*
Emerging from Antibes, follow the coastal route, well signposted from the town, right round this little pine-forested peninsula.

Cap d'Antibes

Cap d'Antibes is the haven of the rich *par excellence*, graced with splendid villas in superb sub-tropical gardens. If you have time, visit the strange little Sanctuaire de la Garoupe which stands by a lighthouse in

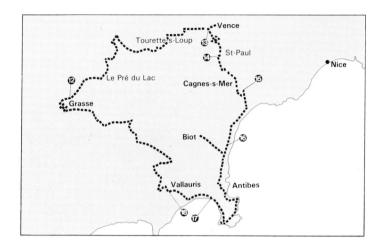

the middle of the peninsula. Its walls are hung with touchingly naïve ex-voto paintings by sailors and others rescued by Our Lady from death or other fates. Next to the chapel is an exceptional viewing point.

La Gardiole, *(hotel-restaurant, Cap d'Antibes)* The route round the Cap leads past the famous Hôtel Cap d'Antibes and its equally illustrious restaurant, the Eden Roc. Those with more modest tastes might like to try the Gardiole, with its sandy beach nearby and family atmosphere. This little hotel is on the way up the Garoupe sanctuary. *Chemin de la Garoupe; tel 93.61.35.03; closed mid Oct-mid Mar; price band C.*

Leaving the peace of the Cap, enter garish Juan-les-Pins.

⑰ *Follow the signs to Cannes and continue west on the N7 to Golfe-Juan, then turn right for Vallauris.*

Vallauris Pottery has been important to Vallauris since ancient times, but only after Picasso himself came to live and work here for six years did it become a world name in ceramics. Pottery on sale at every turn.

Musée Picasso *(Vallauris)* The artist's haunting *War and Peace*, painted on plywood panels in his Vallauris studio, covers the entire walls and ceiling of this little chapel at the top of the main street. Opposite is his bronze of a man holding a struggling sheep. *Open 10-12, 2-6 (2-5 Nov-March), closed Tues*

⑱ *At Vallauris take the D135 signposted Grasse. Then follow signs to Valbonne, first on the D35, then left on the D103.*

After Vallauris you drive up through Cannes' opulent hinterland. In contrast, 2 km along the D103, note on the right the ambitious Scientific Park of Sophia Antipolis, a modernistic industrial zone which displays the Côte d'Azur's developing role as a location for high-technology companies. Continue following signs for Grasse.

Languedoc:

MONTAGNE NOIRE AND THE MINERVOIS

The famous city of Carcassonne attracts thousands of visitors each year; most leave by the same motorway which brought them and few stay to explore the beautiful countryside just a few miles from the city walls. This relatively short tour has been devised to add an extra dimension to an outing to Carcassonne by tempting you to explore two adjacent and little-known areas, the Montagne Noire and the Minervois (you could visit the city in the morning and drive just one loop in the afternoon if time is short).

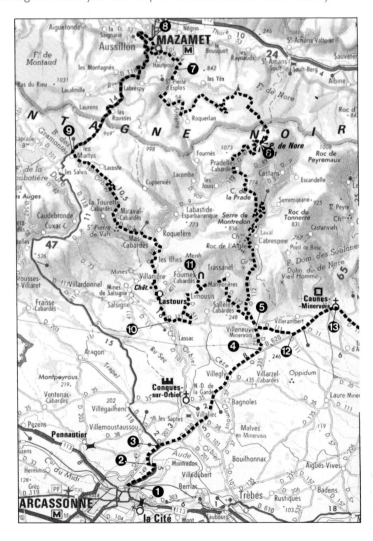

This is indeed a backwater: the landscape has great natural beauty and moments of drama, but beyond that there are few frills and the unassuming people work hard to earn a living from the land. Restaurants, even colourful village cafés, are scarce, and the local shops are unexciting, but for a picnic, who needs more than a fresh *baguette*, some salami and cheese, and a bottle of the ridiculously cheap Minervois?

The two loops contrast the Montagne Noire, far south-western corner of the Massif Central, scored with deep gorges, and the Minervois, a rocky limestone region dedicated to wine growing wherever it may. The routes have frequent reminders of Languedoc's medieval past, particularly of its stubborn religious dissension. In the early 13thC the Pope ordered the Albigensian crusade, led by Simon de Montfort, to ruthlessly eradicate the Cathars, whose religion had taken root in Languedoc; many retreated to inaccessible fortresses, often to be starved to death during long sieges.

████ ROUTE ONE: 90 KM

Carcas-
sonne
The town is in two parts: the historic walled *Cité* on its hill, and the newer bustling town on the banks of the Aude. In the latter you will find good shops and food markets, including a large and colourful open-

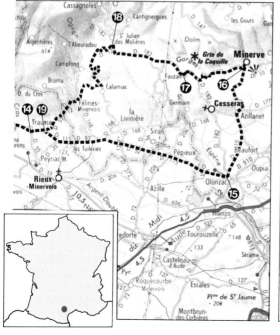

The fortified outer walls of the Cité, Carcassonne.

air fruit and vegetable market in the central Place Carnot. Park on one of the main Boulevards surrounding the maze of inner streets and walk from there.

For the *Cité*, car-parks are situated just outside the ramparts at the entrance, Porte Narbonnaise. If there is a strange feeling of unreality inside the *Cité*, it is because it is not, as it appears, a perfectly preserved medieval walled city, but a brilliant, if somewhat over-enthusiastic restoration. The restorer was the architect Viollet-le-Duc, who rebuilt the crumbling *Cité* in the 1840s.

Carcassonne has a suitably hectic and colourful medieval history, both in legend (you will doubtless be regaled with a fanciful story concerning a certain Lady Carcas and a bloated pig) and in fact. It played its part in the Albigensian crusade, being under the control of the dreadful Simon de Montfort while he pursued his campaign to stamp out the Cathars.

The Porte Narbonnaise, with its double line of ramparts, gives on to narrow, very *touristique* streets which lead up to the Château Comtal. From there visit the *Cité*'s architectural *tour de force*, the church of St-Nazaire with its wonderfully graceful Gothic choir and transepts, and superb stained glass and statuary. Then on to the Tour St-Nazaire with a view north of the Montagne Noire, where the route now leads.

① *From the middle of Carcassonne, follow the signs for Mazamet; this can be confusing and difficult in the heavy traffic. There is one rather inconspicuously marked junction soon after leaving the central square, at the end of a short stretch of road flanked by plane trees: be sure to continue straight on, soon turning right.*

Canal du Midi

The road out of Carcassonne follows for a short, rather impressive stretch the banks of the Canal du Midi. Of France's network of inland waterways, this is perhaps the loveliest and certainly the most popular for an idle floating holiday, though it is still very much a working canal. Stretching from the river Garonne near Toulouse to the Mediterranean at Sète, this engineering feat was begun in 1666 and completed a few years later by Paul Riquet, Baron de Bonrepos.

After crossing the canal the road soon ② turns sharp right. In about one km be ready for ③ the right turn on to the D620 signposted Caunes-Minervois.

④ *Turn left signposted Villeneuve-Minervois on to the D112. If you happen to miss this turning take the next left - the D111.*

⑤ *In Villeneuve-Minervois follow signs for the Pic de Nore.*

Villeneuve-Minervois - Cabrespine

The route climbs into the Montagne Noire, following the Clamoux gorge towards the range's highest point, the Pic de Nore. At first the road runs along the bottom of the gorge, cultivated first by allotments and then vineyards, planted wherever there is space. Then as the gorge deepens, the road climbs upwards high above its rocky sides.

Carcassonne from the plain.

Auberge du Roc de L'Aigle
(restaurant, Cabrespine)
One of those out-of-the-way country restaurants which can produce delightful surprises when one is least expecting them. Service is prompt and willing and the *patron*'s food, though simple, shows imagination - *mousselines* of fish, good chicken dishes, fresh crayfish. Eat for preference on the pleasant terrace overlooking the street. *Tel 68.26.16.61; closed Sun evening and Mon; price band B.*

Cabrespine - Pic de Nore
Though the road is comfortable, with little traffic, driving becomes increasingly slow round the many hairpin bends, while the scenery becomes increasingly dramatic. Lining the road are sweet chestnuts (*châtaignier*), magnificent when in summer flower. Towards the top the landscape flattens out and suddenly one is on a country lane among corn fields.

At Pradelles-Cabardès there is a filling station, and splendid views. *Follow signs for Pic de Nore in the village;* they warn that the road can be snowbound in winter.

Pic de Nore
The *Pic* itself is hardly a pretty sight: its huge television aerial looks like a rocket ready for launch, but the views (orientation table) to south, east and west are impressive.

233

**Pic de Nore
- Mazamet**

⑥ *From the Pic de Nore follow signs for Mazamet. In about 5 km, where the road divides, bear left.* The route now descends the humid northern slopes of the Montagne Noire which, in marked contrast to the Mediterranean side, are thickly wooded with spruce, fir, beech and oak. Towards Mazamet, which has a large textile industry, forest gives way to factories, making a rather grim and malodorous descent.

⑦ *Turn left signposted Mazamet. Follow the D54 into suburbs and*
⑧ *at the main road turn left (Avenue Georges Guynemer). Staying on the main road, which bears round to the left and becomes the D118, follow signs for Carcassonne.*

**Mazamet -
Mas-
Cabardès**

The suburbs of Mazamet are soon left behind and the scenery recovers; soon after leaving the town there is a viewpoint on the left of the road overlooking Hautpoul to the south and Mazamet to the north. Further on, a turning to the right leads to the Lac des Montagnés, a reservoir where you can fish and picnic.
⑨ *Just outside Les Martys turn left signposted Miraval-Cabardès on the D101.* The route now descends through the picturesque Cabardès region which is dotted with ruined reminders of medieval times. A sensational road follows the Orbiel river through a narrow gorge; though the landscape is small scale, it is punctuated by dramatic rocky outcrops and sharp hairpin bends. At Miraval-Cabardès are the remains of its château, associated in the 13thC with a famous troubadour, Ramon de Miraval - Languedoc was the land of the wandering poet and musician troubadours. After Miraval-Cabardès, notice on the right the ruins of the 16thC church of St-Pierre-de-Vals.

**Mas-
Cabardès**

You pass a huge 16thC stone crucifix, standing at a vantage point above the road, and a tiny bar/café on the river.
    For an amusing diversion, especially for those with children, and the wherewithal for a deliciously fresh meal, *turn right 0.9 km outside Mas-Cabardès* signposted *Pisciculture.* Here you can fish your own trout from storage pools (the owner will do it for you if you are short of time, though with worm and float it does not take long). You pay for those you take; live crayfish also on sale.

Lastours

As the road approaches the village of Lastours, the stark ruins of the Châteaux de Lastours come into view high above. If you want to visit them on foot there is parking on the right, and a path which leads up (allow about three quarters of an hour in all). The four châteaux, looking barbarous in their wild setting on a huge rock pedestal, made up Cabaret, a 12thC Cathar fortress which held out against the attacks of Simon de Montfort until 1211, the year after the fall of Minerve (see Route Two), but then bloodily capitulated. Pierre-Roger de Cabaret only surrendered after an agreement on territories had been struck.
⑩ *About 1.75 km beyond Lastours turn left over a bridge, signposted*

Villeneuve-Minervois, and in 1.5 km turn left on to the D511. Follow signs for the Grottes de Limousis.

Grottes de Limou-ssis
From the first chamber of this deep limestone cave the calcified formations are impressive, and as you penetrate further and further they become increasingly interesting - delicate crystalline structures as well as stalagmites and stalactites. The party is led from chamber to chamber, cleverly lit, via narrow defiles, finally arriving at a darkened cavern. When the lights are thrown on they reveal the cave's *pièce de résistance... By guided tour, daily June-Oct, Sun and national hols Oct-June.*

⑪ *To complete the route, retrace to the D511 and return to the D620 (Carcassonne road) via the D172 and Villeneuve-Minervois.*

ROUTE TWO: 50 KM

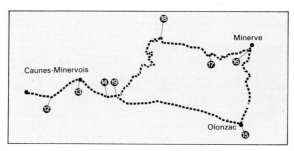

If joining Route Two from Carcassonne, follow directions 1, 2 and 3. Once on the D620 continue straight on for Caunes-Minervois.
   If joining Route Two from Route One, leave Villeneuve-Minervois on the D111 and ⑫ at the D620 turn left.

Caunes-Minervois
Like many villages in these parts, Caunes presents a rather blank face to through traffic, but if you stop and wander around you will find some rather fine 16th and 17thC houses and a Benedictine abbey.

Hotel d'Alibert
(restaurant, Caunes-Minervois)
Popular with the few local tourists since there is a dirth of restaurants in the neighbourhood, the Alibert can be relied upon for adequate if unexciting cooking - *pâté maison, charcuterie, pintade* (Guinea-fowl), *côte d'agneau* and so forth. If you visit the restaurant, be sure to step out into the Renaissance courtyard at the rear - like suddenly being transferred to 16thC Italy. *Tel 68.78.00.54; closed 23 Dec-1 Feb, Fri evening and Sat midday in winter; price bands A/B.*
   ⑬ *Continue straight through Caunes, following signs for Trausse. Outside Caunes, detour if you wish by following the sign on the left to Notre Dame du Cros, a chapel of pilgrimage in a picturesque setting.*

Caunes-
Minervois -
Olonzac

⑭ *At the entrance to the village of Trausse, fork right on to the village bypass road and soon follow signs for Pépieux and Olonzac.* The route now heads into the heart of Minervois wine country. This important wine producing region is a pocket within Languedoc-Roussillon, a prime source of the everyday wines of France, mostly without character or

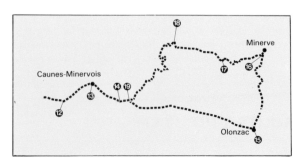

quality. Minervois also produces sound light red wines of VDQS quality, as well as some rosé and white. *Vente direct* factory sales counters abound in these parts; you need to take your own bottles to be filled. The *vente direct* at Peyriac-Minervois, south of Trausse on the D55, is excellent: reds, whites and a good rosé on sale.

The road to Olonzac runs through a broad flat-soled vale which is a sea of vines. To the left, the hills adjacent to the Montagne Noire, to the right, the distant foothills of the Pyrenees.

Olonzac

A pleasant little town, in the midst of the Minervois wine industry and a useful stopping point for the bank or post office, buying film, stocking up for a picnic, or filling the tank. There is a small archaeological museum. The Caves du Minervois (signposted on the right as you approach the middle of the town) offers a cross-section of local wines. ⑮ *From the middle of town retrace to the Caves du Minervois (ie heading west); continue 30 metres and take the right turn signposted Minerve and Azilanet (junction also marked by a conspicuous Auto Ecole sign). Note: the signpost at this junction is difficult to spot if approaching from the east.* Thereafter keep following signs to Minerve through increasingly spectacular scenery with frequent opportunities for picnic stops.

Minerve

Leave your car in the roadside parking area and cross over the bridge to Minerve by foot. This is a remarkable place, built on a spur in the Cesse gorge at the point where it meets the Briant gorge, and just before the Cesse disappears underground for some 20 km. On the far side of the spur, two tunnels have been dug by the Cesse out of the riverbed; in summer, when the riverbed is dry, you can walk to them.

Minerve itself has never forgotten the horrific events of 1210 when Simon de Montfort laid siege for seven weeks to this fortified Cathar

Grape picking in the Languedoc.

stronghold. Using a fearsome catapult sited on the far side of the gorge (there may be a replica there for you to see) he succeeded in destroying the town's only water supply and burned alive more than a hundred '*parfait*' men and women who preferred to die rather than renounce their faith.

As well as a little museum of archaeology, and the ruins of its fortress, Minerve also boasts the oldest altar in Gaul, dating from 456, in its little church.

Relais Chanto-vent
(restaurant, Minerve)

After a stroll round the ramparts and down the narrow Rue des Martyrs you could have a drink and a snack at the bar/café (plenty of seats oustide) where you may also make use of the swimming pool. Alternatively, try a simple but hearty lunch at the Chantovent (may be crowded and noisy in summer) *Tel 68.91.22.96; closed 15-30 Oct and Mon except July and Aug; price bands A/B; a few rooms to let.*

Minerve - Fauzan

⑯ *Returning to the car, head down what looks like a road back into town: it leads off downhill, just by the bridge. At the bottom stay with the main road, ignoring a turning to the right. The road climbs a hill; in about 0.5 km, at a junction, follow the signpost for Fauzan straight ahead. At the junction with the D182, turn right for Fauzan. A marvellous drive, this, following the Cesse gorge through the rugged landscape*
⑰ *In Fauzan follow signs for St Julien des Molières. The road now offers distant views over the plain below. Driving it at night, with the lights of villages twinkling beneath, is almost like flying.*

⑱ *In St Julien des Molières follow signs for Félines-Minervois, and from Félines follow signs for Trausse.* ⑲ *Turn right for Trausse and continue to Caunes-Minervois returning to Carcassonne on the D620.*

Pottok *pony.*

This single loop is in the lesser-known part of the Basque country, the inland provinces of Basse Navarre and Soule. The coastal province of Labourd, which includes Biarritz, Bayonne and St-Jean-de-Luz, is jam-packed for much of the year.

The drive offers something for everybody. You can trace the route of medieval pilgrims on their way to Santiago de Compostela in Spain - it traverses several villages on the tour. Or, setting aside matters spiritual, you could visit one of France's top restaurants, the Hôtel des Pyrénées, in St-Jean-Pied-de-Port.

Then there is natural beauty: the final section of the drive takes in the amazing Gorges de Kakouetta and the heights of the Forêt d'Iraty. You probably will not encounter one of the 20 or so Pyrenean bears that have survived on the French side of the border with Spain, but you do have a fair chance of spotting one or two uncommon birds, including the water pipit and the griffon vulture. In summer, the mountain slopes resound to the delightful tinkle of bells worn by cows (the handsome Blond d'Aquitaine breed), and are dotted with shaggy black-faced sheep (which produce the tasty *fromage de brebis* available from some farms) and stocky *pottok* ponies (which used to be wild, and are depicted in cave paintings).

The Basqueness of the Basques manifests itself in several ways: in their popular and highly spectacular game of *pelote*, their love of festivity and dancing, their (to outsiders) outlandish language and proper names, and their strong sense of national identity and desire to keep themselves to themselves - reflected in a sometimes infuriating lack of signposts - which of course is remedied in the route directions.

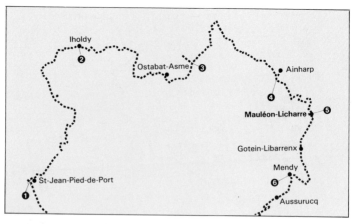

Iholdy ❷

Ostabat-Asme ❸

Ainharp

❹

Mauléon-Licharre ❺

Gotein-Libarrenx

Mendy

❻

St-Jean-Pied-de-Port ❶

Aussurucq

ROUTE: 163 KM

St-Jean-Pied-de-Port

Once an important staging post on the road to Santiago de Compostela, St-Jean-Pied-de-Port is now invaded each summer by a different, less energetic breed of pilgrim. Although a town of only 1,800 inhabitants, it has ample tourist facilities in the form of hotels, restaurants and cafés, and so makes an ideal start for the tour.

Stroll round the tiny old town, or *ville haute*, with its 14thC Gothic church, two gates (Porte Navarre and Porte St-Jacques), and handsome 16-18thC houses built of maroon sandstone (most of these bear the date of construction, plus ornamental details, on the lintel of the front door); climb the 15thC battlements; admire the view from the old bridge over a waterfall and down the backs of the old houses that line the Nive river.

Hôtel des Pyrénées
(hotel-restaurant, St-Jean)

Imagination and simplicity are the hallmarks of Firmin Arrambide's exceptional culinary talents. If you don't take his cheapest menu, which consists of straightforward Basque specialities, you are faced with an *embarras de choix*. Especially good are his jumbo-sized raviolis (which may contain anything from *langoustines* to *cèpe* mushrooms), *pigeon à l'ail confit*, *rognons de veau aux échalotes confites* (with a touch of orange peel), and superb soufflés and chocolate desserts. Most extraordinary in this class of restaurant is the value for money offered by both the menus and the wine list. *19, Place Général de Gaulle; tel 59.37.01.01; closed 5-25 Jan, 25 Nov- 22 Dec, Mon evening Nov-March and Tues 15 Sept-30 June; price bands C/D.*

Pécoïtz,
(hotel-rest., Aincillé)

It is well worth the trouble of driving 7 km out of St-Jean (*on the D933 to St-Jean-le-Vieux, then the D18 and D118 to Aincillé*) in order to enjoy this restaurant's verdant setting, its honest local fare and the friendly

welcome of its owners, Jean-Paul and Michèle Pécoïtz. *Tel 59.37.11.88;
closed Jan, Feb, and Wed, Dec-May; price bands A/B.*

St-Jean -
Iholdy
① *Take the St-Palais road (D933). As you leave Ispoure, a suburb of St-
Jean, turn left on to the D22. Bear left in the first village (no signpost) and
continue past the Padera restaurant (signposted) to the junction with the
D422. Keep straight on to Irissarry,* a village with typical broad-based
Basque houses sporting red-painted shutters and timbers, *then turn right
on to the D8 to Iholdy*

Iholdy
The important position of the game of *pelote* in Basque society can be
judged from the fact that the *fronton* (the wall against which one
version of the game is played) is often located next to a place of
worship - as in Iholdy, whose church has an elegant and
characteristically Basque open wooden gallery on one side.

Garat
(hotel-rest.,
Iholdy)
This place is an institution: renowned locally for her sharp tongue,
deadpan sense of humour and golden heart, Anne-Marie Garat manages
single-handedly, and simultaneously, to serve customers both in the bar
and in the huge beamed dining room. Each of the five courses on the
single menu arrives unannounced eg, excellent soup, *langue sauce
piquante*, roast lamb, a mammoth cheese platter including roquefort
and *brebis des Pyrénées*, and *katalembroche*, a Basque cake with walnuts
that is rarely made nowadays because the process is so long and
difficult: it is cooked on a spit in a special wooden contraption. You are
expected, by the way, to help yourself to the magnum of *hors d'age*
Armagnac that is unceremoniously plonked on your table at the end of
the meal. *Tel 59.37.61.46; closed Mon and Oct; price band B; rooms
available July-Sept.*

Iholdy -
Mauléon-
Licharre
② *Take the St-Palais road out of Iholdy. At the next main junction turn
right on to the D508 signposted Ostabat.* This road runs between neat
drystone walls, then up through heathland to the Col d'Ipharlatze, from
which there are great views east and west. *Bear right in the next village
(Ostabat, no signpost) to the T-junction with the D933. Turn left.*

Haram-
bels
(detour)
About 3.5 km after the left turn on the D933, turn left ③ *for this
detour* to the tiny hamlet of Harambels which, like St-Jean-Pied-de-Port,
lies on one of the main routes to Santiago de Compostela. The present
inhabitants of its four houses are direct descendants of the *donats* who
used to offer hospitality to pilgrims.

Chapelle
St-
Nicolas,
Haram-
bels
An undistinguished building from the outside, it has brightly painted and
gilded woodwork and a superb 15th-16thC reredos within. The
chamber above the entrance, reached by a step-ladder, used to be the
pilgrims' dormitory. Since the French Revolution, the chapel has
belonged to the four families of Harambels, who are responsible for its

upkeep; so contributions to the collection box are welcome. *Open 2-5, Mon-Sat; apply to the house with the green shutters.*

Return to the D933 and continue to the junction with the D242 signposted Mauléon. Turn right on to this road, which climbs through pleasant countryside. About 4 km after Lohitzun-Oyhercq, at the point where good views open up left and right, the D242 seems to continue straight on up the hill; in fact, at a dangerous unmarked crossroads, it turns half right.

Ainharp
(detour)

④ *This typically Basque village is a 3-km round trip.* It is, like Harambels, on a route to Compostela; its most interesting feature is its church (the pilgrims' dormitory is now occupied by the *mairie*. Both outside, in its well-kempt cemetery, and under the shelter of its porch, it has a fine collection of old Basque tombstones, many of them disc-shaped.

Return to the D242, turn left, and wind down to Mauléon-Licharre.

Mauléon-Licharre

Once world capital of the *espadrille* (but now facing severe competition from the Chinese), Mauléon is increasingly turning to tourism: it is conveniently located near the mountains, gorges and fast-flowing rivers of the Haute-Soule area (covered later in the drive). Actually, it is worth exploring parts of Mauléon itself - in particular the old town, with its Chapelle de Nôtre-Dame (note the characteristically Basque three-pronged bell-tower), ruined medieval castle and market place (market: Tues morning). *Pelote basque* is much-played in Mauléon, some of it against the huge *fronton* opposite the Château d'Andurain.

Château d'Andurain, Mauléon

Harmoniously proportioned and with several unusual features, over the centuries it has remained in the possession of the De Maytie family, who built it at the end of the 16thC. It is one of the few buildings in France whose roof is covered with wooden tiles (made of chestnut, which resists woodworm); and it is also remarkable for its sculpted doors, fireplaces and *mascarons* - grotesque masks on the walls with a hole in the middle through which a musket could be pointed. *Guided tours 11, 3, 4 and 5, July-15th Sept; closed Thur and Sun morning.*

Bidegain
(hotel-restaurant, Mauléon)

Housed in an old building alongside the Château d'Andurain, this cosy hostelry offers, in addition to some charming and tastefully furnished rooms with beamed ceilings, a number of Basque culinary specialities such as *pipérade*, trout in Jurançon wine and *poule au pot*. Other plus points include smiling service and a garden that gives on to the Saison river. *13, Rue de la Navarre; tel 59.28.16.05; closed 24-30 Nov, 15 Dec-15 Jan, Fri evening and Sun Oct-May; price bands A/B/C.*

Mauléon - Gotein

⑤ *Leave Mauléon on the Tardets road, the D918. As you approach Gotein, the massive peaks of the Pyrenees can be seen ahead. Turn into Gotein.* As at Iholdy, a *fronton* adjoins the church, a recently restored 17thC building with one of the finest three-pronged bell-towers in the

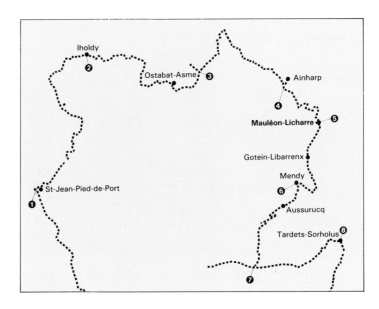

area. As always in the Basque country, the seats in the gallery, which rise in tiers as in a theatre, are reserved for male worshippers. There is a curious statue of the Virgin and Child: the infant Jesus has his index finger stuck in his mouth.

Gotein - Tardets-Sorholus

Continue along the D918. Shortly after it converges with the Saison river, turn right on to the V2 and then over the river to Menditte. Here follow the signs to Mendy, forking left near the top of the hill.

(6) *Turn left at the junction with the D147 for Aussurucq,* which has several old Basque houses. The road (room for improvement) then plunges into the vast Forêt des Arbailles, which consists mainly of beeches interspersed with large boulders and attractive glades. You climb steeply, emerging eventually on to an almost bare hillside near a *cayolar* - a shepherd's hut - the first building since Aussurucq.

Col Burdin Olatzé *(detour)*

To make this detour, 3.5 km each way, (7) *keep straight on up the mountain valley.* The sensuously smooth grassy slopes - and occasionally the road - are dotted with sheep, cows and *pottok* ponies from May to Nov. Park at the next road junction, the Col Burdin Olatzé, and admire the panoramic view over the Pyrenean peaks that run along the border with Spain. The Pic d'Orhy directly to the south is only 12 km away as the crow flies; the Pic d'Anie, to the south-east, rises to 2,504 metres. If you feel energetic you can walk up past the house on the hill to the Fontaine d'Ahusquy, whose waters have medicinal properties.

Returning from the Col, take the road that leads off to the right by the

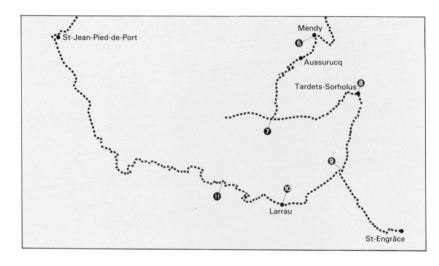

cayolar *and make your way down to Alçay on a sometimes very steep road, not marked on map. At a fork by a house signposted Tardets both ways, bear right, then, by a fronton, turn right and keep straight on down to the T-junction with the D247. Turn left for Tardets.*

Tardets-Sorholus

This *bastide* (fortified village) founded in 1280 holds a celebrated festival of Basque dancing and *pelote* on the *Sat, Sun, Mon and Tues following the public holiday of 15 Aug.* At this point, check your fuel gauge: there are no filling stations between Tardets and Chalets d'Iraty.
⑧ *Take the Oloron road out of Tardets, shortly forking right on to the D26 to Larrau.* After an enjoyable 8.5-km stretch beside the Saison, you reach the turn-off to Ste-Engrâce, which you take if you wish to make the following highly recommended detour.

Uhaytza Valley (detour)

This is quite a long detour - 22 km there and back - but definitely worth it. ⑨ *Climb the narrow D113 past the sign to Gorges de Kakouetta (which you can visit on the way back) and continue up the valley of the Uhaytza. Soon Ste-Engrâce is seen set against the dead end of the valley. There is a huge cleft in the mountain side to the right - the beginning of the Gorges d'Ehujarré.*

Ste-Engrâce

Keep straight on through the hamlet to its asymmetrical church, formerly the chapel of an abbey founded in the 11thC. This is one of the few Romanesque buildings in the Basque country not to have been tampered with. In the choir behind the 14thC wrought-iron grille there is a 17thC reredos depicting the life and martyrdom of Ste-Engrâce in the 3rdC. But the most interesting feature is the series of lively, and in one case erotic, painted and sculpted capitals.

Gorges de Kakouetta.

Gorges de Kakouetta

On no account miss these justly celebrated gorges. The river waters have sliced an incredibly thin wedge out of the soft limestone mountain: at some points the defile is only 3 metres across and more than 200 metres deep. As you follow the riverside path into the ever-narrower, darker and gustier cleft, whose walls are covered with rare mosses, ferns and lilies, you feel something like a Rider Haggard hero being led to a lost kingdom. At the end of the negotiable part of the gorges, there is a sinister cave, a waterfall that shoots straight out of the cliff face (it is in fact a resurgence) and some thoughtfully provided picnic tables. Although there are handrails, planking and numerous little bridges over the stream, it is advisable to wear non-slip shoes. *Open 8 until dusk, Easter-Oct; apply for tickets at the café by the entrance.*
    Continue on the D26 to Larrau.

Etche-maité
(hotel-restaurant, Larrau)

This is a useful place for an overnight stop before tackling the highlands and the Forêt d'Iraty when they are at their best (ie in the morning). The cuisine is simple and relies on local produce such as trout and tasty moutonnet (eight-month-old lamb). *Tel 59.28.61.45; price bands B/C.*
    ⑩ *Leave Larrau on the D19.* This starts as a leafy road beside a rushing stream, but in just 8 km climbs to 800 metres to the Col Bagarguiac, revealing the Pic d'Orhy in all its splendour.
    ⑪ *Turn left at the Col,* past a chalet that calls itself a *centre commercial* (you are in part of the Châlets d'Iraty ski resort), and drive down through stately beech forest to a lake. *Turn left on to the D18 signposted St-Jean-Pied-de-Port.* This good, if narrow road tends to be strewn with rock fragments, so take care. It runs along a mountain ridge, with breathtaking views in every direction, before plunging down through Estérençuby to St-Jean-Pied-de-Port.

East Pyrenees

Like many border areas, the part of France covered by this tour has had a troubled history of invasion (by Arabs and Spaniards) and internecine warfare (between the Albigensians and the Roman Catholic church). This is reflected with extraordinary vividness in its architecture: the castles of Peyrepertuse and Quéribus, like the abbey of St-Martin-du-Canigou, are located in almost absurdly inaccessible spots, and churches often resemble fortresses, with arrow slits instead of windows, letting in little light.

Today the only invaders are tourists, which is why July and August are months to be avoided, unless you want to attend the celebrated Pablo Casals Music Festival in Prades. Visitors are drawn to the area by its exceptionally balmy climate, summed up by the local saying: ''If it's cloudy here it must be raining elsewhere.''

The climate can be explained by the region's geography. The two big valleys included in this tour, which roughly correspond to the areas known as the Haut-Conflent and the Fenouillèdes, run in almost straight lines from east to west, and are thus protected from the north wind. The warm waters of the Mediterranean have more influence on the climate than the Pyrenees.

The startling proximity of those peaks is another major attraction of this tour. On a clear day, the Mont Canigou is visible from almost any viewpoint. Sometimes it just peeps over the horizon, at other times it seems to fill the whole sky - as from the village of Eus which is only 14 km as the crow flies from the mountain's summit.

ROUTE ONE: 87 KM

Sournia

Sournia is a large, sleepy and unspoilt village set among vines and *maquis* in the rocky uplands between the Fenouillèdes and the Haut-Conflent. Although it springs to life in summer when its camp site and *gîtes* are filled, it has hardly been affected by tourism. Sournia has no hotel (though it does have a filling station).

Auberge de Sournia *(restaurant)*

The Auberge is an oasis in an otherwise gastronomic desert. Jean Morero and Cosima Kretz are inventive and very precise cooks; try their delicious *feuilleté* of goat cheese with a tomato *coulis* and fresh basil, pork in a sauce of almonds, cream and Roquefort, and a not oversweet honey and hazelnut cake. The décor is resolutely rustic (mangers, halters, ploughshares) without being kitsch. *Tel 68.97.72.82; closed Sun evening and Mon; price bands A/B.*

Chapelle St-Michel *(detour)*

(1) *For this short detour, take the D2 out of Sournia and turn left on the edge of the village to the* 10thC *Chapelle St-Michel, forking left soon afterwards away from Le Puch.* After one km, park by the signpost to the chapel. A three-minute walk up a narrow path through woodland will bring you to the building, which although in ruins is in the process of being restored by the *Monuments Historiques*.

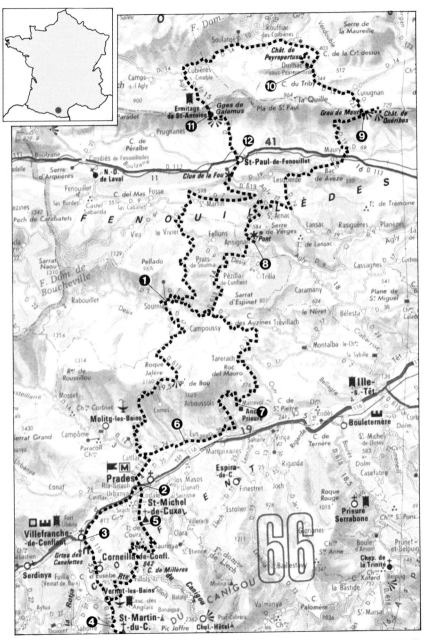

Capitals in the church of St-Jacques, Villefranche-de-Conflent.

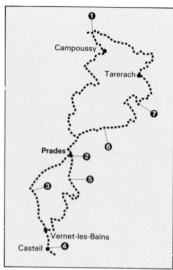

Sournia - Campoussy

Return to Sournia and take the D619 towards Prades. It wends its way up and up an increasingly desolate and chaotic landscape of boulders and scrub. *Turn left shortly on to the D67 to the hamlet of Campoussy,* whose tiny square is dominated by a large central lime tree. From behind the church there is a staggering view to the east over the whiter than white Roc Blanc, the Corbières mountain range and the sea.

Campoussy - Prades

Continue out of Campoussy and rejoin the D619. About 4 km later, there is a well-preserved dolmen a stone's throw from the road (signposted). The incisions on it are thought to represent wild boar. After passing the Roc Cornu (a huge boulder doing a balancing act on another one) and driving through landscape that looks increasingly like that of the Wild West, you will see down below to your left an exceptionally large menhir, about 6 metres tall, known as the Pierre Droite (signposted). Unfortunately it is not very accessible.

At the Col de Roque Jalère, the pass that leads over into the valley of the River Têt and the Haut-Conflent, the colossal Mont Canigou and its sister peaks heave into view with breath-taking suddenness. Prades, below, seems close - but this is an illusion, for the D619 takes its time to zigzag down the mountainside.

Prades

The geography of this part of the Pyrenees means that the little Catalan town of Prades has the misfortune to have to cope with all traffic from Perpignan to Font-Romeu and Andorra (a bypass is planned...). Its straightforward one-way system is, however, well signposted.

Prades has a pleasant, tree-dotted central square away from the traffic; its pink marble paving stones come from local quarries. On one side is the church of St-Pierre, whose 12thC bell tower is a typical example of the local Romanesque style. Its dark, Spanish interior contains a striking baroque reredos. Prades' main claim to fame is its Pablo Casals Music Festival, started by the renowned cellist in the 1950s. It is held from 24 July to 15 Aug in the nearby abbey of St-Michel-de-Cuxa (see below).

L'Etape
(restaurant, Prades)

The best place to eat in Prades is a *Restaurant Routiers*, L'Etape, near the bus station on the N116. Jolly Denise Joer takes plenty of trouble over local specialities (not easy to find in the area): *beignets de calmars, escargots à la catalane*, and a wonderfully aromatic jugged boar. The fruit tarts and caramelised baked apples are also recommended. *Tel 68.96.53.38; closed Sun and May; price bands A/B.*

Prades - Ville-franche-de-Conflent

② *Leave Prades on the N116 in the direction of Font-Romeu.* Soon you will see what appears to be a large castle ahead of you: this is the fortified 'town' (it is minuscule) of Villefranche-de-Conflent, once the area's capital. Park the car outside the walls.

It is well worth visiting the 11th-17thC ramparts *(open June-Sept 9-12 and 1.30-6; rest of the year, telephone 68.96.10.78).* Protected by the ramparts is a maze of quiet streets containing many medieval houses and the church of St-Jacques, which has two remarkable 11thC marble portals with interesting capitals, and a powerful recumbent Christ.

Hôtel Vauban, Villefranche

This peaceful, spotless inn, opposite St-Jacques, offers a tempting alternative to hostelries in the tourist hub of Vernet-les-Bains or Prades. Booking advised; *5 place de l'Eglise; tel 68.96.18.03; price band C.*

Les Grandes Canal-ettes

③ *Take the D116 towards Vernet-les-Bains.* Soon you will see the sign for the Grandes Canalettes (and car park) on the right. The white concretions in these caves are remarkable. *Guided tours hourly 10-6 May-Oct, and 2-5 Sun Nov-Apr.*

Corneilla-de-Conflent

Continuing along the D116, turn left for the church when you arrive in Corneilla-de-Conflent. This fascinating Romanesque church, which is being extensively restored, contains some superb works of art: an entombment (a group of five 15thC painted statues), a vivid sculpted reredos made of Carrara marble, a 13thC Spanish chest of drawers, a fine marble portal with a sculpted tympanum, and some interesting windows bordered both inside and outside by four small columns with capitals. *Guided tour by M. Perez (house adjoining church) 3-6 or at other times by appointment - tel 68.05.60.64.* The tour is free, but a small contribution to the restoration fund is welcome.

Vernet-les-Bains

A small spa town (speciality: ear, nose and throat) with little to offer except its quaint old quarter, and a congenial position.

St-Martin-du-Canigou
(detour)

④ The detour to this extraordinary abbey involves a return journey of 5 km, plus a strenuous 50-minute walk each way. Take the D116 to Casteil. Parking may be difficult, so keep going right into the village, then turn right up the C2 signposted Col de Jou, where there should be room by the roadside. Those who relish a really steep walk up a cool valley with a spectacular view of the abbey from below should continue on foot up the C2, bearing left and left again. If you prefer the easier climb, follow signs to the Abbaye from the middle of Casteil.

The original building, started in the 9thC, was perched on its mountain eyrie, 364 metres above Casteil, in order to be invisible to invaders. When it grew into a monastery in the 11thC, its original chapel became a crypt and the present church was built on top of it. Although the abbey was comprehensively restored at the beginning of this century (when it was little more than a ruin), its stark architecture, unusual pagan motifs and unique lofty position give it an undeniable magnetism. *Guided tours daily at 10,11,2,3,4 and 5.*

Bell tower, St-Martin-du-Canigou.

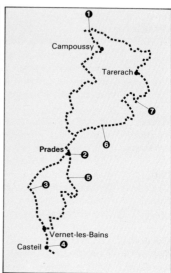

Vernet - St-Michel

Leave Vernet by the D27, which winds its way through a valley of conifers, chestnut trees and alders. Prades can be seen laid out far below.

St-Michel-de-Cuxa

Much of this abbey, too, where the concerts of the Prades music festival are held, had to be rebuilt (half the capitals of its original cloisters found their way to America). The main church is one of the very few extant examples of Mozarabic architecture in France. *Guided tours June-Oct 9.30-11 (except Sun) and 2.30-5.*

St-Martin-du-Canigou and abbey.

St-Michel-de-Cuxa - Eus

⑤ *Continue on the D27 to Prades, get into the one-way system and follow the signs to Molitg-les-Bains. When you get to Catllar, whose church has a curious wrought-iron bell tower, turn right along the D24, and later bear left along the D35 to the hilltop village of Eus.*

Eus

On the outskirts of Eus, fork left to the car park (you cannot drive into the village itself). Although undergoing an inevitable process of gentrification (quite pricey restaurants and a growing number of arts and crafts shops) its labyrinth of little streets and alleys has great charm, and there is a magnificent view of Mont Canigou.

Eus - Marcevol

⑥ *Return to the D35 and continue in the direction of Marquixanes; the road coasts along the orchard-filled valley of the Têt (take care when crossing the narrow little bridges over streams flowing into the river). Ignore the turning on the right to Marquixanes and keep on the D35 as it* climbs the almost vertical-sided Ravin de la Combe Perdrix, passes the village of Arboussols and takes you to Marcevol.

Marcevol

As you approach this hamlet, whose Lilliputian houses huddle out of sight as though still fearing invaders from the south, you pass a peaceful, ruined 12thC priory with a well-proportioned pink-marble porch.

Marcevol - Sournia

⑦ *Continue on the D35. At the various T-junctions, follow the signs to Tarerach and then to Sournia on the D13, D2 and D619.* This last stretch along the Desix valley is a pleasant, easy drive, with fleeting views up side valleys. It offers a delightfully secluded waterside picnic spot by the ruined chapel of Ste-Félicité: about 1½ km after joining the D619, park near a weather-beaten sign to the chapel on the left, and walk down the track to the chapel; just beyond it, the River Desix forms a pool in the shade of the trees.

ROUTE TWO: 91 KM

Vineyards
near
Ansignan.

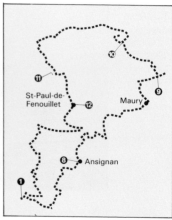

**Sournia -
Ansignan**

Take the St-Paul-de-Fenouillet road out of Sournia and fork right
immediately along the D619. This road will take you all the way to
Ansignan along the valley of the Desix.

**Société
Coopér-
ative
Agricole
d'Ansig-
nan**

The most important feature of Ansignan, apart from an obtrusive
water tower, is its Société Coopérative Agricole (turn left in the middle
of the village), which sells excellent red and rosé Côtes du Roussillon
and an aromatic white Côtes d'Agly at unbeatable prices; there is also
a spicy, far from ordinary vin ordinaire, suitable for picnics. Tel
68.59.00.89; open Tues-Sat 10-12 and 2-5.

**Ansignan -
Maury**

⑧ Beyond Ansignan, the D619 goes through a narrow fractured gorge,
which shows patches of the pink marble used in so many buildings in the
area. Turn right over a bridge on to the D77 to St-Arnac and straight
through the village in the direction of Lansac. There are views of
neighbouring peaks in every direction. Before reaching Lansac turn left on
to the D79 signposted Maury. At the junction with the D19, turn right. The
flattish landscape here is subject to fierce winds, hence the dense rows
of cypresses acting as windbreaks to the vineyards.

Further on there is a superb view across the Maury valley, which is
dotted with curious dome-shaped hillocks and overlooked by the jagged
white ridge of the Grau de Maury. At the top of the ridge, the clean-
cut outline of Château de Quéribus can be made out against the sky.

**Maury -
Château de
Quéribus**

Turn right in Maury (whose only claim to fame is its pleasant eponymous
fortified wine), then shortly turn left along the D19, passing a boule
playing area shaded by plane trees. Follow the signs to Cucugnan. The
road climbs straight up the flank of the mountain.

Château de Quéribus *(detour)*

⑨ *At the top of the pass, turn right for a 1½ km detour to the Château de Quéribus,* the last of the Albigensians' hilltop castles in the region to fall to the crusaders in 1255. Superb views. *Open daily Apr-Sept, Sun and holidays Oct-Mar, 9.30-12.30 and 2.30-7.*

Château de Quéribus - Cucugnan

As you drive down the D123, you can see Cucugnan, the pleasant little village immortalized in Alphonse Daudet's *Lettres de Mon Moulin*, nestling in the valley below, with the vast and rugged forests of the Corbières stretching out behind it. To the left, you will spot another Albigensian stronghold, the Château de Peyrepertuse - if you know what to look for since from this distance it is virtually indistinguishable from a rocky crag. *Turn right into Cucugnan at the junction with the D14.*

Auberge de Cucugnan *(restaurant)*

This well-known restaurant (not to be confused with a newcomer to Cucugnan, the Auberge du Vigneron) is housed in a former barn that is partly hollowed out of the rock. It serves unchanging menus of straightforward local dishes with local wine at reasonable prices. *Tel 68.45.40.84; closed 1-15 Sept and Wed from Jan to Mar; price band B.*
   On leaving Cucugnan, take the D14 towards Duilhac; as you come into the village turn left ⑩ *up the road signposted to Château de Peyrepertuse.*

Cucugnan - Château de Peyrepert- use (detour)

This 7-km return journey really is worthwhile. The fortress, a colossal construction, strung out along a high mountain ridge, looks like a rocky excrescence rather than the work of man until you are right upon it. *Open at all times.*

Château de Peyrepert- use - Gorges de Galamus

Return to the D14 and continue through the narrow streets of Duilhac, following the arrows on the road, then turn left out of the village. From here there is a view of the Château de Peyrepertuse, which from this side looks much more like a castle. *After driving through Soulatgé and Cubières-sur-Cinoble, turn left on to the D10.*

Gorges de Galamus

⑪ The D10 seems to be going straight into the hillside, but amazingly it follows the River Agly, which has sliced a passage through the rock. The road, which winds its way timidly beneath overhanging cliffs, is so narrow that it is impossible to park. *Drive through to the exit on the far side, where there is a car park,* and explore the gorges on foot.
   Continue down into St-Paul-de-Fenouillet, turning right at the rail crossing. ⑫ *In St-Paul-de-Fenouillet, go straight over the traffic lights in the direction of Sournia.* You soon come to the Clue de la Fou, a perpetually windswept gap cut through the rocky ridge by the Agly. *Turn right over the bridge, then fork right immediately along the D7 in the direction of Prats-de-Sournia.*
   As you continue on the D7, *ignoring the turning to Fosse,* you can briefly glimpse to the right the massive, sinister mountain of Pech de Carabatets. *Turn left at T-junction into Le Vivier, bear left in the village, and keep going on the D7 via unsightly Prats-de-Sournia to Sournia.*

Index

Includes: towns, villages and hamlets given a substantial mention; major, identified châteaux and manors; notable landmarks, viewpoints, cols, defiles, rivers, gorges and valleys.

Acknowledgements

Picture Credits
Stephen Brough 31, 35, 40, 45, 49, 53, 55, 60, 63; **Andrew Duncan** 212; **John Farndon** 1, 15; **Fotobank** Cover, 144; **Leslie and Adrian Gardiner** 74, 78, 94, 101, 113, 127, 129; **Chris Gill** 135, 137, 143; **Peter Graham** 148, 152, 183, 185, 188, 190, 198, 201, 248, 250, 251, 252; **Susan Griggs Photo Library** 26, 106, 233; **Robert Harding Photo Library** 158, 237; **Richard Platt** 107.

Editorial and Design
Copy editing **Gilly Abrahams**; proof reader **Linda Hart**; editorial assistance and index **Rosemary Dawe**; art editor **Mel Petersen**; designer **Lynn Hector**; illustrations **Mike McGuiness**. Our thanks also to **MJG**, without whom this book could not have been written.